The
GREEN MAN
and the
DRAGON

*The Mystery behind
the Myth of St George
and the
Dragon Power of Nature*

PAUL
BROADHURST

MYTHOS

First published on
St George's Day 2006
by

MYTHOS
Box 888
Launceston
Cornwall
PL15 7YH
United Kingdom

ISBN 0 9513236 6 0

Designed by Gabriele Trso, Cornwall
Printed by Gomer Press, Llandysul, Ceredigion

Illuminated capitals by Typographer Mediengestaltung

Other titles
by
Paul Broadhurst

Secret Shrines
Tintagel and the Arthurian Mythos
The Sun and the Serpent
The Dance of the Dragon

ACKNOWLEDGEMENTS

Of the many people who have helped with this project,
providing inspiration and support over a number of years,
the following, in no particular order, are due special thanks:

Bruce Mace, Graham King, Gabriele Trso, David Elkington,
Colin Bloy, Kit Broadhurst, Rob Lloyd, Teresa Lloyd, Joyce Froome,
John Michell, Robin Heath, Tricia Heath, Simon O'Rourke, Dave Ward,
Kerriann Godwin, Hassan Hassan, Wilma Dierkes, Vivienne Shanley,
Hamish Miller, Michael Omejer.

Heartfelt thanks in particular to
the Angel Gabriele,
who came from Heaven
to help guide us back
into the Light.

List of Illustrations

Original photography by Paul Broadhurst; thanks to Gabriele Trso for colour photographs of the Dragon energies at St Nectan's Keive, St John's Cathedral, Trogir, Chalice Well, Glastonbury, the chevron at Fourknocks, the stained glass Bull of Co. Cork and the illustration of the Knowth Stone bowl; Vivienne Shanley for the map of Tintagel's 'Round Table', Horus as a Roman centurion, Wodewoses at Christchurch and Chester Cathedral, the bench ends at Altarnun and the St Michael & Apollo alignments; The Museum of Witchcraft, Boscastle, for access to its library and illustrations from the Richel collection.

Contents

For
the Queen of Heaven
and
the Lords of Light

Prologue

Green Roots, Green Shoots

At the heart of the greatest megalithic temple complex in Britain, built from the shattered stones of its vast henge, lies the village of Avebury. In many ways it is the classic English country village, with its ancient manor house tucked within the steep earthen banks, a vicarage, pub and post office. The cottages that line the narrow street are well-tended, with roses and creeping plants blending with the mellow stone that speaks of another time altogether; a time when Neolithic people constructed cyclopean temples that reflected the movements of the heavenly bodies.

On a Sunday morning it is idyllic, yet strangely surreal. The church bells ring, people walk their dogs to collect the newspapers, blinking in the sunshine and greeting their neighbours with cheery good mornings. In between the cottages the remaining great standing stones of the Henge are glimpsed, staring impassively at the scene, as they have done for at least 5000 years. The local priest appears and vanishes along the path into the churchyard, amongst the birdsong and bells.

Inside the small church there is a powerful atmosphere of antiquity, even though the building is virtually new compared to its stone-age precursor outside. One's attention is immediately drawn to the oldest object of all, standing

directly beneath the tower. It is a remarkable font around which generations of Avebury folk have gathered for the rites of baptism during the last 800 or so years. The deeply-carved images cut into the stonework are heavily defaced but they are striking. Two early bishops in an archaic Celtic style hold a book in one hand and a crozier in the other with which they spear dragons writhing underfoot. The dragons appear lively and playful, nibbling the vestments of the bishops as they are taunted by the tips of the spear-like rods which hover over the dragon's eyes, whilst curliques of foliage wrap themselves around the old stone bowl, worn and discoloured by a thousand stroking hands. Half-hidden behind the rood screen is another ancient carving: The Green Man.

When the antiquarian William Stukeley first came across Avebury in the 18th century whilst exploring the Wiltshire countryside on horseback he

One of the Avebury dragons

was mesmerised. He saw what he took for a Druid Temple, the scale of which was bewildering. The great Henge was constructed of stones so big he could hardly imagine how they were moved and lifted into place. All around were other gigantic monuments. Just over the ridge was Silbury Hill, the largest prehistoric man-made mound anyone had ever seen. Another collection of stones called The Sanctuary was joined to the Henge by a serpentine avenue of megaliths. The entire landscape was studded with such remains. The most notable thing within the circles of stones that formed the centre of the complex was a massive erect stone known as The Obelisk.

Stukeley became so fascinated by Avebury that he spent some years visiting it, talking to the locals and immersing himself in its mysteries. At the time the villagers, encouraged by the Church authorities, were doing everything they could to destroy it forever by lowering the great stones into fire-pits and smashing them with hammers. The Obelisk was broken up and the fragments used to build a chapel within feet of where it had once stood. Fortunately Stukeley made a series of sketches of the Great Temple before finally, the locals gave up, the size of the stones and the scale of the task having defeated them.

Having explored Avebury from every possible angle and recorded it in detail, Stukeley came to a conclusion about its original purpose. He was convinced it had been built as a 'Serpent Temple' to worship the sun, moon and the powers of fertility of the earth, and that a network of such temples that he called 'Dracontia' existed across Britain. The plan of Avebury suggested to him that of a great serpent fertilising an egg. He believed ancient priests gathered there at Mayday, surrounded by large numbers of the inhabitants of south-west Britain, and performed rites that honoured the fertile principle in nature and the cycles of life upon which everyone depended.

Dragon-stabbing bishops? Stone-age serpent temples? What could it all mean?

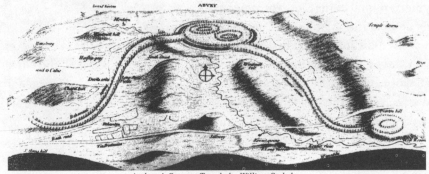
Avebury's Serpent Temple by William Stukeley

The Cornish May morning is laced with the salty tang of the sea as you descend the narrow steps to the town below. From somewhere within its radiating web of narrow streets the distant sound of a slowly beating drum, wafted here and there by the breeze, resonates within your being, stirring something deep. It echoes through the streets and alleys like a heartbeat, the insistent rhythm making the hairs on the back of the neck curl, hypnotically summoning you onwards. An ancient shiver of recognition runs along the spine, and your emotions quicken. A strange sense of mystery seeps into your soul. The drum beckons.

With the Sun streaming through the boughs of greenery that festoon the whitewashed buildings, flags flapping wildly in the wind, you are entranced. The Padstow folk are all dressed in spotless white with bright red or blue sashes and scarves, and sprigs of cowslips and bluebells tucked into their hats. A lively scene confronts you, with the crowd animated by the joyful music. People are laughing and prancing around the gaily decorated maypole which stands in the square, and the thrilling cadences of the singing and accordions pumping out their vibrant tones is somehow familiar, as if from a time far away. Somewhere, in the middle of the thronging crowd, the Oss is dancing, led by the wild cavorting of the Teazer waving its magical wand.

The 'Wee' or Children's Oss begins the May morning celebrations at Padstow

You catch a glimpse for the first time and it is an extraordinary moment. The great whirling disc of the Oss's body seems almost out of control, and indeed, the crowds have to defend themselves by steering it away from doing serious damage with its thick oak frame, under whose black skirts maidens will soon be gathered, to emerge flustered, red-faced but exhilarated. Girls scream with both delight and terror as it drunkenly reels and lunges towards them. Will they be caught by the Oss and subjected to its wild and frenetic rite of spring? Inside, a burly youth gyrates with all his might, sweat stinging his eyes so that he could not see even if the mask did not obscure his vision. The tall conical head evokes ancient witchery, with its wild tassled mane flashing coloured ribbons in a strange and urgent frenzy. The mask is dragon-like and nothing whatever like a horse. One moment it appears fearsome and threatening, the next smiling and benign.

Is this just some quaint rite that gives expression to pent-up emotions as winter becomes a memory and summer returns? Or does it signify something more? The whirling Oss is the most dramatic and extraordinary thing about the entire spectacle, and suggests a memory of the cosmology of the spinning cycles of the sun, earth and universe—Creation itself. Why else does it call so strongly to some atavistic instinct? The mesmeric beating of the drum suddenly stops, the Oss sinks down and everyone is stilled as the slow strains of an eldritch lament evoke a melancholic mood. The Oss is dead, and a low dirge lamenting his demise is sung: *'Oh where is St George, where is he-o? He's out in his longboat all on the salt sea-o!'*

A collective mourning sweeps through the crowd, moving some to stifle back the tears. There is a pause, the air charged with the fizz of expectation. Suddenly, alarmingly, the crowd erupts into ecstatic shouts as the Oss leaps up to resume its wild dervish-like dance, bringing with it a surge of fresh emotion that is filled with vital energy. Everyone feels uplifted as the Oss is reborn, and with it a sense of profound belonging, a sharing of that primal energy that somehow connects us with our ancestral roots. Then the resonant banging of the drum breaks out, the accordion players pump their squeeze-boxes, the singers strike up, and a great wave of joy sweeps away all shadows. The Teazer is teazing, the Oss is spinning, the air is charged with a joyous celebration of Life, and Summer is come!

Can this powerful evocation of the dying and rising forces of Life be anything other than a dramatic rite of the regeneration of Old Gods?

On the edge of the steeply-wooded valley of the River Esk a few miles south of Edinburgh stands one of the most enigmatic of all medieval Gothic buildings. Reputedly built by the Knights Templar, the legends and air of mystery that surround this remote chapel have spawned many theories and much speculation: Is the true Stone of Destiny concealed within? Is the Holy Grail buried beneath its flagstone floor? Or even the Ark of the Covenant? Is the head of Christ himself secreted within its richly-ornamented interior? Or secret scrolls dug from the vaults of Solomon's Temple at Jerusalem by the Templars? The outside of the building bristles with flamboyant pinnacles, flying buttresses, gargoyles and other more inscrutable carvings that all add to the mystery of the place.

Yet it is only when one enters through the deeply set doorway that the true magnificence of Rosslyn Chapel becomes apparent. It is like stepping into a different world. It is a world that takes the breath away with the opulence of its decoration. But this is not embellishment for its own sake; the lavish carvings in white stone that cover the interior are full of variety and profound esoteric symbolism. It is a treasure-trove of the arcane and magical that has no equal in Europe. Angels are sculpted from the columns and walls, many seemingly engaged in ritualistic activities, impossibly ornate bosses hang from the arches like pendulous incrustations, and strange eyes peer out from every corner, along with figures of men and women telling some story that has long been forgotten.

A macabre dance of death runs around one of the arches, with a procession of skeletons taunting the living. Yet the joyousness of the hundreds of other carvings speak of vibrant life in all its myriad complexity. Dozens of different plants are depicted, trailing like stone creepers across arches and capitals. Many tantalise the imagination. What are cacti and Indian maize doing here in a Scottish chapel?

The carvings exhibit a striking vivacity that is rarely encountered in church decoration. Their liveliness has a hypnotic effect, as if they sing to a part of the mind that recognises the power of symbols. A veritable orchestra of angelic musicians pluck and blow their instruments with such enthusiasm that the entire place seems to resonate with rich music that is just, but only just, out of reach. Horns, viols, pipes, harps, all are depicted with characteristic flair to remind us that such places were once not silent and sombre, as so often today, but filled with the love of life that music represents. One particularly lively angel plays the bagpipes from the top of a column deeply incised with stone greenery. Either side, half-hidden in the luxuriant growth, are two Green Men, with strands of foliage curling from their mouths. Another, impishly grinning from a protruding boss between two altars, looks down directly at the observer, as if challenging any preconceptions we may hold. These Green Men are everywhere within the interior of the building, in astonishing diversity. They are usually thought to represent the pagan Nature God of fertility and regeneration. Curious, then, that this small Christian chapel at Rosslyn has the largest number of Green Men found in any medieval building.

Another recurring image in this welter of the stonemason's extravagance is equally intriguing, for yet again it is challenging to modern notions of what Christianity means. Crawling from the columns and darkened recesses are a menagerie of dragons. It is obvious at once that the great majority of these are in no way satanic, for their expressions are disconcertingly benign. Dragons' heads form the main feature of many lintels, their mouths gaping open and spilling forth great wreaths of serpentine foliage. These are not creatures of evil and retribution: they are symbols of the renewal of the natural world, for they breathe forth the Breath of Life.

Within this wondrous netherworld, which seems to have drawn its original inspiration from some sacred grove with its luxuriant forested columns and drooping boughs, is an extraordinary work of art. A large pillar, known as

the Apprentice Pillar, stands out as the focus for the entire building. So called because of its legend of a murdered apprentice (widely believed to indicate initiation rituals used in Templarism and Freemasonry) it commands the attention by the exquisite nature of its ornate carving. Around the base are eight intertwined dragons. From the mouths of four of them issue vine-like branches which sweep up around the pillar to grow into a fourfold spiral of rich foliage.

Green Dragons?

On the northern edge of the Quantock Hills in Somerset stands Shervage Wood, once part of a dense forest that covered the region in prehistoric times. Lying here and there, fallen trees make comfortable resting places for wanderers as they wend their way homewards amongst the leafy paths. But take care. Twilight descends and curious rustlings are heard; odd noises that sound vaguely unnatural. Did something move in the shadows? Was that a twig breaking?

Travellers who find themselves in this woodland as night falls can perhaps be forgiven for feeling a little nervous. For Shervage Wood is the site of one of the many thousands of dragon legends that are to be found thickly populating folklore and mythology across the world. The Shervage Dragon, or 'Great Vurm' in the local dialect, was said to have had a girth greater than three oak trees, and also a considerable appetite. It slept by day with its great body coiled around an old earthwork, but at twilight it awoke and began to search the woods for prey. Villagers began to notice that their sheep and ponies were going missing. A shepherd and two gypsies who had approached the Vurm's lair whilst gathering bilberries, for which the woods were famous, were never seen again. Everyone avoided the area, including the deer and rabbits who moved to a nearby hill.

One old lady from the neighbouring village of Crowcombe, who made her living selling bilberry pies, feared that if she could no longer gather berries, she would herself starve. No-one could be persuaded to venture anywhere near Shervage until a stranger from Stogumber, about three miles away, appeared, and, apparently ignorant of the lurking dragon, agreed to go and find some ripe berries, or 'worts'. The Crowcombe woman gave him some cider, bread and cheese in return, and he set off in search of the fruits of the forest. The folklorist Katherine Briggs, as she chatted to the locals about the legend, recorded an amusing version of this old story in the days when every conversation with countryfolk was in traditional dialect and laced with wit and good humour:

'Being a Stogumber stranger he wasn't used to Quantock Hills and by the time he'd a-walked into Shervage Wood and seed a wonderful fine lot of worts on the way, he were feeling 'twere quite time for his cider. He'd just got nicely started on his mummet when the log begins to squirmy under'n.

'Hold a bit!' says he picking up his axe. 'Thee do movey do thee? Take that then.' And he raised the axe and cut it in two and both ends of the log began to bleed. Then the one end it up and run as hard as it could go to Bilbrook and t'other end it runned to Kingston St Mary and since they two halves went t'wrong way to meet, the gurt vurm couldn't nowise grow together again so her died.

Folks down to Bilbrook, they call the place Dragon Cross and folk to Kingston St Mary, they boasts about the same old tale of a fiery dragon—might be as they got the head end of our gurt vurm—but he were all Quantock to start with.'

The woodsman, on his return with a large hatful of wild berries, naturally mentioned that he had experienced a bit of bother with a dragon. Feigning surprise, the woman said she wondered why no-one had mentioned it to him. They had, replied the woodsman, but they had been from Crowcombe, and everyone knew that they were liars!

Crowcombe Church, raised on its ancient mound, is fairly typical of many Westcountry churches except that it still possesses a fine collection of Jacobean bench ends, which have miraculously survived the passage of the years. Once, almost every old church would have had such a collection, carved by local men whose skill in depicting the folklore of the locality provided an important link with pre-literate times. Unfortunately the great majority of such bench ends and rood screens were ripped out and burnt by Victorian restorers, so depriving future generations of a glimpse into the mythological folk art which their ancestors had grown up with. At Crowcombe, however, this link is still there. The carved oak panels, darkened by the centuries, depict striking images. On one, a double-headed winged dragon rises out of the forest and is being speared by two naked men in what must be one of the best-preserved images of its type. A few feet away another bench end has carved upon it a Green Man with branches loaded with berries exuding from his gaping mouth and two club-wielding figures rising from his head. Another depicts a lively Green Man with tendrils coming from his mouth and draconic creatures issuing from his ears.

Were the Green Men and Dragons merely childish stories invented by credulous countryfolk? Or could they allude to something more, some archaic understanding that has, in the modern world, been almost entirely forgotten?

Old Cairo, as it is known today, is an outlying area of the sprawling city that has long since taken its name. Now a run-down collection of ancient churches and narrow alleyways, it was once a great centre of Egyptian religion, referred to in the Bible as On. It was later called Babylon, for it was recorded by the classical historian Diodorus Siculus that around 2000 BC prisoners from the great Mesopotamian capital found their way here and erected a fortress. Persians and Romans were also to leave their marks, but perhaps the most intriguing thing about the place is a long-standing tradition that the Holy Family, Joseph, Mary and Jesus, sought refuge here when they were driven out of Israel during the time of Herod.

Old Cairo is also called Coptic Cairo, after the earliest form of Christianity that was the transmitter of much Egyptian religion from Pharaonic times. Many of the myths from the earliest centuries parallel those of the old gods of the previous millennia, for in the Coptic Church we find a richness of mythology and symbolism that comes from very ancient times indeed.

Through an entrance in the old walls of the Roman fortress and down a narrow dusty alleyway stands the Convent of St George, set back from a small courtyard garden behind a gate over which is a figure of the illustrious saint taunting a dragon. It is a lofty building reputed to be at least 1000 years old. One immediately senses an intense energy and atmosphere. The enormous wooden doors decorated with carved panels are thought to have belonged to the original building, and inside is a beautifully painted ceiling from the 15th century.

Entering this place is a strange experience. The sound of a Coptic priest intoning a prayer floats above the haunting tones of singing nuns, rising and falling in spine-tingling cadences. This is accompanied by the rather alarming noise of rattling chains. Here, a devotee of St George is undergoing one of the most curious rituals of Christendom.

Within a small shrine the pious devotee has an iron collar around his neck, fixed to the wall by a chain. It is claimed by the 30 or so nuns who live here that it was part of the original torture equipment when St George was being persecuted by the Emperor Diocletian. Worn shiny by continuous use, it looks anything but antique.

Nevertheless, they claim that the blood of St George ran over the chain and collar, that many miracles have been observed after their use, that evil spirits are driven out of those who are possessed, and that the spirit of St George is here. An old, wrinkled nun clutching a crucifix unlocks a door to an inner sanctum, ushering a lone penitent within for special prayers. Another removes a rich red velvet bag embroidered with an image of the saint from an adjacent wooden shrine, apparently containing relics, and touches it against the forehead of a small child. Icons of the saint are everywhere, glowing in the reflected candlelight within the twilit shrine. One in particular is prominently displayed, and this tells an unfamiliar version of the myth. A young boy, called after the saint, is being attacked by a serpent. His parents had prayed to St George after being unable to conceive, and God had granted them a son. The saint himself is mounted on his white charger, and tickling a dragon's tongue with the point of his spear. The painting is surrounded by a flowing, voluminous design of greenery, vine leaves heavy with grapes.

Is St George here, in this great centre of ancient religion, more than a saint and healer? Is he the embodiment of something much older than Christianity, an old god deeply connected with fertility?

*St George as a central figure in British Mythology, by George Cruickshank, from Thomas Keightley's **Fairy Mythology**, 1850.*

1

A Legend Obscured

here to start our quest for the truth behind the story of St George? To begin at the very beginning would certainly prove a difficult and taxing task, impossible even, for he has undergone such revolutionary changes over so many centuries that we may not initially recognise him for who he really is. Better, perhaps, to start from where we are now, with our understanding, limited though it may be, firmly rooted in the received wisdom. Then, page by page, age by age, we will gradually penetrate the mystery, and see how the traditions have been adapted according to the demands of each time, reflecting the prevailing attitudes and needs of humanity.

So we will begin at the end, and cast around for information that might naturally present itself before anyone wishing to start such a quest. The first and most obvious place to begin would therefore be to go to any reasonably well-stocked bookshelf and consult one or more of the numerous standard works that mention the famous saint and his exploits. These are invariably based upon official biographies that have been carefully (but sometimes exceedingly carelessly) compiled by the early Church scribes, those in the hot dusty regions where the stories are set and those who later copied them in the dark candle-flickering scriptoria of medieval monasteries.

A short study of these sources will quickly lead us to the conclusion that there is far more to ponder on than might appear at first sight, and will set us wondering how and why such a figure could gather around him such an intriguing body of lore. For on the face of it, St George was merely one of the many early converts to Christianity who directly challenged the prevailing paganism of Rome, paying with his life. Indeed, in the earliest accounts, especially if we read between the lines, there is little to suggest that he was anything other than a classic martyr, even though his early life is unashamedly embellished by the enthusiastic zeal of the official writers. This can leave the enquirer with a curious nagging feeling of dissatisfaction. Questions immediately arise, and we are confronted by an enigma right at the very beginning: how did a man who died for his beliefs so suddenly ascend to virtual godhood, becoming the illustrious hero of so many nations and such diverse countries? The list of places of which he has become the spiritual protector could fill many pages. Perhaps most famous as the heroic champion of the Crusader Knights, he has become the patron saint of so many states, including England and other places far removed from his Middle Eastern roots, that he appears to us as a universal figure, omnipresent throughout a great area of the world.

Wherever we travel, we find the image of St George before us. Some of the earliest churches, such as the ancient Coptic and Greek monasteries in Jerusalem, as well as other examples scattered all over the Middle East, speak of his ancient and enduring popularity. When searching for the remains of the True Cross the Empress Helena erected a church dedicated to him near the Holy Sepulchre in 326 AD, the traditional site of the entombment of Jesus Christ. Countless cities, towns and villages are also under his protection and guidance, for he became the special guardian of the Byzantine Empire and eventually the whole Roman Church.

The Oxford Dictionary of Saints tells us that George died in 303 AD, tortured and killed by the Emperor Diocletian as the Roman Empire sought to defend itself against the spread of Christianity. He was, according to classical tradition, born into a wealthy family in the Roman city of Diospolis, the local centre of the worship of Jove, known as Lydda in Aramaic. This place, situated in the midst of the green plains of Sharon, just over 20 miles from Jerusalem, had been an important centre from remote antiquity, renowned for its fertility, and was known as 'The Garden of Palestine' in the Arabian world. Extensive vineyards, groves of olives, figs, pomegranates and a host of other fruits were in abundance, and seemingly there was no more fertile place in the Middle East to sow the seed of the legend of St George.

According to the body of work known as the 'Encomiums', Coptic texts translated by E.A.Wallis Budge[1] (former keeper of Egyptian and Assyrian Antiquities at the British Museum), George's father was originally from Cappadocia in modern-day Turkey. He had risen to become the wealthy governor of Palestine, but died when George was just 10 years old. The owner of considerable hordes of gold and silver, hundreds of servants, vast herds of cattle and flocks of sheep, the family's great riches and reputation for good works reads like a fairy tale. In fact the entire mythology of St George follows on in the same vein; perhaps we may begin to appreciate even at this stage the blossoming literary skills of the early Church propagandists. The manuscripts, without question, were compiled centuries after the events referred to apparently took place, and even so had been translated from Greek, so it is entirely natural that certain aspects of the tales would have been enhanced for popular consumption.

The Coptic texts tell us that the new Governor of Palestine was an exceedingly pious man who, having heard of the boy's situation, sent for him, showered him with kisses and wept deeply for the death of his father. His mother, a native of Palestine, was beseeched to hand George over so that he might become his adopted son. Later, even at such a tender age, George was despatched with a hundred soldiers to the King, who was so impressed with his bearing and character that he immediately appointed him General over 5000 men and granted him a generous salary, plus expenses. Celebrations ensued; the charmed life of the handsome young George continued with much pomp and feasting, to which the whole city was invited. The poor, especially widows and orphans, received gifts of money, and the people of Lydda praised their great good fortune in having such a worthy champion. At the age of 20 George was said to be one of the strongest and most valiant soldiers in the entire region; *'And the Grace of God was with him, and He gave him such beauty and strength that all those that saw him marvelled at his power and youth'.*[2] When in battle, he only had to declare who he was and his enemies' weapons miraculously fell from their hands, at which point he vanquished them mercilessly and carried off the spoils.

Surprisingly, almost nothing of George's later military career and exploits appears to be recorded in the extant manuscripts. What a story they might have told considering the wondrous events of his earlier life. It is left for us to surmise that he would probably have taken a key role in the Egyptian and Persian wars, which are generally well documented, yet strangely no mention is made of George's involvement. We could also hazard that it was entirely possible he could have travelled to Britain during this time, for military leaders of such brilliant genius and overwhelming popularity would almost certainly have toured the other hotspots of the Roman Empire.

Everyone might have lived happily ever after if it had not been for the fateful edict by Diocletian in 303 AD to exterminate Christians throughout the crumbling Empire. We are told that his orders caused such consternation in George's heart that he immediately laid down his arms, returned to Lydda, freed his slaves, sold all his possessions and distributed his vast fortune to the needy. He then prepared to challenge Diocletian directly, and set off for Nicodemia, on the south shores of the Bosphorus, which the Emperor had made his capital.

Appearing in front of Diocletian and Galerius, (who is noted in the Coptic texts as particularly cruel and ruthless), along with 69 other governors in the Roman Basilica, George detailed the nobility of his birth and how both he and his father had always been Christians. His plea for them to cancel the edict unsurprisingly fell on deaf ears. Instead, he was offered rulership over ten cities if only he would accept the pagan faith.

The narrative continues with glowing accounts of George's character:
'And what are the qualities of this brave soldier of Christ, Saint George? His upright and unwavering faith in God; his certain hope; his sincere love; his compassion for every one and the whole human race; his gentleness to all creatures, both great and small; his benignity; his goodness; his zeal; his patient endurance of the cares of this life; his good disposition and the joy of his soul; the blamelessness of his heart and his taking his stand at the tribunal boldly...'[3]

Another Encomium, this time written by Andrew of Crete, tells of the inevitable outcome when George is summoned for a last time before the tribunal and refuses to bow to their demands. On the sentence of death he prays for his persecutors before suffering a week of the cruellest torture culminating in his beheading on April 23rd 304 AD. Ironically, a year later Diocletian abdicated and war against the Christians ceased.

An account said to have been written by his servant Pasikrates also tells of these final days. Entrusted with the mortal remains of George, Pasikrates prepared a tomb, but the fortunate appearance of a merchant ship at Jaffa gave them the opportunity to take the body back to the place of George's birth and fulfil his last wish to be buried in his home city. Amidst much weeping and marvelling at the story of how he challenged the authorities and withstood terrible tortures, George was laid first in his old house, and then buried in a simple shrine at a nearby church.

And so the story apparently gathered such a remarkable momentum that it was to result in George becoming something far greater than simply a 'local hero'. He was soon to be transformed into a world-renowned inspirational figure whose mythology created a saintly aura of universal truth and courage, a character that was now to step out of the fairy tale and leap into even greater mythical dimensions. He was set to become the great archetypal hero of a new incoming religion, second only to Jesus Christ.

Old Gods, New Gods

It may seem surprising to us today, in a world rent by religious sectarianism, that until the early 4th century Christians and pagans had co-existed harmoniously alongside other religious traditions; they frequently lived side-by-side, honouring each other's beliefs and convictions. Mithraism was the principle state religion ever since a declaration by the Emperor Aurelian in 274, but all forms of paganism were tolerated, creating an inclusive belief system that accepted virtually every god and goddess as aspects of the Divine. Thus Christian, pagan, Jew and Arab were merely followers of the same all-encompassing God/Goddess, seen through different eyes and cultural backgrounds. The churches and temples were full of their respective worshippers, intermarriage was common, and some of the highest born, including the emperor Diocletian's wife and daughter, were followers of the new Christian faith.

But then, as now, there were undercurrents of hostility between rival factions, especially those of a subversive nature who wished to challenge the oppressive Roman rule. There were plots and counter-plots, and a number of soldiers were executed. Then a conspiracy against Galerius (who was the real author of the fearsome Christian persecutions later continued by Diocletian) suddenly brought swift and relentless retribution that was to shatter the peace between the different religions. All soldiers were required to make sacrifices to the pagan gods, and on 23rd February 303 AD the Praetorian Guard unexpectedly destroyed the Cathedral of Nicodemia, burning all the holy books. The next day Christian gatherings were banned forthwith, and all churches and scriptures ordered to be destroyed. Any Christians were immediately removed from official positions and deprived of citizenship, and a wave of destruction swept through the empire. The persecution engulfed the furthermost regions, including Britain, where a number of devout followers were killed, including St Alban.

This is the backdrop that the official account of the martyrdom of St George is set against. The chronicler and Bishop of Caesarea, Eusebius, records in his version that immediately after the edict to destroy Christian churches and books was displayed, a certain high-ranking official in the district of Lydda (named after the Hebrew King Lod or Ludd) tore it down and destroyed it in public. In Roman soldier's armour, he is said to have stormed into the Temple of Bacchus and thrown down the god's statue. Unrepentant, and stubbornly refusing to honour the pagan gods, he was arrested forthwith and dragged before the authorities. Imprisonment and torture only increased his determination, and he bore both with a calmness of mind that impressed itself upon all present. He was finally executed on April 23rd, and so the official legend of the heroic St George began, with his feast day eventually incorporated into the Christian calendar. He was also given the epithet 'The Rose of Sharon'.

There is, though, one surprising inconsistency in this record. Eusebius, under whose jurisdiction Lydda came, whilst mentioning that this independently-minded soldier was the first to be martyred in this district (and therefore of particular significance) does not refer to him by name. This seems very curious. Why, we may find ourselves asking, if the details of George's life as recorded in the Encomiums are so definite, does one of the foremost chroniclers of the time (and generally considered to be one of the most reliable) not give his name?

The 4th century was a critical time for the Roman Empire. The reality was that it was in a process of steady disintegration, having expanded and centralised to a degree that it was unwieldy and increasingly impossible to govern. Roman military might was being challenged on many fronts, and there was an urgent need to consolidate the sprawling Roman world. How to do this? It would take the brilliant genius of a military general who rose to become Emperor, Constantine the Great, to formulate the solution. It was at once an audacious and original idea: to create a state religion.

This was not as difficult as might be imagined from our modern perspective, for both early Christianity and paganism shared much in common, having grown from universally extant traditions of great antiquity. The great Mystery religions of pre-Christian times were based on a number of central issues; among them were the cyclic nature of the seasons which bring fertility to the Earth, and the mystery of human spiritual awakening, symbolised by the birth of the divine child within. The Mithraic and Dionysian religions were replete with such symbolism, rooted in prehistory and yet readily adapted to a new emphasis. Thus Mithras, the Sun God, was born at the Midwinter Solstice, and his successor Jesus Christ now took over the role. The fragmenting Roman Empire was thus to find its salvation in a new creed that would eventually create the greatest bureaucracy the world had ever seen, imposing its strictures not just by force of arms, but through more subtle means, the control of hearts and minds through the religious impulse.

Constantine became a Christian himself after a vision; shortly before the decisive battle with Maxentius at the Mulvian Bridge he dreamt he saw a great shining cross of gold in the sky, across which was written 'By this sign you will conquer'. This is usually interpreted as being a Christian symbol, yet it was also a sign of Sol Invictus, the Invincible Sun, a pagan Mithraic cult widespread throughout the region. This story was seized upon by the early Church as a divine revelation that the new religion was to sweep the Empire, and was accordingly heavily publicised as the point at which paganism was replaced by official Christianity.

One of Constantine's first acts upon coming to power was to grant toleration to all Christians in the edict of Milan, 313. The following year he held a synod at Arles attended by bishops from throughout the Empire. It was at this council he proposed that the martyred George of Lydda be chosen as the model saint of the fledgling state religion. George was canonized, and referred to as the 'Champion Knight of Christendom' or 'The Victorious One', a hero figure worthy of the new political and religious world view. George's future mantle of 'Victory' seems to have derived specifically from Constantine's own favourite appellation of 'Constantinus Victorus', thus linking Saint and Emperor in a way that would remind everyone that they had both fought for the Christian ideal.

Whether we see in this the zeal of a genuine religious convert or the machinations of a politician is a matter of interpretation or personal belief. Even Constantine's sycophantic court historian expressed his doubts about the much-publicised vision. It seems clear that Constantine was motivated by political considerations as much as visions of flaming crosses in the sky, for his grand strategy was nothing less than to forge a new imperial order, military, economic, political and spiritual. It was in 325 at the Council of Nicaea (Greek for 'Victory'), a prosperous Hellenistic city 80 miles from Istanbul, that Constantine, in an ill-tempered discussion that drew much opposition from the assembled bishops, ordered them to fall in line. Many of them had been previously tortured for their faith, having had their eyes plucked out, or otherwise maimed. Eusebius, an eyewitness, commented on how his fellow bishops were fearful at the 'glint of arms' as they went about their business, the memories of their recent sufferings at the hands of Constantine's soldiers still all too vivid.

On the Emperor's arrival he was handed a bundle of objections to his plans: dressed like a Persian king in silk robes and jewel-encrusted shoes, he threw them into a burning brazier and ordered his bishops to accept a uniform doctrine that would profoundly affect all aspects of life for many centuries to come. He introduced Sunday as a day of rest (something that would appeal to the Sun-worshippers as well as the followers of Christ), and also unified the calendar, settling once and for all the disruptive question of when Easter should fall. This question, one of the most divisive of its times amongst the various sects, had come about because no-one at the time had thought to write down exactly when Jesus had died. Constantine's new world order said that henceforth it was to fall on the first Sunday after the first full moon after the Equinox, but never at the beginning of the Jewish Passover in order to make a clear distinction between the faiths. He himself wrote that 'By the unanimous judgement of all it has been decided that the most holy festival of Easter should be everywhere celebrated on the same day'.[4]

In like vein, the sacred writings from antiquity were to be heavily edited and in many cases re-written by sympathetic authors whose brief was to denigrate or ignore pre-Christian religions in favour of the officially sanctioned state system, as personally approved by Constantine. The doctrine of reincarnation that was so important in early Gnostic Christianity was ignored completely.

Because of the total opposition of pagan Rome, Constantine was obliged to found a new capital, Constantinople, which became the heart of the Byzantine Empire, and the seeds of spiritual dominance were sown for more than sixteen centuries throughout the western world. Christianity, founded on timeless principles derived from former mythologies, was to become in many ways a fearsome tool of oppression very similar to the regime it replaced, as well as the world's first centralised religion, eventually to touch every corner of the Empire. Opinions vary about the benefits of this, with some regarding it as a great leap forward in humanity's development. Others consider it to have been the greatest political scam in history.

The new system demanded that the credibility of the incoming religion was buttressed by as many pagan elements as possible. In this way the entire edifice of previous beliefs and practices was converted, stage by stage, to one that supported Constantine's vision. Many former pagan gods and goddesses were assigned new roles, often by a subtle change of spelling or the introduction of the prefix 'saint'. The old temples were adapted or rebuilt as churches so that worship could carry on as before, as were the rites, centred on the formerly Dionysian and Mithraic observances of eating the god's body, in the form of bread, and drinking his blood, in the form of wine.

Another essential requirement was to introduce some popular characters to the new religion, to absorb the pantheon of pagan gods and goddesses that had been worshipped for centuries across many diverse lands. Constantine, who became King of Britain and Emperor of Rome in 306 AD, just three years after the death of the Roman soldier referred to by Eusebius, proceeded to build a magnificent church at Lydda to honour the heroic martyr. Could this have been the time that the name George was first definitively linked to the nameless character mentioned by the Bishop of Caesarea? We seem confronted by two distinct possibilities. Firstly, that Eusebius was particularly badly informed about significant events in his own diocese, or was unaware of the name of an important Roman general who had already become famous in his homeland. The second possibility is that Constantine found it particularly expedient to create a new myth in which the central hero was given the name George. If this was the case, then there would have been a compelling reason.

A Magnificent Shrine

And so the roots of the official version of the life and death of St George began to take hold. Fostered by official patronage, many different versions of the stories began to circulate, and the cult soon spread across the region. Churches were built as far away as Armenia, with others springing up in Syria, Mesopotamia and Egypt. Constantine himself was believed to have built no less than 21, none of which have survived.

After George's body was said to have been interred at Lydda (by a member of his close family called Andrew), his relics apparently began to undergo that curious process common to such artefacts, whether fragments of the True Cross or the bones of saints. They began to magically multiply to fulfil the demands of those bishops who believed that some physical relic would bring more business their way.

The attendant miracles also became ever more wondrous, and eventually his head was removed to Rome to be preserved as one of the foremost relics of Christendom, until it was lost, only to be rediscovered again in 751 AD (although during this time a prominent bulge in the church at Lydda was also pointed out to pilgrims as concealing the saint's head). The original simple church created by his family on the site of his tomb was later rebuilt in grandiose style by Constantine, becoming a great centre of pilgrimage as George's fame began to spread.

The earliest account is by the pilgrim Theodosius, in about the year 530 (that is, over two centuries after George's death), who referred to 'many wonders being wrought'. By the 8th century the chronicler Adamnan was describing this richly decorated building along with its magnificent marble statue of the saint, and it was being visited by a great number of devotees. The city eventually changed its name to St George, with other ports along the coast adopting his special guardianship. By this time the great hero was known for his protective powers over the maritime realms too, as wielding a power 'from whom all demons of the deep, all monsters of storm and flood shrank back in dread'.[5]

Across Europe during this time the cult of St George became a vehicle for the expansion of the new religion, and the *Martyrology* of the Venerable Bede records him in several early records from this period, centuries before the various eponymous *Acts* were written in Greek, Latin, Armenian, Coptic, Syriac, Ethiopian and Turkish. With Constantine's enthusiastic support for someone who had been a great champion of early Christianity, St George had quickly become one of the most popular figures in the new state religion, and received official sanction throughout the Empire. Within a few hundred years he had swept to widespread fame across the Roman and Byzantine world.

The remains of the old church at Lydda.
From a photograph taken in 1875.

The church itself, destroyed first by Persian invaders and then by the Saracens three hundred years after its construction, was in total ruin when the Crusaders, under Godfroi de Bouillon, one of the founding fathers of the Knights Templar, reached Lydda in 1099. There is much mystery surrounding the beginnings of the Templars, as well as the true reasons for the Crusades themselves. Godfroi was accompanied by Peter the Hermit, who was linked to a mysterious group of monks from Calabria, and was one of the first to call for a Crusade. It was as if they knew a great secret, and had to capture Jerusalem for some purpose beyond the usual political reasons.

But when they arrived at Lydda, Godfroi, whose brother Baldwin was later to be crowned King of Jerusalem by a shadowy group of nobles, was amazed to discover that the sepulchre of the saint was untouched. After celebrating a festival to him they installed St George as their patron saint in recognition of his miraculous intervention at the recent siege of Antioch. At this battle, the saint was said to have appeared and aided them to victory carrying the red cross banner which was to become their own special symbol of courage and victory.

The destroyed church of Constantine was, according to Crusader chroniclers, later rebuilt by Richard the Lionheart, and by long-standing tradition repaired with oak from the English royal forests until the time of Edward VI, but even this is now long gone. The last remaining fragments were captured in rare photographs taken by the Palestine Exploration Society in 1875 before it vanished forever.

Anyone visiting the site of St George's tomb today will probably be greatly disappointed unless they happen to be there during one of the times of pilgrimage, when the adjacent mosque is filled with devotees. The area around it is desolate and run-down; nothing stirs except mendicant dogs and the odd face peering out of a cracked window. Seemingly the local people are so unused to visitors that the appearance of a lone pilgrim creates a bewildered curiosity and some surprise that anyone should wish to come to such a remote and inhospitable place. The heat of the afternoon sun beats down on a place that has an unmistakable air of dereliction; gone are the palm trees that would once have provided welcome shade, gone is the magnificence of one of Christianity's most treasured places of pilgrimage. Can this really be the same place, once frequented by emperors and kings, the object of so much devotion down the centuries?

The Greek church that now dominates the place is plain and unassuming; only an image of St George over the door gives a clue to the former significance of the site. It is locked, but knocking at a door opposite elicits the appearance of a parchment-faced nun, who blinks as if disturbed from an afternoon snooze. She unlocks the door and inside is the vague smell of incense, and some pictures of the saint. Nothing impresses the senses with the one-time importance of this place, and the atmosphere is distinctly gloomy.

In a small crypt beneath the church is the tomb itself; unassumingly cut from marble and almost as plain and uninteresting as its surroundings. Is this really the resting place of one of Christendom's most famous saints, who has become the patron of so many nations and the inspiration of generations of nobly-minded individuals? A Greek priest appears, makes the sign of the cross, stands silently for a few minutes, and vanishes as quickly as he appeared.

The once-miraculous aura of St George is nowhere to be found. His shrine is desolate, the spirit has flown, its energy dissipated.

Other St Georges?

Even though Constantine did everything in his power to publicise his own version of St George, it is apparent that certain other figures in history also laid claim to his fame. In fact it seems there has been considerable disagreement in the past amongst chroniclers and historians as to who exactly was the original St George. The historical veracity of such a character is therefore much disputed, and scholars have tied themselves up in labyrinthine knots trying to establish the truth or otherwise of the various claims. Such is the confusion that even in relatively recent centuries there has been disagreement about his origins.

Edward Gibbon, in the *Decline and Fall of the Roman Empire*, comes to a very different conclusion than that promulgated by Constantine. He has St George as an Arian Archbishop of Alexandria, who rose from lowly conditions to become a rich and ambitious man with precious few of the heroic qualities we would associate with the illustrious saint.

A one-time purveyor of army provisions, he had, through guile and fraud, become so wealthy that his corruption caused his enemies to threaten his life, and he took refuge in Cappadocia. There he became an Arian Christian, a member of an heretical sect that denied the equality of Christ with God. They eventually became powerful enough to undermine Constantine's ideas for a Roman state religion. It is one of those curious turns of fate that if the Council of Nicea had resulted in a different outcome, this 'heresy' would have become orthodoxy, and consequently our view of Christian belief very different indeed.

As Archbishop this particular George plundered the temples and taxed the people heavily whatever their religion, until he was forced from power and imprisoned. Murdered by an angry mob, his body was paraded through the streets and then thrown into the sea. Can this really be the George who has come down to us as a hero of both royalty and the common man, a semi-divine figure who inspires courage and brings natural justice to prevail? It seems very unlikely. Chronology bears this out, for the date of his murder was 362 AD, whereas churches such as those at Ezra in Syria bear a dedication to St George from 346, sixteen years earlier. Was Gibbon hopelessly mistaken? Even his own biographer believes he was, and yet the great historian seemed convinced.

Perhaps we should not be too surprised at the level of scholarly angst in this particular case. It serves to illustrate the level of confusion that surrounds the subject, even amongst those who have studied it in depth. This is not simply a modern phenomenon. Disagreement amongst Church authorities has been a hallmark of the George question.[6] Even Alfric, Archbishop of York in the 11th century, in his poem *The Passion of St George* referred to this baffling state of affairs. In the opening lines he wrote that one of the reasons for his work was to 'preserve the faithful' from the various heretical accounts circulating within the Church of his day; 'Misbelievers have written misbelief in their books...'

Since that time, these heresies have been progressively eradicated from the official manuscripts until only the orthodox version remains. One of the most curious things about looking at the origins of St George is how often totally different characters and stories appear to have attached themselves to the legend. There is a plausible reason for this, as we will presently discover. Legend-making is, besides other things, a political art. Whatever characteristics may be useful to the desired objective are readily absorbed to create an amalgam of ideas that can be very difficult to disentangle. There are in reality many St Georges, who all appear to have taken on the mantle of local saints and pagan heros. Consequently there are a number of candidates historically who may attract our gaze, yet they all hark back to something deeper, some underlying enigma at the root of the mystery. The question we are left with after looking at the official accounts is surely why should a Roman soldier (a common theme throughout Christian hagiography) become one of the most prominent saints in Christendom, and the great hero of so many countries? Tradition also tells of St Demetrius who was said to have been a friend with the Roman George, and martyred at about the same time, yet he is obscure by comparison. What was it about St George that gave him such power?

A Course in Miracles

As Constantine's cult of St George grew and developed, so did the stories that attended his martyrdom. In the 6th century the Greek *Acts*, and two hundred years later their Latin equivalent, both dwelt heavily upon the inhuman tortures he was forced to endure, and even more heavily on his amazing powers of survival. In the medieval *Passions of St George* the most imaginative tortures are described in fabulously gruesome detail, yet George, The Victor, survives almost every one due to the intercession of supernatural help. As the folklorist Christina Hole notes:

'His body was broken on a wheel and restored to life by St Michael Archangel. He was transfixed by spears, crushed with heavy stones, buried in a cave, thrown into a well, and burnt by molten lead. He was hurled over a precipice in an iron box set with sharp nails, and roasted over a slow fire inside a brazen bull. His feet were shod with shoes of red-hot iron; he was cast into a pit of quicklime, beaten with sledge-hammers and forced to drink poison, as well as a draught intended to destroy his reason. From all these ordeals he emerged unscathed, not only alive but perfectly whole. His broken limbs were restored to their original state; the marks of burns and scourgings disappeared as soon as the punishment was ended, and all his wounds were immediately healed. Only when God permitted it were his tormentors able to kill him, and they were given no time in which to enjoy their triumph. At the moment of his death his chief enemies were struck by lightning or, according to one version, swept away by a fiery whirlwind.'[7]

Clearly, George was an exceptionally holy character if we are to believe the legends, someone who could count on the help of God and his hierarchy to alleviate his suffering right until the end. Even accounting for the embroidery and fertile imagination of writers and storytellers, though, it begins to look as if we are dealing with no ordinary human being here. His attributes and influence would appear to exceed even that of a mythologized character, plucked from the pages of history and used for political propaganda. The Victorian chronicler of the *Lives of the British Saints* Sabine Baring-Gould pondered the records of George's miraculous ordeals and came to the conclusion that his trials were never meant to be anything other than mythic accounts. They were, he believed, later transformations of the various martyrdoms and resurrections that took place in the temples of Babylon and Assyria, symbolically re-enacting the sacred rites of Tammuz, the vegetation god who was continually reborn.[8]

The fabulous legends that cluster around the figure of St George cannot really be explained by the alleged historical facts. Already there is more than a suspicion that what we are trying to unravel here is a thread that takes us far beyond the limits of a story about a martyred Roman soldier, and leads us back to a time before those early centuries of Christianity in which these events are set. The miraculous nature of his ordeals echoes those of another order of being entirely, like so many pre-Christian myths, almost as if he were a God in his own right.

16th century woodcut from the frontispiece of Sir Thomas Malory's Le Morte d'Arthur

2

Lord of Sun and Earth

hroughout the myriad of images found in Christian iconography, St George is almost invariably depicted with a shining solar halo around his head. In the classic Mystery Wisdom this signifies two things. The first is that he represents the principle of the Sun, the life-giving force that nurtures all growth on the planet, and the second is that as a human representation of a god-like principle, he has achieved a level of consciousness where he is at one with nature.

These words are being written at dawn on St George's Day, April 23rd. The early morning mists that were wreathing the folds of the land as the first shades of daylight crept over the darkness are becoming transparent, revealing the shape of the blue-washed monochrome countryside. A bank of cloud appears on the horizon, out of which the ethereal ghostly figures of old trees emerge, their arms and frozen fingers raised skywards. From behind this is rising the effulgent orb of the Sun, as yet invisible, but whose presence is heralded by a luminous golden glow.

Now the Sun emerges from its cocoon of mist, which quite suddenly reclaims the sweeping fields, making the trees appear as if they are floating above the Earth. A rainbow halo is reflected in the moisture around the gathering intensity of the Sun as it slowly dances across the horizon. It leaves a strong after-image when the eyes are closed, ever-present in the mind. A few moments later it is impossible to gaze upon it, just like the Face of God. The land is bathed in glory. The shining Sun God has returned.

Those who feel moved to observe the Sun rising at certain times of the year, and especially at certain places, cannot fail to be deeply affected by the experience. They are without doubt some of the most intensely spiritual events of one's life; moments that somehow last forever in the inner recesses of the spirit. Particular days especially seem to possess a magical potency, and one can sense a mood of profound celebration at these times, as if the whole secret world of Nature rejoices. St George's Day is one of those moments in the Sun's annual cycle that speaks of a special mystery.

There can be no doubt that the ancient festivals practised for so many thousands of years were set at times when the Sun and the Earth have a special relationship; points in the annual cycle when the energetic influences between them are at their most potent. Solstices mark the high and low points of the year, and Equinoxes the times of balance, when light and dark are equal all over the world. Other festivals and celebrations each have their own characteristics. In former times they were determined by the priesthood who studied the heavens minutely. The early Christian Church naturally took over these special times, calling them after saints whose names often conceal immeasurably ancient roots. St George's Day is one of these. As Rudolf Steiner observed:

> 'Festivals are not merely the commemoration of historical events or personalities. They are in and of themselves, each year, spiritual events that grow and deepen with the developing phases of human evolution.'[1]

It may seem very curious, even amusing, to us today that in the 18th century, when the calendar was reformed and the Gregorian version introduced, there were riots in the streets of Britain. The common people, unschooled in the sophisticated concepts of Church elders, believed that eleven days were being stolen from them. Suddenly, it seemed to them, the Pope had issued an edict that deprived them of eleven days, shortening their lives accordingly and forcing them to pay eleven days extra rent. Across the land mobs gathered and shouted 'Give us back our eleven days'. In Bristol, people were killed during chaotic scenes. The Glastonbury Thorn, however, which was famous throughout the land for blossoming on Christmas Day, was noted as 'contemptuously ignoring the new style' when it 'burst into blossom on the 5th January, thus indicating that Old Christmas Day should alone be observed, in spite of an irreligious legislature.'[2]

It had been Constantine who had first laid down the agenda for a uniform calendar when he replaced the former traditional Roman one. It was supposed to have originally been invented by Romulus, the founder of Rome, and then adapted by his successors until Julius Caesar decided to stamp his authority on how time was measured. Through his infatuation with Cleopatra and Egypt Caesar was introduced to the great centres of learning as well as some of the greatest luminaries and philosophers of the time. When he returned to Rome in 47 BC he made one of his boldest attempts to centralise power by introducing the Julian calendar, demonstrating that, like a god, he was even capable of re-ordering time itself. This new time frame was based on the science of Ptolemaic Egypt, focused at the time around the academies and libraries of Alexandria, famous for its stargazers and astrologers. It had been Ptolemy III, in 236 BC, who had devised the system of three 365 day cycles, with a 'leap' year added every fourth one to compensate for the gradual drift of the Earth/Sun cycle.

Constantine, some three and a half centuries after Caesar, likewise realised the godlike power of ordering Time. At Nicea he fixed the time of Easter, introduced the seven-day week and moved the day of worship from Saturday, the Jewish Sabbat and the day of Saturn of the pagan world, to Sunday. He knew what priests and politicians have known from time immemorial; that the calendar was a potent political tool that governed festivals and religious holidays as well as market days and the cultural and legal framework of everyday life. The calendar was thus responsible for the efficient functioning of the economy as well as determining which days people could worship, affecting every aspect of existence.

Some twelve hundred years later, an even more fundamental change was to take place across the Roman Empire that was to throw it into utter confusion. On October 4th, 1562, by order of Pope Gregory, ten days were suddenly stolen from the calendar, and those that awoke the next day were understandably perturbed to have lost ten days of their lives as well as paying extra rent. In Frankfurt rioting mobs blamed mathematicians and the Pope for changing their saints' days, believing that the seasonal cycles of fertility would no longer operate as they had done for centuries.

In the end the Vatican's reforms were adopted only in a few countries, with Italy, Spain and Portugal losing their ten days outright, for opposition to Catholic control was gathering. Protestanism was growing across Europe, with independence being declared and wars fought against the Catholic tyranny. In Britain, Queen Elizabeth, at war with Spain, declined to co-operate and accept the will of Gregory, even though her advisor John Dee reckoned it scientifically valid. Although other European countries eventually adopted the changes because of threats and political pressure from Rome, Britain's independent status meant that it would be another 170 years before it fell into line, despite strident attempts to enforce it on an unwilling public. As Voltaire wryly observed, 'The English mob preferred their calendar to disagree with the Sun than to agree with the Pope.'[3]

Parliament eventually passed an Act on May 17th 1751 after Lord Stanhope convinced it that 'the Julian calendar was erroneous, and had overcharged the year with eleven days.' Eleven, because those already following the Gregorian way had not observed a leap year in 1700 and added the necessary day.

In early times, the festivals were determined by cosmology and the natural order of the heavens. Careful observation of the skies and the precise use of stone calendars, of which Stonehenge is the most famous example, was the core of the ancient wisdom. This gave the priesthood vast power to order their respective cultures, but there was a deeper purpose; to harmonise events on Earth with those in Heaven. *As above, So below.* In the Roman world the calendar had been determined by an alliance of priests and politicians in secret, which gave them great advantage over commercial transactions which were only permitted on certain days. In 304 BC this priestly monopoly on time had suddenly ended when Flavius, who was later elected to high office, stole a copy of the secret codes. He posted them in the middle of the Forum in public view, and thus ended a long tradition of the manipulation of Time. In contrast to the civilised Roman world, in other regions the progression of the Sun from Solstice to Solstice had always been observed and measured against the horizon. Each community had its 'Sun Temple' or stone circle that linked the people to the cosmic cycles of which they naturally felt a part. An endless round of religious celebrations, embedded into the annual rhythm, was at the core of earthly life.

The Gregorian calendar shift must have threatened this connection with nature in a way that we can hardly imagine. People felt that they were quite suddenly de-linked from these cosmic cycles, even though the real reason for the calendar's introduction was the exact opposite. In future, the days of special celebration, the saint's days, the times to sow and reap, were to be reckoned by the Church, and few would hereafter recognise their original function; that they were originally moments of cosmic significance in the heavenly drama of the cycle of life.

To reclaim this ancient understanding, we must also reclaim the knowledge of those eleven days that were 'stolen' by the Church authorities. When we begin to see the patterns that reconnect us with our true birthright as children of the Sun and Earth, we rediscover a wisdom that has been all but expunged in the modern world. One of the most illuminating examples of this is the curious story of the 11th of November, Armistice, or Remembrance Day. Another is the day allocated to St George.

November 11th, the day when fallen soldiers are remembered and honoured, is no arbitrary date. We can see that if the eleven days of the calendar shift are tracked back, we arrive at a very significant date indeed, October 31st, Hallowe'en, the Celtic Samhain. This is the time when traditionally the spirits of the dead can be most easily contacted, for the veil between this physical realm and the Otherworld is gossamer-thin, and communication between them can take place more naturally than at any other time of the year. In antiquity it was also the beginning of the New Year, the mark-point of the annual cycle. It was a time of remembering what had passed in the preceding year, and especially those ancestors who, it was believed, were not actually dead but alive in a different dimension.

In this way the modern world unwittingly keeps a tradition alive that has its roots in prehistory, perpetuating a religious and spiritual function that has been part of life for many thousands of years. When we remember our fallen, we are thus also recalling the spirits of the dead warriors of prehistoric times. November 11th is in a mystical sense thus the 'true Samhain'. Curiously, the modern poem/prayer we use today at this time, 'At the going down of the Sun, and in the morning, we will remember them' even sounds like a Celtic incantation. Perhaps, in a strange way, it is, for the lines were written by Laurence Binyon just weeks after the outbreak of World War I whilst meditating on the cliffs of North Cornwall. The spot that inspired him, between Pentire Point and The Rumps near Padstow, with distant views of Tintagel, is studded with prehistoric barrows. Here we touch on an important theme, of how certain places have the power to inspire us with timeless concepts as if they are somehow caught in an energetic matrix. This idea will become ever more significant on our journey to discover the real meaning behind the St George myth, for the land is a repository of an ageless wisdom.

In the same way as the old Samhain, other ancient festivals that mark the Sun's annual cycle also reflected the Cosmic order. At one time, not so long ago, before modern society became inward-looking and resentful of these ancient 'superstitions', great bonfires were lit to honour the Sun God, as an act of sympathetic magic to bring his beneficent influence streaming into the Earth. They were invariably kindled on holy hilltops, sometimes later being moved to more appropriate locations for practical reasons. These Baal Fires were once to be seen throughout Britain and Europe, sparkling against the darkening horizon as night gathered, in an extraordinary display that made the landscape come alive. Can we imagine the effect on an observer as hilltop after hilltop burst into life in a great ritual marking the dance of the Sun and Earth? Contemporary reports make moving reading, as witnesses describe the effect of seeing the living landscape burst into flame, as if each sacred site became an energetic focus in a web spread out across the land in a celebration of earthly life, linking people powerfully with their ancestral spirits. These fires also had a protective and healing function, as one traveller to Ireland in the 18th century recorded:

'I saw, on a radius of thirty miles all around, the fires burning on every eminence. I learned from undoubted authority that the people danced round the fires, and at the close went through these fires, and made their sons and daughters, together with their cattle, pass the fire; and the whole was conducted with religious solemnity.'[3]

At Whalton in Northumberland the Baal Fire is still lit on the 4th of July, (Old Midsummer Eve), for if we again add eleven days to June 24th, the traditional Midsummer Eve when the Sun God is at the peak of his powers, this is the date at which we arrive. Similarly, Old Christmas Eve now falls on January 5th, which used to be celebrated until Victorian times with the traditional wassailing ceremonies where bread was hung in apple trees and they were doused with cider. In mythological terms the apple is a symbol of the Earth itself, and so giving back food and drink has always been an important part of rituals associated with the turning of the year. This day relates to December 24th, the evening sacred to pagans and Christians before the Sun God is reborn. The old links with the land and our timeless traditions are still there, heavily disguised and often forgotten in the midst of the alienation from our roots that characterises the 21st century. And what of St George's Day?

Rites of Spring

The answer to this question reveals much of the true character of the original St George. One of the most significant dates in springtime is Mayday, the 1st of May, or the Celtic Beltane, which was traditionally the first day of summer. This was in former times a joyous celebration of fertility, whose ancient name is likely to have derived from the Celtic/Phoenician Sun God Bel or Baal and his consort Tanit, who, conjoined, fused the male and female principles into Bel-Tanit.

Tanit, Tan or Taine, (whose name in Celtic regions also meant 'sacred fire') later became Christianised as St Anne (known as the Mother of Mary), and her special places can be found wherever the centres of the old pre-Christian ways existed, although today perhaps in name only. Tan Hill, or St. Anne's Hill, near the great megalithic henge of Avebury, is a sacred hill where celebrations were held on old St Anne's Day (August 6th) from time immemorial, until the introduction of motor vehicles made the old trackway impassible, and consigned the ancient festival to the pages of history.[5] This date was another mark-point of the year, the mid-point between the Midsummer Solstice and the Autumn Equinox.

Throughout the ancient world every town and village had its May rites, when young men and maidens would couple in the greenwoods, bedecked with flowers and burgeoning foliage. May Eve was also a time when the sacred fires were lit, illuminating the land with points of light against whose flickering flames could be seen the shapes of dancing figures. This impressive spectacle must have reminded everyone of their dependence on the fertility of the Earth, and the return of the Sun which made it all possible. The following day the festivities continued, with garlanded processions, dancing in the streets and around the maypole—which represented the dancing of the planets around the central Sun—and the symbolic marriage of a May King and Queen, the God and Goddess incarnate. These celebrations continued for a week or so in the manner of all ancient festivals.

Sadly, where once every city, town and village had its May revels, only vestiges of this once-universal practice remain. Much of the real life of the countryside was drained away during the Great War, when the menfolk were transported into a more malign world that was the antithesis of the gentle nature of their roots. Killed in their thousands by an unforgiving and unrelenting war machine, they were never to return to re-enact the rituals of their youth, and the women who remained, mourning the loss of their men, felt little cause for celebration in future. Thus the life and ways of the countryside that had been sustained for millennia were lost, becoming either footnotes in history or merely quaint customs whose original vivacity was no longer apparent.

Yet these May rites give another glimpse into the mystery of St George, for if we count back eleven days from the modern date of May 4th (as the central point of the week-long celebrations), we find ourselves at April 23rd – *St George's Day*. This links George with the May Rites in a way that seems to be very significant, as if he were the presiding deity of this time of renewal and regeneration. The further we look into the last remaining relics of this once widespread tradition, the clearer it becomes that this was indeed the case. St George features prominently in both song and the symbolic enactments that were at the root of these ancient festivals, whereby the cosmic events that governed Life on Earth were ritualised into folk art and theatre in a way that perpetuated an understanding of Man's place and purpose in the mysteries of Creation.

Some of the most vibrant vestiges of this once universal tradition still exist in Cornwall, a land that has jealously preserved the old ways when so many other areas have been overtaken by the rationalism that denounces such activities as merely quaint and superstitious. This attitude has swept away the yearning we once had to honour the seasons and the natural wisdom which guided our ancestors, and has left us the poorer, bereft of the community spirit and the inexpressible magic that partaking in such activities creates. Perhaps it would be no bad thing to reclaim that old memory of our continuity with Nature that has been so effaced by the depredations of time.

Hallowe'en
Oct 31st/Nov 1st, plus 11 days = Remembrance Day, November 11th

Christmas
Dec 24th/25th, plus 11 days = Old Christmas Day, January 5th

Midsummer Eve
June 24th, plus 11 days = Old Midsummer Eve, July 4th

Michaelmas
Sept 29th, plus 11 days = Old Michaelmas, October 10th

St George's Day
April 23rd, plus 11 days = Mid-point of May celebrations,
Old St George's Day, May 4th

Yet at two places in Cornwall, the potency of the old spring festivals can still be experienced by everyone, and at both, the figure of St George is central. This gives us yet another clue to the true nature of St George, the old God of the Earth whose solar halo recognises the magical powers streaming from the Sun at this time of year.

We have already sensed the emotionally-charged atmosphere of the Mayday ritual at the port town of Padstow on the North Cornish coast, right at the beginning of this book. This is probably one of the most moving ceremonies left in Britain, for it preserves an innocence and a primeval potency that touches the soul, awakening old memories.

This is best experienced in the early morning, before the crowds descend on the narrow streets and turn it into a jostling scrum of snapping cameras and claustrophobic mayhem. But before it became a popular tourist attraction, it was purely for the locals, and would have had a very different effect on people who enacted this truly ancient rite.

The song that they sing speaks of the coming together of men and maidens, echoing the fertility of the Sun and Earth at this time, and of the unity that is behind Creation;

Unite and unite and let us all unite,
For summer is acome today,
And whither we are going
We will all unite
In the merry morning of May

And as the joyous throb of the drum stills, and the dragon-like Obby Oss sinks down, the tune changes to a melancholy lament in a minor key that is charged with emotion;

O where is St George,
O where is he, O?
He's out in his longboat
All on the salt sea, O

When the Oss crouches down to drink at a pool of water, a definitive feature of such rituals, St George is invoked again, but this time with even more passion;

O where is St George
O where is he, O?
He's in his longboat
Upon the salt sea, O
And for to fetch the summer home,
The summer and the May, O
For summer is acome, O
And winter is agone, O

Here is a direct allusion to St George as a god of fertility and the Lord of the Summer Sun. For in the Mystery traditions of prehistory the Sun God travels the heavens endlessly in his solar boat, bringing the cycle of the seasons and the lush green growth of Spring and Summer.

As if to emphasise the religious origins of the event, the Oss eventually returns to Prideaux Place, now a manor house but formerly a monastery. The main door points directly to the sacred mountain of Roughtor on Bodmin Moor, visible in the far distance, a Neolithic place of Sun worship with the ruins of a chapel to St Michael (the Christianised Sun God) on its summit. Here we can sense the extraordinary continuity that is behind the Padstow celebrations, and perhaps why they may evoke in us such a deep response.

Another well-known Cornish tradition also reveals the strong links between St George and the fertility of Spring. At Helston Furry Day, held a week later on the Feast of the Apparition of St Michael, we are initiated into the close relationship between the Archangel and St George, both aspects of the same principle, represented iconically by the slaying of the dragon.

The foundation legend of Helston is interesting in this respect; St Michael, hurling a great stone at the Devil from St Michael's Mount, missed his target and the stone fell short, landing in what is now the centre of town, where the Angel Hotel was built around it. Unfortunately the stone was apparently destroyed during renovations in the last century; whether this has anything to do with the very odd atmosphere in the hotel, which is often commented upon by visitors, is open to question.

On Furry Day (or Flora Day) it is again the early morning that gives a glimpse into the real meaning of the rites, when what is known as the Hal-an-Tow, the oldest part of the celebrations, is enacted. As the crowds begin to assemble in the streets there is suddenly a cacophony of whistles and shouts; up the hill dances a crowd of gaily festooned revellers, dressed in green with flowers and leaves tucked into their hair. The shops and cottages are likewise bedecked with colourful greenery and boughs brought in from the countryside the night before.

The theme of the proceedings is very ancient, and revolves around the eternal battle between Light and Dark. Prominent amongst the dancing green men and women is St George, clad in shining silver with a Templar-like surcoat displaying the red and white flag of the saint. Curiously, this particular year, as often in recent times, the character of the Saint is played by the local Member of Parliament, Andrew *George*!

The dragon is dancing too, and rushing about through the crowd, taunting his adversary, until after a tussle he is defeated by the sword of St George. Then it is St Michael's turn, dressed in scarlet and gold, to finish him off, yet of course the dragon is still very much alive, and the actors in this cosmic drama move off to another location before the rest of the day's festivities get under way. The song they sing is reminiscent of the Mayday song of Padstow, with its curiously antique cadences, and once again there is a powerful verse referring to the triumphant saint:

As for that Good Knight, St George,
St George he was a Knight O
of all the Knights in Christendom
St George he is the right, O
In every land, O
The land where e'er we go

Here the shining knight is apparently more than an actor in a local spring rite, for he is 'in every land, O'. This hints at the widespread power of St George, and acknowledges the universality of a tradition that has come echoing down through the centuries. The old God of Fertility was once everywhere, the presiding spirit of the return of summer, the source of the Light.

In former times this was the season when the entire country celebrated the awakening of the Earth and the mystery of fertility. The snowy-white blossoms of the May trees signified the most magical time of the year, when life was bursting forth wherever one looked. In every town and village the cosmic drama was enacted by young couples in the woodlands, teams of dancers showing their exuberance for the wild energy they felt pulsing through their veins, and all manner of anarchic revels. In many places the spirit of the vegetation god was personified as a living tree or bush, and a specially-chosen individual was completely submerged in greenery, encased in a wickerwork frame threaded with leaves, and led a procession of dancers and revellers.

Can we imagine the joys of one of these ancient springtime festivals? Every community would come together as one, caught up in the preparation for a ritual of life-enhancing celebration as old as time itself. The evening before May Day was of special significance, when countryfolk would vanish into the woods to emerge with bundles of greenery with which to bedeck their houses and streets. Thus their place of habitation became transformed, drawn into the magic spell to become one with nature and the life force that coursed through the land at this time.

The sound of childrens' laughter on the wind—the excitement and atmosphere of a rite that encompassed the entire country, the knowledge that the spirits of your ancestors were close, that beguiling feeling of consciously becoming part of nature's harmony—these are things which we have all but lost, and are the poorer for their passing. But still, the memory of those distant days is lodged firmly in our being, and can be re-awakened if only the evil enchantment that smothers our spirit can be banished.

Rebirth of the Sun

As winter approached, mumming plays took the place of the celebrations of springtime and were performed from Hallowe'en to Easter, the time of the Spring Equinox, but most notably at Yuletide or the Midwinter Solstice. The word mumming comes from the old Greek 'mommo', meaning 'masked', and the characters in the play wore heavy makeup or masks becoming archetypal characters who enacted a common theme that involved music, dance and sword-fighting. The central heroic personality was, like the May rites at Padstow and Helston, almost invariably St George.

As the original concept of theatre was derived from the Mysteries of Dionysos, an earlier version of the spirit of Nature, and performed for instruction and initiation purposes, these performances were based upon ritualistic themes that reflected a preoccupation with the life cycle.

St George, representing the Light as the Sun dies at the Solstice, is challenged by various adversaries, the dark forces that threaten his existence. The saint, dressed as a Crusader Knight, here exchanges his dragon for a Turkish foe (a style of folk-theatre that reflected the medieval preoccupation with the Crusades):

> *'Here comes I, St George, a knight of courage bold,*
> *If any Saracen is near, I'll make his blood run cold.*
> *I fought the evil dragon and brought him to the slaughter*
> *And that is how I won the King of Egypt's daughter.*
> *Where is the foe that bids me stand?*
> *I'll cut him down with my right hand!'*

After a fight, he is sometimes killed. Enter then a miracle-working doctor who revives him with the aid of a magic potion. In some versions of the play, including one recorded at Christmas in Cornwall, the dead Turkish knight is also brought back to life by a magical infusion. Saint George is often referred to as King George, reflecting his royal nature.

These plays are the oldest dramatic entertainment in Britain, more ancient than the mystery plays of the Middle Ages, passed on from year to year in an unbroken sequence until recent times. Yet underneath this quaintness we can discern the figure of St George impersonating the dying god of the Vernal Equinox and the Winter Solstice.

Here St George is the central figure in both the Maytime revels, when he represents the gathering strength of the Sun, and also the Midwinter celebrations, when the Sun dies and is reborn anew. These days we can see that St George, like so many other icons of archetypal power that have become debased by rationalism, has been transformed from a sacred concept to an image that has become institutionalised, almost redundant. It has taken on the air of a corporate logo belonging to an organisation that has long gone bankrupt. But in his true and timeless form, he typifies the sacred power that flows through the land, the fertilising inner Light of the Earth.

Lost Times

'Beating the Bounds' is an ancient ceremony that magically marks out the area of a parish, to promote fertility and as a protection from wayward influences, similar perhaps to the magic circle cast by a magician transposed onto the land. It was the custom until fairly recently for a party, led by a priest or bishop and attended by a group of schoolboys, to set out on Rogation Sunday at the end of May to perform a pilgrimage around the parish bounds. They would often carry slender wands of willow, perhaps decorated with a knot of flowers, and proceed to certain well-known landmarks that marked the boundary—a bridge, stile, ancient tree or old stone where the party halted and a litany or rogation was said. The tree or stone was then beaten with the willow wands, and with much joy and amusement this mystical whipping was transferred to the boys themselves, who thus became sacrificial victims, sometimes bumped on a boundary stone and often rewarded with a shilling for their pains.

Such rustic entertainments performed many-layered functions, blessing the fields and wishing for good harvests amongst them. It also, in an age before maps, conveyed to each new generation exactly where the ancient boundaries were: being ritually beaten at a particular place would invariably impress upon the boy's minds the exact location of such revelry, and so communicated the extent of the traditional territory in an unbroken fashion down through the ages.

Within the land, and within every human being, there is an essential and eternal innocence that creates fun, joy and magic. In former ages people possessed a sense of divine joyousness and their rites celebrated it. The holiness of life was acknowledged, so different to current times when we have mutilated the innate, quintessential joy of existence by focussing our collective attention on the darker and more destructive sides of human nature.

Yet still, within the land and within our own beings, is a sanctifying and transforming power that quickens apace, and calls us back to that time of lost innocence, a place of strange but familiar dreams that speak to us through nature. Increasingly, St George is beginning to seem synonymous not only with the Sun God, but also with the God of Vegetation, celebrated in his various guises as Robin Hood, the May King, Jack-in-the-Green, and that foliage-sprouting face that haunts our collective imagination, the Green Man.

3

Green George

'The historical mystery surrounding St George is not to be explained by his Christian career, nor his appearance in nature ritual due to his crusading popularity. The secret of St George is that he is a pagan divine image.'

R.J.Stewart
'Where is St George'[1]

ll over Britain and Europe, the Green Man still haunts the land, staring down from the dark recesses of churches and cathedrals, and inviting us to imbibe his intoxicating gifts at pubs and inns, thereby abandoning ourselves to the spirit of wildness, wit and wisdom that he represents. The images found in religious buildings throughout Europe and even further afield are amongst the most archaic and striking examples of ecclesiastical sculpture. They peer down at us from across the centuries, from a vanished world where magic was everywhere, and the mysteries of creation manifest in human nature. The Earth was green and teeming with life; everywhere the laws of Nature ruled.

This face, speaking to us of renewal and abundance as the leaves curl from his lips, sprouting life from his mouth, nostrils and ears, is a direct link with humanity's primeval past. The plain fact that he is so omnipresent reminds us of his power; the power of the land on which churches are built. It is a very telling fact indeed that, according to a number of researchers, images of the Green Man vastly outnumber those of Jesus in European churches and cathedrals.[2] This sounds extraordinary, for it appears to acknowledge that there is another god beyond the Christian rites reminding us that behind everything is the Force of Nature.

As every town and village once had its rites celebrating the death and rebirth of the Green Man, and every church was the focus of this inheritance, those same churches now reflect the current state of our society. They are frequently locked to stop thieves stealing and vandals desecrating, and this surely marks the absolute nadir of our modern godless civilisation. The sacred centres of the life of the land are fast becoming soulless relics from a past that few understand, or even care for.

Yet still they harbour secrets of human existence and our relationship with the ancestral spirit of the land. The sacrificed God of the Greenwood has been crucified on the cross of rationalism, but his piercing glare and mischievous grin tell us that although he may have died, he is always ready to be reborn anew; the once and future King of the Green.

As late as the end of the 19th century the remnants of timeless rituals that once took place in every town and village were still in evidence, and at Lewisham (now a suburb of London), the May ritual of 1894 typified the celebrations. A man was encased in a wicker frame (shades of Druidic rites here) wound about with ivy and crowned with paper roses. In what was probably an allusion to the planets circling the Sun, the Jack-in-the-Green slowly revolved on his axis whilst the May Queen and her maidens danced around him. In 18th century London, chimney sweeps danced through the streets led by their own version of the Green Man, hidden again inside a frame covered in holly, ivy, flowers and ribbons.

One of the most lifelike Green Men, at Sutton Benger, Wiltshire

The wild nature of these celebrations can leave no doubt that, although the archaic faces watching us from the columns and roofs of old churches and cathedrals may appear frozen in time, the energy they represent was always untamed and licentious. All the more surprising then, that there are literally thousands of them across the land, half-concealed in the twilight of those buildings that should be the very embodiment of propriety.

Robin Hood, another mask of the Green Man, was prominent in many old British ceremonies also noted for their vibrant character. The legend suggests he was also a figure of justice and cosmic order, freely giving the poor the gifts of his realm. He and his Merrie Men, living within the Greenwood and dressed in Green, typified the beneficent force of Nature that bestows its abundance so freely. The legend was once widespread and the rites performed in many locations. These days though, popular tradition associates him with Sherwood Forest, a small country park near Nottingham, and the district of Sherwood is but a suburb of the city where the Green Man may well feel the need to hide from the traffic and flickering TV screens.

In other parts of the world such as Russia, the Balkans and across central Europe, the same god of Nature was, and still is, called Green George.[3] The Russian Green George was the focus of a ritual where a specially chosen tree was felled and then decorated with flowers, before being carried in procession behind Green George, who was clothed in birch branches. He then processed to a stream or pond where he was ritually submerged to ensure rain would be plentiful in the summer. The elements of all these rites hark back to an immemorial past, and the carrying of the tree and baptism suggest that these elements were incorporated into early Christian religion.

George as Spirit of the Year

'Gawain is ostensibly the same knight who was the original Grail hero of an earlier literature. This, many believe, was firmly based on pagan ritual.'

Brian Stone
Sir Gawain and the Green Knight[4]

Beside Green George being the central figure in the May fertility ceremonies, he was also one of the prominent protagonists at the high and low points of the year, the Solstices. The Midwinter Solstice especially is a time of ancient magic, when the Sun God is reborn and the greenery that issues from the Spirit of Nature is brought inside the home.

This is a time when things appear to stand still as we are poised on the threshold of the birth of a new year, naturally inducing a childlike reverence. For mythology is not simply a thing of the past but an ever-present state of mind that one can tune into; a living entity that exists outside and beyond us.

In medieval times, the Oak King killed the Holly King at the Midwinter Solstice, their roles being reversed at the Summer Solstice in an eternal and ever-renewing battle. After the Crusades this developed into the mummers' plays where St George defeats the Turkish Knight and then declares he has slain his brother. The Knight's restoration through a magic potion meant that he was miraculously reborn, and would probably have gone on to slay St George at the Summer Solstice had this not been modified by the Church who would no doubt have been very uncomfortable at the sight of St George being slain by a Turkish infidel.

This memory of the battle between the Light and the Dark is universal and all-encompassing, and references can be found throughout early literature. However, in later times Light and Dark became synonymous with Good and Evil, and came to mean a very different thing. One of the most intriguing examples is the 14th century poem *Gawain and the Green Knight*, which although medieval, preserves many elements of the rites of pre-Christian times. This is the earliest mention extant where George, the Green Knight and King Arthur can be seen as elements of the same archetypal Sun God myth, for Gawain in Welsh is *Gwalchmai*, meaning *The Hawk of May*, a reference to the return of Spring.

Gawain is the eldest son of Morgause, nephew and heir of Arthur, and one of the earliest and most important figures associated with him. Later versions have him as a womaniser and showoff but in the original stories he is a knight of the Goddess, the Sovereignty of the Land. His strength grows towards noon, when the Sun is at its strongest and he becomes the classic Solar hero. The Green Knight is a giant green-skinned, green-clad figure who comes crashing into Arthur's court mounted, naturally, on a green steed, in his hand a gleaming green steel axe.

He also carries a holly bough to show that he comes in peace. Significantly, the court at Camelot is preparing to celebrate the feast of Christmas, so the myth is concerned with the mysteries of the Winter Solstice. He challenges those present with a 'Christmas Game', to cut his head off with the axe, as long as he can return the compliment the following year. When the assembled knights and ladies appear reluctant King Arthur seems about to accept the challenge when Gawain steps forward. With a mighty blow, he strikes off the Giant's head, only for the great Green Man to pick it up and ride off with it. As he gallops away, he reminds Gawain that he must seek him out in a year's time at the 'Green Chapel' to claim his return blow.

The year passes, and Gawain, in search of the Green Chapel, comes across the castle of Sir Bertilak, where he is warmly entertained, especially, as it happens, by Lady Bertilak, who is intent on seducing him. Chivalrous to the end, Gawain declines her advances even though a few kisses pass between them. On the third day she gives him a protective baldrick of green lace (a type of belt for holding a sword or dagger) to protect him from all harm.

The next day as he approaches the Green Chapel Gawain hears the sound of an axe being sharpened on a whetstone. Then the Green Knight appears to claim his return blow. Twice he almost brings the axe down, and mocks Gawain for flinching. On the third stroke he nicks the hero's neck, whereupon Gawain jumps up and claims that the bargain has been fulfilled. The Green Knight now reveals himself to be none other than Sir Bertilak, who has become the Giant through the enchantment of Morgan Le Fey, who was also behind the challenge of the Beheading Game and the attempted seduction of Gawain.

The elements of this mythic scenario are also to be found in at least eight other Arthurian texts, and according to a number of scholars probably originated in an earlier Irish story known as Bricriu's Feast from the cycle of Cuchulainn, another Celtic solar hero with a shining halo of golden hair. But perhaps what is most interesting is that the ever-renewing Green Man, whose death and resurrection are brought about by the youthful Sun God personified by Gawain, has as his weapon an axe. This is a thinly veiled metaphor for that other axe, the *axis* of the annual cycle.

Axis and *axes* mean the same, and are linked to *axle*, the central point of a wheel, the still point around which everything revolves. So, in the punning way of early legends, the Giant's axe alludes to the wheel of the year which turns endlessly in order to replenish the Earth.

This axis, created by the positions of the Sun as it rises and sets at the times of the Winter and Summer Solstice, is of crucial significance not only in the earliest legends but also the layout of temples, their positioning and wider significance in the landscape.

The Temple of Man

Since the earliest times, in all cultures, temples have been constructed according to cosmological principles. Stonehenge, pyramids and every sacred building always conform to such requirements. The axis of Stonehenge is aligned to the rising Sun at the Summer Solstice, (the word Solstice means 'Sun standing still') and the setting Sun at the Winter Solstice. The pyramids of Egypt and those of South America are positioned with such amazing precision that their faces lie exactly North, South, East and West. Newgrange in Ireland is carefully aligned to accept the first rays of the rising Sun at the Midwinter Solstice. Thousands of other monuments throughout the world follow the same patterns, from stone circles to the great Egyptian temples of the Nile, as well as those of Greece and Rome. This is such an essential discipline that even church architecture continued the tradition, with many Gothic cathedrals like Chartres having built into them a special aperture through which the Solstice Sun can shine.

This is more than a convention; it signifies that the church or temple is located and designed according to cosmic principles. Even modern-day Freemasonry continues these traditions whenever a new temple is built. No such temple can be constructed without laying out the site according to the diagonal axis of the Solstices, whose angles vary according to latitude. This creates a double-headed axe shape that was widespread in antiquity (especially associated with the Bronze Age civilisations of the Mediterranean), and it may be no coincidence that a prehistoric carving of exactly this design has been found on one of the great standing stones of Stonehenge.

But before one can do this, it is essential to orientate the structure to the four cardinal directions, to centre it according to the wider universe, forming a cross. And here we come face to face with St George, or rather his predecessors, for the symbol of St George's Cross is one of the oldest in human existence. Even in ancient Sumeria gods and kings are depicted wearing the 'Sun-Cross' on their arms, rather like a prototype wristwatch. The same symbol forms a common Egyptian hieroglyph, and in the Celtic world there are many thousands of examples carved in stone. These equal-armed 'Celtic' crosses often predate the introduction of the Christian cross by thousands of years. They are also found on megalithic monuments such as Knowth in Ireland, which is over 6000 years old. It cannot be coincidental that the flag adopted so enthusiastically by the Templars signifies the essential requirements for constructing *a temple*.

This cross pattern, especially in the case of St George where it is coloured red upon a white ground, may also be a symbolic representation of a sunrise or sunset. If we imagine it as an image in the landscape before us, with the horizontal line as the horizon, the vertical line linking the observer to the Sun and then connecting with the highest point in the heavens, it becomes a talisman of the Earth. It is like an abstract painting and an alchemical glyph rolled into one, for to determine the elemental directions the easiest way is to observe sunrise at the Spring Equinox. This gives us true East, and the other directions can then be readily added. It might be interesting to mention here that if we accept that George is a god of the Spring Equinox, his heavenly counterpart is Michael, whose feast day of Michaelmas falls during the time of the Autumn Equinox. These two saints thus convey the axis of the agricultural year, from sowing the seed to harvesting, the fertility cycle of the Earth.

In Cornwall, (whose original patron saint was St Michael), the red and white cross of St George becomes the flag attributed to its more recent patron saint, St Piran, and a symbol of the county. Here a white cross is blazoned on a black background. Yet it is still precisely the same symbol. In Cornish tradition it represents white streams of molten tin issuing from the dark ore, a powerful image of Light from the Earth. Considering the ancient connections of this land with the Phoenicians, who came to Cornwall for tin in remote antiquity, it seems more than likely that it originally harks back to those times when they established trading colonies, providing much cultural exchange between the west of Britain and North Africa, the land of Baal, Tanit and later, the legendary St George.

Another important cross derived from cosmology is the cross of St Andrew (from *Andros*, meaning man). This is likewise a very ancient symbol which, like that of St George, can be found throughout Egyptian tombs and temples. It represents the diagonals drawn on the surface of the land marking the directions of the solsticial axes. The cross of St Andrew is thus the *axe* of the Green Knight, whose segments or blades show the repeating movements of the Sun as its power waxes and wanes.

It is interesting in this context that no-one apparently recorded St Andrew dying on a cross until the 12th century.

St George's cross, combined with the cross of St Andrew thus creates the ground plan for any sacred structure that conforms to the Hermetic axiom *'As above, So below'*. In this way every temple becomes a microcosm of the greater universe, its divisions marking the axis of the north pole, the rising and setting places of the Sun at the Equinoxes, the Sun's most southerly and powerful position, and the solsticial axes that determine the moments of the solar hero's decline and rebirth. It is significant, too, that the term *patron* saint comes from the same root as *pattern*.

It is probably no coincidence that the British national flag is a composite of those of St Andrew and St George, overlaid one upon the other.

It is one of the ultimate symbols of the guardianship of the land in the esoteric traditions of former times, indicating the eightfold division of the annual cycle. Little wonder, perhaps, that St George and Britain have had such a special relationship in the past, and that his presence is still felt in the national psyche.

It is difficult therefore not to conclude that the Green Knight and St George are essentially one and the same, one appearing to us out of the strangely magical mists of the Celtic twilight, the other standing before us as a Christian hero who has taken on the mantle of his mystical ancestor. They are both the Green Men of the endlessly renewing cycle of fertility, on which all earthly life depends. Eating the traditional 'hot cross buns' at Easter could be thought of as a sacrament to the God of Spring, and is probably far older than Christianity.

The Devilish Green Man

The Green Man, as the personification of our pagan past, has had a long and mysterious history as the guiding spirit of humanity. The story of how his image became so widespread in church architecture will prove to be enlightening, especially the role played by the Knights Templar. But as the medieval Church became ever more centralised and controlled, what had formerly been accepted as a natural part of life was to become demonised. The devil was abroad, lurking in the dark corners of humanity's soul, waiting to snatch and torture you for eternity. Fear was the ultimate tool of the Church, and nameless horrors awaited those who did not heed the warnings. At any moment an unwitting sin might catapult you into a terrifying future.

So desperate were the authorities to force their flock to obey their orders unflinchingly that anything that had previously been associated with pre-Christian ways was declared the work of the devil, and he came in many forms. Certainly a popular choice was that of a dragon, even though it was formerly a royal symbol and rooted in a culture that never associated it with evil. But he was also easily recognisable as the force of nature that could still threaten the all-encompassing bureaucracy of the Church. And so, during the late Middle Ages, the Green Man became associated with the Devil himself.[5]

Yet we can clearly see that this was not his original function, otherwise why would he be so prominently displayed in old churches? No bishop or priest would allow images of the devil to adorn his buildings, except perhaps as a warning to those with sinful thoughts. The only conclusion can surely be that he had previously been seen as the face of the spiritual force which animated the sites on which the churches stood, giving them that special quality inherent in all sacred sites. Even though he was immortalised within the fabric of the buildings themselves, he was to be banished to the realm of the demonic and shamefully abused in an attempt to divest him of his ancient power. Like his giant ancestors of millennia before, he became the ultimate bogeyman with which to terrorise small children and credulous countryfolk. The Templars had attempted an alchemical blending of both paganism and Christianity, for they knew that they were derived from the same truths, but now the Crusades were long gone, and the Church was in the ascendant. The myth of the dying and rising god of the natural world had been almost completely eclipsed and absorbed by Jesus, but his alter ego the Green Man came to represent a darker side of religion. Churches were painted with hellish scenes to remind the congregation in the most vivid way of the fate that awaited them should they lapse back into the old ways.

As the ubiquitous Green Man became ever more devilish, many of his more positive characteristics were re-aligned with those of his officially-approved persona, St George, the champion of Christendom in its battle with paganism, whose worship was not only acceptable but consequently greatly encouraged. As the old foliate faces glowered in the dark corners of medieval churches, the new god became the invincible hero of the new age.

The Green Man of the fields and forests was also skilfully made to blend with the 'Red Man', or Satan, a vestige of the Egyptian Set, whose red colour signified the chaotic aspect of nature. Thereafter, the Devil's favourite colours were to be a mixture of red and green, and he lurked in remote wild corners of the countryside, especially at megalithic sites which were now renamed after him. The Devil's Quoit was his plaything, the old rude standing stone was sure to be impregnated with evil, and that damp gloomy cave was almost certainly his likely lair.

The old stones, once centres of a living force, still preserved a power over the countryside, for they had always been known as places of fertility. Many were reputed to make both men and women fruitful, and all were linked to the seasonal cycles that determined the patterns of natural abundance. They also could link people with their ancestral spirits, the protectors of the land, and their own spiritual heritage. They were places where the people, the Earth and the Sky became one. For this reason the Church did its best to proscribe them, issuing a series of dictates warning people against their use. Legends were re-written or invented to frighten people away, suggesting the devil would turn them to stone if they dare to dance or play music or enjoy themselves in any other way whatever. The deadening hand of puritanism was creeping relentlessly over the land.

Of course the Church had very good reason to do its best to remove the powerful aura surrounding the old sites. They preserved arcane knowledge from a time when spiritual science was paramount, and also gave individuals the opportunity to comprehend something of the Mysteries of Creation through gnosis, a direct personal connection with the Divine, enhanced by the natural power inherent at such places. If such a thing were to be tolerated, the priests would soon be out of work.

And so the old gods of the land became the adversaries and devils, yet still they retained their power against the odds. A common legend tells how churches that were being built had stones moved to another spot by the devil himself during the night. A well-known example is Brentor, on the edge of Dartmoor, Devon, where villagers wished to build a church at the foot of a steep crag so that it was easily accessible. Every morning the stones were found to have been moved to the summit by the devil. Visitors to the place today will immediately see that in the end he had his way, and that the church of St Michael crowning the rock is certainly one of the most inaccessible in Britain.

Also in Devon is the village of Shebbear, where a stone outside the church is known as the Devil's Stone. This, according to ancient ritual, must be turned every year on November 5th (probably originally Hallowe'en, the start of the Celtic New Year) by local men with the aid of crowbars. This was religiously performed until 1938, when, in the rapidly gathering climate of rationalism, it was felt to be little more than superstitious nonsense. The following year World War II broke out, the menfolk of the parish were off to fight, and the harvest was exceedingly poor. The next year the ancient ritual resumed with even more gusto than before. Every year still witnesses the power of the spirit of the stone as it is turned and the church bells ring in a wild and cacophonous manner to dispel any evil forces. Meanwhile an embarrassed clergyman reads a sermon and rails against the belief that the old demonised god of the land still lives on in the minds of locals. The truth is that the devilish Green Man, Green George, is still with us even though we have forgotten who he really is.

Green Man at Kilpeck, Herefordshire.

4

The Name of the God

ne of the most useful tools for discovering the truth behind the development of ideas is the study of the Word. Whenever we are perplexed about something all we have to do is look at the etymology, and threads leading us back to very remote times give us striking clues which illuminate our understanding. For all language is a sound-picture of thoughts that crystallise in our minds, and similar sound-pictures have been growing ever since we have inhabited the Earth. The similarity between *Jesus* and the *ysus* in *Dionysus* is a telling indication of their common origin; to this could be added *Hesus*, the messiah-like figure spoken of by the Druids. The root word is in fact a common theme that runs through all major world religions.[1]

In the original Greek, the word George means a farmer or tiller of the soil, literally 'earth-worker' (*Ge* = earth, *ergon* = work). This seems a long way from the sainted soldier with whom we are familiar, for no Christian legend speaks of him as a farmer in tune with the seasons, ploughing his fields, sowing his seed and tending his animals. But it gives us a potent clue to the labyrinthine path we are treading in endeavouring to discover his true origins. To follow it we should realise firstly that the word is made up of three syllables in its original pronunciation, spoken with a hard G; *Ge – or – ge*.

We can see immediately that the initial syllable is repeated at the beginning and end of the word, and so this appears to be the most significant component. Where does it come from? What does it mean? To discover this we should time-travel back to ancient Sumeria some six thousand years ago. It was here that the word *Ge* was first known (pronounced *Gey*), which is thought to mean 'Land' or 'The Earth'. This root component is also found, slightly altered in English, as the first syllable in *Gilgamesh*, whose famous *Epic* is one of the earliest Creation Myths known. His name is variously interpreted as 'The Plant of Youth' or 'The Old Man who is still a Young Man'. He was the 'King of the Underworld' who pronounced judgement on behalf of the Sun God Shamash.[2]

Words may change their emphasis but their roots are amazingly resilient even over long periods of time. We may not be surprised to learn that the Egyptian God of the Earth was called *Geb*. He was the son of Shu and Tefnut, the gods of air and moisture. He is depicted as a giant figure reclining on the Earth, a symbol of the planet itself, with an erect phallus. Arched over him is the great body of Nut the Sky Goddess, the vault of the heavens, as they copulate to bring forth the other principle gods of the Egyptian pantheon: Osiris, Horus, Isis and Nepthys. This personification of the Earth as distinctly male, with the sky as female, is uncommon, yet it demonstrates an aspect of the Egyptian deities that is often neglected; that each possessed both male and female attributes.

Geb, the father of the Egyptian Green Man, Osiris, later shape-shifted into the Greek pantheon where he became the feminised Earth Goddess *Ge, Gaea* or *Gaia*, which represented the essence of the Spirit of the Earth and its creatures and plants. Born of Chaos, she was one of the first goddesses, and famous as an underworld deity of oracles and caves. Delphi first belonged to her before it was taken over by Apollo the Sun God, and was considered to be her navel, the very centre of the world.

The extraordinary thing is the power and longevity of this root word *Ge*. We still, often unwittingly, use it in everyday speech whenever we speak of the Earth, each time we mention Ge-ography, Ge-ology, or the old Earth-magic, Ge-omancy. Curious, too, that until recently, the word *Gay* (French *gai*) indicated a bright, merry and irrepressible mood that lifted the spirits, and was as infectious as the laughter of the gods. Of course these days, like so many traditional words, its meaning has been changed to imply something else altogether.

The remarkable fact is that we are still using a sacred word, often in total ignorance of its origins, many thousands of years after it signified an Earth deity. This line of enquiry will bring further revelations when we examine the word *George* in classical and English mythology. But the letter *G*, in its original essence, is a God-letter, a glyph of divinity, being constructed from a circle (an ancient sign for God, being continuous and all-encompassing) and a central dot (the individual consciousness) connected to the circumference by a straight line. It was also used to depict the Sun. We may even be tempted to see it as a symbol of the individual experiencing direct communication with the divine.

And what of the middle syllable? Can this shed any light on the mystery? The *or* in George in fact signifies Light, as in the Egyptian *Horus*, the God of Light. It is the same in Hebrew, where the word *Har*, meaning Light, is pronounced as *or*. In French it means gold, with its intimations of shining, incorruptible splendour. In the English *ore*, it means unworked metal, taken from the Earth, and again indicates Light created out of the dark body of the planet. In the word *Oracle* it hints at some form of divination linked with special sites located on the surface of the Earth. Does this all stem originally from the temples of ancient Sumeria and Babylon? Was the original meaning of *Ge-or-ge* to do with the honouring of the Light within the Earth? An invocation?

The story of the transmission of this primeval Earth God down through historical times is one that reveals a great amount of information about the roots of religion, and the way they entwine their tendrils across the centuries. In many ways it is the untold story of the human race itself. But as the story unfolds, it will become even more clear why Constantine chose the figure of St George to herald the birth of Roman Christianity. It is a possibility that the soldier-saint we are told was the original George shared the same name, and as such was an ideal candidate for this role.

Or it may be that the name was merely grafted on at a later date, as suggested by the fact that Eusebius neglected to mention it in his otherwise detailed account. Either way, it would seem that Constantine calculated that to make his state religion successful, he would have to incorporate at its heart one of the fundamental and timeless tenets of pre-Christian beliefs.

Giants in the Earth

In Salisbury Museum, not many miles from Stonehenge, resides the mouldering effigy of a 12-foot tall giant with a dark complexion and a black hairy beard. Named after the biblical giant St Christopher, who was supposed to have carried the baby Jesus across a river, it was an object of peculiar veneration in the locality in times past. At moments of national rejoicing this huge figure was paraded through the streets of the town accompanied by much music and merrymaking. It was particularly associated with celebrations at Midsummer, as is the great henge nearby, which in British tradition was also built by a race of giants. It is probably one of the last remnants of an earlier age when giants ruled mythology and the landscape.

In prehistoric Britain, they were believed to have been responsible for the formation of the land, sculpting the mountains, hills and rivers. In this way they were a metaphor for the Giant Forces of the Earth itself, as if they were great sentient beings behind the forces of nature.

At the beginning of the 12th century the medieval chronicler Geoffrey of Monmouth, in *The History of the Kings of Britain*, records what are some of the last memories of the old Celtic ways.[3] As the oral tradition declines, soon to disappear forever, he writes of Merlin and Arthur and the vanished world of the oldest legends. He tells of the founding of Britain by the Trojan Brutus, who landed at Totnes in Devon (the stone on which he is said to have set foot is still to be seen in the high street). When he arrived he found a land that was until recently inhabited by a race of giants; but now only one remained, from Cornwall. His name, according to Geoffrey, was Geomagot.

Brutus' general Corineus, whose favourite sport was apparently giant-killing, fought a battle with him on Plymouth Hoe and won, hurling him from the cliffs into the sea. Henceforth there were to be no more giants in Cornwall, or anywhere else for that matter; Brutus' new land was to be called Britain and

Corineus' men became Cornishmen. Brutus' descendants were to become the royal line of Britain, and the old giants were dead.

These old giants were prehistoric personifications of the Sun and Earth Gods, for Geoffrey's books were never really meant to be anything other than a mythological history of the land of Britain. Even in the 12th century this was far removed from the old bardic traditions of Druidism from which they originated, but nevertheless the stories contained essential truths that had been handed down for many generations. It would be easy to dismiss much of the material as fantasy, but that would be to throw out the giant with the bathwater, for there is much truth yet to be discovered within the ever-intriguing details of the old stories. Places like Cornwall had always been inhabited by giants, as the collections of legends and lore about them testify. Practically all of the places at which they had lived were former centres of the Druid religion, like St Michael's Mount, which, long before St Michael made his appearance, was the home of Cormoran and his wife Cormelian. (A hard *'C'* and *'G'* were interchangeable in old European languages, so again we have the equivalent of *Gor*, the root of the word George).

The giant called Geomagot, the last of his race, has **Ge** as the first part of his name; the word for the Earth. That would be of considerable interest to our quest, yet there is more. As detailed in a previous work, ***Tintagel and the Arthurian Mythos***, the place where the giant was killed was, until the 17th century, marked by two large turf-cut figures called Gog and Magog. These were thought at the time to represent the giant and his foe. This was part of a very ancient and unique British tradition, where giant effigies were cut into the land at places of legendary significance. The Westcountry, as one of the last bastions of the prehistoric ways, is home to many of them, some of which, like the tumescent Cerne Abbas Giant in Dorset, with his erect phallus and club, leave us in no doubt that they represent the power of fertility. This particular mystery deepens, however, when we discover that these figures at Plymouth were linked to another legendary site, Tintagel, on the wild north Cornish coast, by a long straight-line axis laid out on the surface of the land.[4]

This axis precisely marks the position of the rising Midwinter Sun, and part of it is still visible as a remarkably straight road on the northern edge of Bodmin Moor, which may have originally been part of a processional route. It also passes directly through the great Neolithic ritual centre of Stowe's Hill, where the Druidic rock pile known as the Cheesewring stands on its lofty outcrop. In Geoffrey's book he famously records that Arthur was born at Tintagel; the story is too familiar to be repeated here. But what we can see quite clearly is how Geoffrey was preserving powerful elements of an ancient understanding that linked Sun and Earth in the guise of a giant who died on one end of the axis at the Midwinter Solstice, and a solar hero king who was born at Tintagel at the other extremity. The myths are hardly myths after all; they speak of the powerful drama of the renewal of life.

The central feature of this axis is the dramatically-poised Cheesewring on Stowe's Hill. Cornish legend speaks of as a Druid idol rather than a natural formation, which is said to respond to the sunrise by its topmost rock revolving. The suspicion is that this striking feature may be more than a natural outcrop, for it forms the precise centre of a cosmological landscape, and one of the foremost prehistoric ritual centres in the west of Britain. Directly to the south is St George's Island, a short distance off the coast. Exactly due west is a medieval bridge at Wadebridge, which used to have a chapel dedicated to St Michael guarding it. Other features, notably prehistoric mounds, some of which now have Norman castles built on them, suggest a 'Round Table' that reflects the elemental directions and the movements of the Sun mirrored on the Earth's surface.

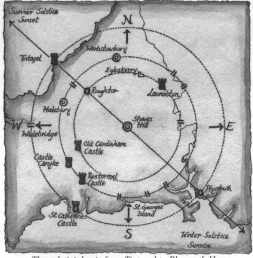

The solsticial axis from Tintagel to Plymouth Hoe, surrounded by a 'Round Table' of significant ancient sites

The Cheesewring is also a marker for that other great countrywide alignment known as the St Michael Line, which travels up through Glastonbury and Avebury to the east coast, taking in a considerable number of sites dedicated to St Michael, the heavenly aspect of the more earthy St George.

Across Europe we find that many prehistoric sites retain the names of the old giants. Mont St Michel in Normandy, (another place of Druid Sun-worship) was once the haunt of **Gargantua**, and Monte **Gargano** on the spur of Italy is also named after its titanic resident. Names such as Mount **Carmel** in the Holy Land remind us that **Gar**, or **Car**, came to mean a mountain that had been created by the geological movements of the Earth giants, and by analogy, a pile or **cairn** of stones. Rabelais explored many of the old legends in his tales of Gargantua, who could swallow an ocean or knock down a mountain in a moment. How far this goes back we cannot tell, but it is certainly of immense antiquity. The prehistoric **Gargas** caves in south-western France are home to cave paintings that are dated back to at least 25,000 BC. Greek legends of the **Gorgons** similarly speak of the great forces that shaped the Earth and are responsible for its fertility. According to Apollodorus they 'had heads twined about with the scales of dragons, and great tusks like those of swine, and brazen hands and golden wings, by which they flew'. These later fearsome demonesses were originally derived from an earlier, single deity. Protective talismans called ***Gorgonia*** were used long before Homer, just like Gargoyles on a medieval church.

We can sense here something far greater in the legends of giants than mere fairy tales. The stories which come down to us have encoded within them a deep wisdom that may tantalise our imagination, yet they are firmly based upon an understanding of the relationship between the Sun and Earth. Only our preoccupation with mundane matters, and our unquestioning mirage that prehistoric people were desperately primitive, prevent us from seeing the truth.

Mythic Geography

An exploration of the root word ***Ge*** can be, as we have observed, very illuminating in our quest for the real meaning behind the St George myth. It seems that George was originally a giant. In fact in the medieval manuscripts such as that of Geoffrey of Monmouth the word giant is spelt ***Geant***.

Further linguistic forays into the world of etymology can be similarly revealing. A whole host of geographical features, sites that have always been central to our mythic connections with the landscape we inhabit, are also part of the mystery. One of the most enlightening is the word ***Gorge***, the true origin of the word ***Gorgeous***, referring to the inner magical realms of the planet. We can see immediately that this word is almost exactly the same as the appellation of our illustrious saint. Its meaning is that of a cleft or sudden opening in the body of the land; an entrance into the interior of the Earth. We have yet to arrive at the point where we penetrate into the deeper meaning of the other aspect of the mystery of George, that of the dragon, but we can at least be aware for the time being that such cave-like features are important to our investigation. It gives a singularly significant pointer to the fact that George is intimately connected with these entrances to the underworld, the lairs of the dragon.

Other words to consider may include ***Orgy***, originally derived from sacred rites associated with initiation and rebirth, designed to encourage the forces of nature to be fertile through an act of sympathetic magic. These rites were held especially during spring, at Beltane, when the Sky God (or goddess) conjoined with the Earth Goddess (or god).

The great giant of Celtic and pre-Christian times was known as ***Og***, probably the earliest form of the word to become eventually ***George***. His name is preserved in hundreds of places throughout Britain and beyond, and it can be of great interest to research them in connection with local mythology. One of the most intriguing village names in the Westcountry is that of Ogbourne St George, a few miles from the Neolithic henge of Avebury. The river Og, the source of the fertility of the area, meanders across the chalk uplands to the north of the great temple, to skirt the land adjoining the village church. The name of the place suggests the direct link between the words Og and George which we might expect in an area that was such a notable centre of the work of giants— the gargantuan megaliths of the henge, and Silbury Hill, the largest artificial mound in Europe. A short distance away is Ogbourne St Andrew, where another Neolithic mound can be found next to the church, half-hidden by trees and vegetation. Curiously, here we have the George/Andrew link suggested by the crosses of the four quarters and the solsticial axes. In similar vein, Ogbury is a village close to Stonehenge, where a sacred hilltop enclosure (now built upon) reveals large numbers of spherical chalk spheres to those who explore the site. These are supposed to be of natural origin, yet it is difficult to see how geology could create so many and deposit them in such a small area. Is it a coincidence that they so closely resemble symbolic Suns?[5]

As this is not a gazetteer of such places we must reluctantly confine ourselves to the task in hand, noting that the landscape is full of such enigmas which confirm our suspicion that at one time the world was indeed metaphorically inhabited by giants. The giant Og is even to be found in the Bible as a survivor of the Flood, evidently living for 500 years until he was slain by Moses. He was so tall that the waters of the inundation reached only to his ankles. He was also said to have perched on Noah's roof, being fed by him in return for promising to be his slave. His daily meal was 1000 oxen (though we can only wonder from where Noah may have got them). Og is also said to have fallen in love with Sarah, Abraham's beautiful wife, but the match was not to be, and he was doomed to be killed by Moses as a mountain crashed down around his ears.

In the Celtic world Og was also known as *Gog*, a word with the rudimentary elements of the word George prominent within it. This giant had a wife, Magog. Here is an acknowledgement of the dual nature of the forces that reside within the relationship between the Sun and the Earth, exactly as the Egyptian gods and goddesses possessed both male and female aspects. The name Magog may be one of the oldest prehistoric titles of the mother goddess, miraculously preserved through millennia by the power of the spoken word. She was predominantly concerned with earthly fertility, whilst her husband represented the power of the Sun. We come across these figures yet again in the Bible, where the names Gog and Magog are mentioned as kings of the land of Bashan, foes of the Israelites. In rabbinical literature they are represented as cosmic bogeymen, and even linked with Satan.

Geoffrey of Monmouth recorded another story about Gog and Magog as the survivors of a race of primeval titans, which gives a further clue to the once widespread nature of these tales. In this version Brutus captures the giants (which were in this case both male) and installs them in London to stand guard over his palace, where they become legendary talismans of protective power; deities whose effigies can still be seen even today guarding the Guildhall.

These modern figures are replacements for more ancient images that were in earlier centuries ritually carried through the streets of London on Old Michaelmas Day, but destroyed during a bombing raid in 1940. These in turn replaced even earlier ones of great age that had decayed beyond restoration. The old giants were brought out at every important royal occasion, where they were made to bow to kings and queens. So persistent was the power of the giants that 18th century coachmen swore 'by Gog and Magog', just as we might today say 'by George', and they were frequently used as a threat to terrify children and apprentices. As Lewis Spence comments in *The Mysteries of Britain*, '...surely a terror so long-established could have survived only on account of an exceptionally powerful folk memory of ancient sacrifices to the deities in question; there can be no doubt that Gog and Magog were deities of fertility.'[6] Another tradition asserts that they were miraculously transformed into the Gogmagog hills at the ancient British camp of Wandlebury, east of Cambridge. Curiously, the archaeologist and dowser T.C. Lethbridge excavated this site in the 1950s and found what he believed to be a huge effigy of Magog, the mother goddess, with a crescent shape above her head, indicating her lunar nature.

In Scotland, the midwinter feast of *Hog*manay is the festival of Og or Gog, celebrating the rebirth of this most ancient of Sun giants. In Irish tradition, some of the most complete legends extant, Og becomes *Ogma*, known as *Ogma Sunface* of the Tuatha dé Danaan, often depicted with hair radiating out from his head like the Sun's rays, perhaps the earliest version of St George's halo. He was a god of poetry, speech and eloquence, and the eponymous inventor of *Ogham* writing, a system of notches (vowels) and consonants (lines) cut into the edges of

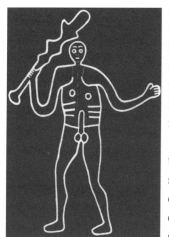

The Cerne Giant,
from a survey by Sir Flinders Petrie

standing stones and other monuments. This was also a system by which priests and initiates could communicate secretly, by using their fingers to replicate the written shapes even during normal conversation, thereby conveying a different meaning altogether. It is said to be one of the reasons the Romans hated the Druids, as this code was used during their meetings in full view, yet they could not understand it.

The same god/giant was present on mainland Europe, with the latinised Gaulish name of *Ogmios*. He had a beneficent smiling face worthy of a Sun God, and the gift of great eloquence. He is depicted with golden chains connecting the ears of his subjects to his tongue. Another, more fearsome, side of his nature was revealed by his image as a Celtic Hercules, garbed in a lion-skin and with a club in his hand, very similar to the image of the Cerne Abbas giant. Is the chalk-cut titan, with his green turf covering, the oldest remaining ancestor of Green George?

The fact that the giant is on the extended Midsummer axis leading from Stonehenge only confirms this idea, for it suggests the Summer God triumphant and at his most potent. Interesting too that Giraldus Cambrensis in the 12th century calls Stonehenge 'The Giant's Dance', surely a mythic metaphor for the giants of the Sun and Earth which endlessly dance with each other through space, with the steps of their dance marked on the land by such monuments.

As Christianity gathered power over the gods of old, Gog and Magog were demonised. Yet the powers they represented could not so easily be vanquished. Even today their spirits can be found in the landscape, and their names attached to places such as the hills at Wandlebury. At Glastonbury exists what is probably one of the last physical vestiges of the old veneration, two ancient oaks known as Gog and Magog. They are certainly of immense antiquity and are believed to be the remnants of a Druid grove. They have become natural shrines, with offerings left to honour the spirits that still seem to hover around them.

Generally the giant forces that created life, so closely associated with the dragons and other monstrous beasts of earlier times, and the megaliths and temples of prehistory, became the fearsome giants with which the Church could terrify its subjects. Like the Green Man who was later to inherit so many of their attributes, they were largely stripped of their godlike characteristics of immense strength and vitality and became pagan adversaries who were always causing mayhem and mischief. They became the Ogres and Ogresses of fairytale, who in future would haunt the collective imagination of humanity. Yet their power could never be completely taken away; it was absorbed into a new ethos where their essential characteristics were retained in a different guise.

In conclusion we must ask if Gog is one of the earliest names of God, with which it shares such similarity, whose half-forgotten memory comes echoing down from prehistory. The replacement of the final *G* may have come about by its blending with another God-letter, *D*. This too is an ancient symbol of Divinity and Deity, and is rooted in the Indo-European base *deyeu* meaning 'light', 'shining' or 'God of the Sky'. It is from this we get the Latin *Deus*, the Sanskrit *Deva*, (both meaning God), and the English word *Day*.

5

The Mystic Way of St George

During January 1961, the poet and mythologist Robert Graves entertained three guests at his island home on Mallorca. One was the founding father of modern witchcraft, Gerald Gardner, the others were Idries Shah and his brother Omar. The two brothers were, so Graves was later to believe, direct descendants of the prophet Mohammed, and possessed the secret wisdom of Sufism, the mystical tradition of Islam. Idries Shah had the easy, philosophical manner of a cosmopolitan mystic, who had spent his life exploring the magical customs of various disciplines. He had, according to his letter asking if he could meet Graves, 'written various books on the diffusion of magical practices' and was currently 'studying ecstatic religions.' He had attended British witchcraft rituals and experimented with hallucinogenic mushrooms. Graves was so impressed with his ideas that he agreed to write the forward to his book *The Sufis*, published in 1964 and destined to become one of the most influential books of its day.[1]

The three men enjoyed each other's company so much that they met again later in the month. Shah was soon to become one of Graves' most trusted and influential friends. Graves was particularly attracted to Shah's interpretation of the Islamic concept of 'baraka', a word that referred, amongst other things, to 'the sudden divine rapture which overcomes either a prophet or a group of fervent devotees…whom it unites in a bond of love.'[2] Graves' first experience of mushrooms had induced exactly this deep feeling of unity and love for all creation, the essence of which was contained in baraka, the Sufic term for the Life Force. According to Graves, this mystical force was present in all natural things, as well as in objects made with a sense of love and creativity that all possessed a 'certain glow of life'. In the creative arts this force was 'of the utmost importance', and Graves associated it with the inspiration of the Muse, when it could be channelled into a poem or painting which consequently became charged with a spiritual power.[3]

Intoxicants held a powerful fascination for Graves, who realised that all ancient religions and mystical traditions saw them as a divine gift that enabled devotees to transcend the limitations of normal consciousness. He wrote of his own experience that mushrooms gave him 'full use of the imaginative senses… it certainly heightened my poetic powers by making me aware of sound and colour and texture as never before since my late childhood.'

This account of Shah's visit to the foremost mythologist of his day may initially seem somewhat out of place in a book on St George. But it alerts us to a crucial aspect of the entire phenomenon, that behind the power of the Green Man, St George, and the former gods and goddesses of the old religions lies a long tradition of the mystical experience of nature. We may wonder why the faces of many Green Men look so wide-eyed; it is something that no-one appears able to explain. Yet such expressions are inevitably the result of the revelation that takes over one's being when a heightened state of awareness is achieved through spiritual practices, or the use of intoxicating sacred herbs and plant substances, gifts of the Green Man himself. The Occult traditions are full of such examples of the imbibing of psychoactive brews and herbal preparations. They are the stock-in-trade of all ancient mystery religions, witchcraft (which Shah claimed was derived from a Sufi word meaning *wise-craft*) and rituals designed to expand the consciousness. Under their influence one can access a level of reality where the participant becomes at one (at-one-ment) with the whole of Creation.

Thus, by quite literally eating and drinking the 'body' and 'blood' of the Green Man in the form of consciousness-changing herbs and plants, wine and others brews, anyone who is initiated into the appropriate techniques can *become* the Green Man. The experience of this unity is a life-changing moment, enough to make one's eyes bulge in astonishment. Could this be the reason why so many Green Men have that look of startled amazement? Are they representations, not of some mythical spirit of nature, but of actual experiences that were once common in a world where hedgerow herbs, plants and mushrooms were known for producing altered states of consciousness? It may be the reason why the old primeval god of nature, Og or Gog, was thought to have huge staring eyes, for his name gives us the words *Ogle* and *Goggle*.

Idries Shah took a particular interest in the mystery of St George. As an initiate into the Sufi wisdom tradition he possessed knowledge that was generally unavailable to outsiders. He believed the reason George had achieved such a widespread following in so many countries during medieval times was not just because of the Church, but due to the mystical traditions of Freemasonry and the Knights Templar. In *The Sufi* he wrote 'The Sufis are an ancient spiritual Freemasonry... Indeed Freemasonry itself began as a Sufi society. It first reached England in the reign of King Athelstan (924-939) and was introduced into Scotland disguised as a craft guild at the beginning of the 14th century, doubtless by the Knights Templar.'[4]

He was also convinced that much of English folk tradition stemmed from the time of the returning Crusaders who had been steeped in the mystical lore of Sufism during their sojourn in the Holy Land. They had certainly become deeply immersed in arcane practices, introducing the concept of Gothic architecture, with its Byzantine arch and use of sacred geometry, and changed the face of Europe forever.[5] They were also rumoured to possess esoteric and occult knowledge, and probably knew more about the true origins of the Church than the Church itself. They lent huge sums of money to the royal families of Europe, a factor that was to help precipitate their demise, as Philip le Bel of France owed them a fortune and conspired with the Pope to destroy them. This eventually led to their ruthless extermination, famously at dawn on Friday the 13th October in 1307, 'the most evil day in history', a day notoriously linked with bad luck. Somehow they had attained a level of knowledge that was deemed heretical by the established Church, a knowledge that could have destabilised the whole edifice of Christianity as it was known, and they had to be expunged.

It is known that certain knights of the aristocratic bloodlines of Europe, themselves deeply immersed in the mysticism of their own lands, mingled freely with their counterparts in Constantinople and Jerusalem, both famous as centres of esoteric learning. The fact that the original Order of the Knights Templar was written by Bernard, Abbot of Clairvaux, reformer of the Cistercians and one of the leading forces in Europe, gives a clue that the Crusades were no ordinary attempt to invade another country, for the mystically inclined Bernard appeared to have had other reasons besides the purely political. The suspicion is there may have been a definite agenda resulting in the formation of the Templars and their subsequent rise to power.

Exactly what the agenda was is the subject of much speculation. Some of the families were deeply involved with the production of the legends associated with King Arthur and the Holy Grail, whose influence was to have such a profound affect across Christendom. What does appear certain, however, is that the Templars were schooled in the Mystery Wisdom of antiquity, and re-introduced an entire body of tradition into a Europe that had lost much of its own due to the depredations of war, famine and plague. They were responsible for an extraordinary renaissance of religion and culture that revivified lands whose own ancient mysteries had waned as the Church grew ever more powerful.[6]

One of the most remarkable aims of the Templars, and one which they largely achieved, was an extraordinary blending of the Christian, pagan, Jewish and Islamic religions. They seemed to be aware that all religions were derived from a common source, and they wished to make a powerful statement to this effect. Evidence of this can be seen in any Gothic building they had a hand in; they established guilds of craftsmen (which eventually developed into the Freemasons) who designed and decorated the interiors and exteriors of their buildings with a vast array of striking carvings. Most prominent amongst this array of images from both the Biblical and the pre-Christian era was the image of the Green Man. One of the other main themes running through the Templar tradition was that of

St George. They had adopted him as their protective deity right at the very beginning of the Crusades. A vision of him on his white charger had appeared to Godfroi de Bouillon at the siege of Antioch in 1098 and become legendary, and was followed by a similar incident to become even more famous at Acre. Richard the Lionheart claimed that this victory was due to the personal intercession of St George, whose apparition was evidently seen hovering over the walls of the Saracen city. During the battle Richard made his men wear thongs of blue leather around their legs so they could distinguish themselves from other Crusaders in the heat of the battle. After his victory, Richard vowed to refound the old British Order of St George and make his fellow knights 'Companions'. The incident of the thongs may have been the original inspiration behind the later Order of the Garter. 'For England and St George' was to become the battle cry for many generations to come.

Returning Crusaders also brought with them many of the mystical traditions of the Holy Land that they had witnessed. As the aristocratic guardians of the land, they introduced, (or re-introduced) much of this into everyday life. One of the most notable rituals to become universally popular was the mumming play, with St George as a central figure. This became an integral part of country life, along with the re-invigorated rites of Beltane, of which the Padstow Mayday celebrations and those at Helston are the lively remnants—both including the god-like presence of St George. Everyone wonders where the Padstow ritual originated, with the wild swirling motion of the dancing Oss. The answer is that it may well derive from the Sufi tradition of the 'whirling dervishes' whose dance is such an integral part of their own rites. Idries Shah makes the point that the riding of a hobbyhorse, (something that was widespread across Britain), is a well-known part of Sufic ritual.

The musicologist Cecil Sharp was in no doubt as to the likely origins of that other great folk tradition, Morris Dancing. This was introduced, he believed, from the *Moorish* regions of Spain, where the great Sufi centres of learning at Granada, Toledo and Cordoba provided the nobility of Europe with unfettered access to Islamic traditions. In his ***Parsifal***, Wolfram Von Eschenbach claims to have received the story during the 12th century from one Kyot, a famous master of Toledo, a celebrated repository of Arabic wisdom.

In these Islamophobic times it may come as something of a cultural shock to realise how indebted the West is to Islamic science and culture, which in early medieval times was extremely advanced by European standards. It was the engine of the great Islamic empire stretching from central Europe right across Persia and the Middle East to Spain and then to the rest of the Continent.

Many of the most important discoveries that have since been attributed to Western science were derived from the Arabic universities, where many centuries of learning had resulted in vast libraries, attracting scholars from across Europe.[7] They were the originators of modern arithmetic, trigonometry, astronomy, chemistry, physics and medicine, to name but a few of the many disciplines. It was the introduction of Arabic numerals, superseding the Roman type (which were unsuited for advanced calculation), that stimulated a completely new era of research. In astronomy, we are taught that it was the likes of Copernicus and Galileo who were the founders of modern thought, yet Islamic works predating their discoveries were translated into Latin and available from the 12th century onwards. This is why all stars have Arabic names.

The names of chemical substances like al-cohol, and the disciplines of the mystical sciences such as al-chemy, were to spread across Europe, creating a great renaissance in the quest for knowledge. Newton's theory of gravitation was in fact a restatement of the findings of the 11th century Muslim scholar al-Biruni (regarded as one of the great geniuses of the Middle Ages by historians), who stated that all particles, no matter how large or small, are attracted to the centre of the Earth through gravitational pull. A later Arab physicist, Ibu Bajjah, refined this by pointing out that when the resistance of air is removed, all objects fall towards the Earth's centre at the same rate.

There are even records of teaching journeys to Britain undertaken by Sufi masters such as Najmuddin Gwath-ed-Dahar Qalandar in the 13th century. Another teacher, Najmuddin Baba, is said to have 'followed in his father's footsteps' in 1338, suggesting that communication was common between the two cultures and indeed had been for some generations.

Thus, in the centuries following the Crusades, the exchange of culture, religious and mystical ideas that had begun in the Holy Land thoroughly permeated the western world and blended with the remnants of the old pre-Christian worship to create a new flowering of European culture. A renaissance in the indigenous religions accompanied that of scientific thought; the energetic dancing that may well have been an important ritualistic element at the stone circles of prehistory now moved into the heart of the villages and towns, where it continued to be the focus for seasonal celebrations of the spirit of nature, the Green Man, now called St George.

The Green One Cometh

'Hail unto thee, George, the Evergreen Green One'

*Invocation made by Christian and Muslim pilgrims
on their annual pilgrimage to the shrine of St George at Lydda*

In the Islamic world the Green Man, Green George, is known as al-Khidr, translated literally as *The Green One* (the root Kh.d.r. means 'green'). He is to be found in many stories and legends as a guiding and inspirational figure, a powerful spiritual presence that can appear at any time. He is blessed with something approaching immortality as well as many miraculous and magical virtues. Being one of the most revered spiritual guides he represents ideals that are also to be found in the concept of chivalry which was spawned by the Crusaders' intimate contact with the Holy Land. Amongst them are the absolute dedication to live up to certain exacting standards, the honouring of the feminine principle and a single-minded determination to further the spiritual growth of humanity. The central theme is that the inner teaching of all religions is the same. These shared ideals create a 'visible elite' just like the Order of the Garter, or the Round Table which is its corollary. Another significant element is that of the central figure who assumes the role of teacher, wise man or sage; he is invested with the attributes of Sufic kingship as the leader of the community.

*The Royal Coat of Arms
of Elizabeth I, with dragon and motto
of the Order of the Garter*

This idea of sacred kingship resonates throughout British and European traditions of the Round Table and the Grail mythos. In a remarkable parallel to the quest for the ever-elusive Grail, al-Khidr is also known in the mystical Islamic tradition as the 'cup-bearer'. His motto in Persian is said by Idries Shah to sound strikingly similar to that of the Order of the Garter, 'Honi Soit Qui Mal y Pense' (Evil To Him That Evil Thinks), a motto that is still to be found displayed in every Court of Law in Britain. Its inner meaning is one of the central tenets of eastern mysticism; it is the quality of thought that determines one's character.[8]

The mysterious organisation known as the Order of the Garter or the Order of St George was founded in England by Edward III, and said to be 'The noblest brotherhood of knights in Europe'. It was the first of its kind, but created such a stir amongst the mystical elite of Europe that it was later followed by the Order of St Michael in France, the Order of the Golden Fleece in Burgundy and that of St Andrew in Scotland. In Sufic terms, the garter is the same as the mystical tie or bond existing between the members of the Order. The true origins are lost; not surprising for a group of chivalric knights emulating the Templars, an esoteric society preoccupied with secrecy and hidden agendas. In their place numerous legends have grown up; in the most well-known the garter is said to have slipped from the leg of a beautiful woman during a dance. These legends contain elements of important themes that have subsequently degenerated into their folkloric aspects. (The woman involved in this case was William de Montecute's wife Katherine. Is it just a coincidence that he was Earl of Salisbury, so close to Stonehenge, the great centre of the mystery wisdom of Albion?)

The figure of al-Khidr, the Islamic Green George, has many of the attributes we might expect of such a legendary lord of fertility. He is clothed in green, the Earth becomes verdant at the touch of his feet, and he leaves a trail of green footprints in the desert wherever he goes. His colour is his most powerful attribute, and has come to symbolise Islam itself, the only contemporary religion (besides perhaps neo-paganism) to have become associated with a particular colour. To the Muslim the Temple Shrine is any patch of ground upon the Earth, thus the whole world is sanctified, and even dry sand and rocks signify the living planet. In this way Islam shares the same fundamental approach to achieving oneness with the Earth as the archaic shamanic teachings and pagan religions before their slide into decadence. The colour green is viewed as a reflection of the divine light itself.

Yet Khidr's popularity extends beyond Islam, and in both the Hebrew and Muslim traditions he is also strongly linked to the priest-king Melchizedek. Khidr/ Melchizedek first appears in the Qur'an as the mysterious guide and companion of Moses, sent by God when he asked if there was a servant of God on Earth more knowledgeable than himself. Another story in the Qur'an tells of Khidr coming across the severed head of a king which is miraculously restored to life, elements of which bear similarity to the British legend of *Gawain and the Green Knight*. There are also surviving cults in the Hindu religion, where he is associated with the euphoria experienced by his devotees who smoke hashish and marihuana, just like the *Assassins* or *Hashishin* with whom the Templars are known to have associated. His principle shrine is on the Indus at Bokhar.

Khidr, said by some to be a son of Adam, is also remembered for being the companion of Alexander the Great, around whom much legendary material gathered. They both set out to seek the Fountain of Life, but only Khidr succeeded in drinking from it, gaining immortality. Alexander learnt from the green prophet that the source of the River of Life was in the North, beneath the Pole Star. The stories are extensive, and an entire book could be devoted to the subject of the Islamic Green Man. According to many Islamic historians the Khidr story is

A gnostic seal of the Earth's energy rising up a standing stone (note the Palm Tree, a Sufic symbol of sacred force, and the spiral growth of the shell).

believed to have been inherited from a much older tradition. Some think that he may have originally come from the Sumerian *Epic of Gilgamesh*, where the hero sets off in search of his immortal ancestor Utnapishtim.

As we attempt to discover the true beginnings of the Green Man or Green George we can but note that al-Khidr is one of the foremost spiritual presences throughout the Islamic world. He is the archetypal figure of the green spirit of nature, a deity of trees and flowers whose feet encourage the growth of plants and healing herbs. Perhaps because of this he is also a great healing saint to whom many miracles are ascribed, and there also seem to be strong links between him and Jesus Christ, who, in Islamic custom, is not the son of God, but one of his many prophets. A town called Al-Khadar can be found close to Bethlehem, and has become a centre for healing pilgrimages where miracles are routinely reported, just as in various churches and chapels dedicated to St George.

As a Lord of Fertility, al-Khidr is not limited to being the essential principle behind the growth of plants and the fertilising waters of the Fountain of Life. Sir James Frazer notes that according to Syrian and wider customs he can do more than encourage fruitfulness in the thin desert soil. Khidr, like Green George, is the favourite saint of barren and childless women wishing for offspring. The most celebrated shrine for this purpose is Kalat el Hosn in northern Syria (which is evidently so efficacious that many Muslims have forbidden their wives to visit it). At this place and others the saint himself is believed to appear and mystically impregnate the childless women. As Frazer comments; 'These modern saints are nothing but the old gods under a thin disguise.'[9]

Al-Khidr is without doubt the oriental spirit of Green George. Both are revered for their special power of protection to travellers and those who quest for the truth, and their respective images can often be found in very remote places. As Islamic tradition says, if you need a guide to cross a desert or unknown land, how much more do you need a guide to venture into the inner world of the psyche, into the depths of the soul? Amongst the many examples encountered on old pilgrim routes in the East, a carving of al-Khidr can be seen over the gateway of a caravanserai on the road between Sinjar and Mosul in Iraq, dated to the 11th century. In the relief he is thrusting a spear into the mouth of a serpentine dragon.

Khidr, with his magical attribute of appearing just when required, guiding travellers or instructing them in the ways of the spirit, is an archetypal allegory for the travelling dervish, the wandering Sufi mystic. Although he is shrouded in mystery, Muslims believe he walks amongst them as a living presence who will guide anyone who is physically or spiritually lost. Many people claim to have met and conversed with him, including one of Islam's greatest scholars and sages Imam Zakariyya al-Nawawi.

Thus it seems extremely likely that the Knights Templar who became immersed in Sufi mysticism during their sojourn in the Holy Land must have known of Khidr as a powerful spiritual presence. He must have reminded them strongly of their own native traditions of the European God of Nature, the Green Man. There may be far more to this than we may ever understand, for they are known to have spent years exploring and excavating below Jerusalem's Temple Mount searching for treasure, whether spiritual or material, or a mixture of the two, we cannot yet tell. Their meteoric rise to wealth and influence seems to indicate that they did find something. Magical artefacts, secret scrolls, the Ark of the Covenant? We will probably never know for sure.

Yet we do know that the Mount is riddled with a labyrinth of ancient tunnels, passages, chambers, caves, wells and cisterns, many of which go back to prehistoric times. One of these, located directly beneath the Mount, is known as Bir al-Khidr, or the Well of Khidr. It seems an appropriate place to find a spring of water named after the Green One, who drank from the Fountain of Life.

Al-Khidr is also the main presiding deity of a number of modern occult groups, who invoke 'The Green One' in their rituals and look to him for inspiration. The late Andrew Chumbley, the head of one such group, has written, 'The subject of al-Khidr is most significant in terms of the 'earth-based' origins of religion. As a power which journeys the world and whose step encompasses all places, Khidr, The Green One, embodies the very essence of the Dragon-path as Man, or as the initiate.'[10] In his book *Qutub*, he states that Khidr 'signifies the bestowal of fertility and may be regarded as the embodiment of the creative force of Spring preparing the 'land' for new growth...'[11] He interprets the root of the word thus: 'To be in deep sleep or trance', inferring the altered state of consciousness symbolised by Khidr, who is traditionally considered to embody the prophetic faculty of the soul: 'From the root KhDR is the word Khadar meaning 'to cut a Palm Tree', that is, to release the force from the form. The Palm Tree is a Sufic symbol of Baraka or spiritual power...'

6

St George and the Mysteries of Albion

hortly after his coronation in 1327 the teenage King Edward III, with his young bride Philippa, visited Glastonbury Abbey, then the wealthiest in Britain. Its magnificence was the product of centuries of patronage by royalty and pilgrims from all over the world, who were drawn by the richness of its legends. These stories were viewed as historical fact, for they had been recorded by many chroniclers and were so deeply woven into the early history of Britain that even the Roman Church accepted them.

The legends stated that Jesus Christ had visited Glastonbury in his boyhood, accompanied by his uncle Joseph of Arimathea, who was 'in the tin trade'. Similar stories clung to many locations in the Westcountry, including St Michael's Mount in Cornwall, which many authorities believed to be the 'Ictis' of the Greek historians, where tin was traded with the Phoenicians. The boy Jesus had travelled with Joseph for a good reason, according to those versed in the mystical traditions. He had studied at the famous Druid colleges of the day, for Britain was renowned throughout the ancient world as the greatest centre of learning in Europe, where the sons and daughters of foreign nobles and royalty were sent to be schooled in the philosophy of their ancestors. Even Caesar had noted that the British Druidic schools were the most influential in Europe, spreading their knowledge of good governance, spiritual truths, and the laws of nature throughout the known world.

The first surviving written record of Jesus' visit is from the 10th century manuscript *The Life of St Dunstan*. Earlier versions had been destroyed or lost in the Saxon incursions of Athelstan when the old libraries of ancient Britain had vanished forever, and the oral traditions suppressed. Certain legends, though, were so persistent that they clung to places as if stored in the memory of the land itself. Many were so ingrained into the consciousness of the British psyche that they could never be eradicated. The Glastonbury legends were amongst these, for they had been passed down through the centuries in the old Bardic traditions. The chronicler of *The Life of St Dunstan* stated that the first church on the site of Glastonbury Abbey, a simple wattle building with a thatched roof, had been built by Jesus himself in honour of his mother, the Virgin Mary. The building still stood at that time, enclosed within a rectangular church, and was one of the great wonders of the country. Because it had been built by Jesus' own hands it had the remarkable reputation of being the first Christian church ever constructed, a fact that was acknowledged by both Eusebius and Constantine.

The fabulous treasures that accumulated within and around the site of this original building became the focal point of pilgrimage. Glastonbury, the oldest and most influential of all the British churches, had a collection of sacred relics that was probably the greatest in the western world, and besides that there was also the tomb of Joseph of Arimathea, (who was said to have brought the Holy Grail with him) as well as those of St Patrick and St David.

The precious but crumbling remains of the wattle church had been carefully preserved in about 625 by Paulinus, Archbishop of York, and parts of it could still be seen until the 12th century, adorned with glittering crosses, jewelled relics and golden censers hanging from the roof. In 1126 the Abbot of Glastonbury, Henry of Blois, commissioned the most trusted scholar in the land, William of Malmsbury, to write a history of the Abbey, and offered him the opportunity to research in the magnificent library, the finest collection of ancient books in Britain. He noted that:

'The church at Glastonbury is the oldest that I know in England, and thus it has deserved its name, the Old Church. In it are preserved the bodies of many saints, nor is there any part where there are not ashes of the blessed. Not only the stone-paved floor and the sides of the altar, but every altar itself both above and within, are crammed with holy relics. That repository of so many saints is justly called a heavenly sanctuary on earth.'[1]

However, the ancient glories of Glastonbury were destined to become but a poignant memory. Just over half a century later, on 25th May 1184, a taper set light to one of the hangings in the Old Church, and within a few fleeting moments it became a raging inferno, destroying every last remnant of its illustrious past. All the dry-as-dust relics were suddenly gone, the library was reduced to ashes, and the Abbey became a smoking, ruinous shell. Within a flicker of the Eye of Time, Glastonbury's irreplaceable trove of mystic treasures had been utterly destroyed.

A century and a half later the young Edward, who had been crowned King of Britain at the age of fourteen, was thus following in a long tradition of royal pilgrims to the most holy site in the country. The rebuilt abbey may not have possessed the atmosphere of antiquity of the previous one, but it was truly magnificent, and the hallowed ground itself was still sacred and imbued with an ineffable ancient power. The teenage king felt it strongly, for he had been schooled in the mystical traditions of kingship and his responsibilities to the land, and the memory of those that had gone before was his guiding light.

The main reason he was visiting Glastonbury was not just that it had been founded by Jesus and Joseph, or even that it was the last resting place of so many saints, but that it was the centre of another order of legend entirely: here lay the mortal remains of the great British hero-king Arthur.

Around the year 1190 the historian Giraldus Cambrensis, a Welshman of partly Norman descent, had accompanied Henry II on his travels and recorded a remarkable event in the history of Glastonbury. Although the fables had long since connected Arthur with Avalon, which people equated with Glastonbury, the stories were indeed fabulous and incorporated much lore from Celtic and earlier times. The great warrior-king of the Dark Ages had drawn to himself a mantle of tradition that was rooted in another age, an age where Divine Kingship reflected a preoccupation with ancient magic and a knowledge of cosmic order. Thus the movements of the heavens were understood to have their effects on Earth, and in the perennial wisdom the king stood for the central power of the Sun surrounded by his Round Table of twelve knights, each representing a particular zodiacal influence. The quest for each of them was to discover their true nature and their place in the greater whole. This inheritance from former times, and an understanding of the ritual significance of certain places in the customs of kingship, meant that the Arthurian stories concealed much esoteric knowledge from the immemorial past.

It was reported that Arthur's tomb had been discovered between two stone pyramids whilst monks were digging a grave outside St Mary's Church, the site of the original simple building erected by Jesus. Sixteen feet down they had found a hollow tree trunk containing the bones of a man 'of unusual size'. Also present within the coffin were the bones of a woman, amongst which, we are told, was a tress of golden hair which turned to dust as it was exposed to the air. The man's bones were shown to Giraldus by the Abbot, Henry of Sully, and included a giant thigh bone and a huge skull exhibiting a large number of scars, one of which had not healed and was assumed to be the death blow. At the bottom of the coffin was a stone, under which lay a leaden cross stating 'Here lies entombed the renowned King Arthur with Guinevere his second wife in the isle of Avalon.'

In these cynical times it is natural to suspect the motives behind such a discovery, and in fact most historians see this story as little more than a huge publicity coup which would result in attracting considerable wealth to the ailing Abbey. Yet the exhumation was said to be attended by many eyewitnesses of note, and there is no doubt that many influential people believed it to be genuine.

Even William Caxton, who printed Sir Thomas Malory's *Le Morte d'Arthur* in 1485, was still convinced that 'Arthur's Grave' was one of the few certain pieces of evidence about him. But our suspicions may be further aroused by other details which are at the very least confused. Curiously two antiquaries of the 16th century, John Leland and William Camden, later saw a cross which they believed to be the one referred to, although the 'barbarous manner' of the lettering made no reference to Queen Guinevere. Was it a later forgery? Did the original ever exist? Since it has now vanished we will probably never know. Whatever the truth behind the story (and can we really be certain that events such as this can never be attributed to divine intervention, where the ancestral spirits of the land intervene in human affairs?) the bones were re-interred in two marble coffers in a chapel next to the great church. It had been Geoffrey of Monmouth who had written that Arthur, mortally wounded, had been borne away to Avalon. Previous chroniclers had called Glastonbury *The Glass Island*, referring to its mythical reputation as a luminous realm of Annwyn, or the Celtic Otherworld.

The spirit of Arthur, that memory of ancestral kingship signifying something more than any historical character ever can, is not to be easily dismissed in such a place as Glastonbury. Its pre-Christian traditions as a great Druid College, the legends from those times, identifying it as an entrance to the Otherworld, and the discovery of the Glastonbury Zodiac in the 1930s by the artist and mystical scholar Katherine Maltwood, who called it *Arthur's Round Table of the Stars,*[2] all point to a body of tradition that is far more than any political history. Who can deny the inexplicable influence still to be found at Glastonbury, and the potent inspirational power exuding from it? Who is to say that the legends of Jesus, Joseph and the Holy Grail are nothing but romantic invention? It would be a very brave or foolish person who would dismiss the magical aura of so many thousands of years.

Edward, then, found himself in Glastonbury as a pilgrim to the shrine of King Arthur. He no doubt hoped for some spiritual connection with his great ancestor, perhaps seeking guidance on the true principles of kingship. What we can be sure of is that he felt it his destiny to re-establish the old Order of the Round Table along Arthurian lines. Here in the heart of Arthur's kingdom, standing before the richly-decorated tomb in front of the High Altar, as he touched the bones of his hero proffered by the Abbot he must have felt a strong spiritual link with the ideals of his illustrious forebear.

St George and the Round Table

'The old order changeth, yielding place to the new, and God fulfils himself in many ways'.

Tennyson, Morte d'Arthur

Edward's visit to Glastonbury resulted in a vision of his own reign as an idealistic reworking of the legendary Arthurian era, to which he dedicated himself wholeheartedly. All the hallmarks of the age of Arthur were to be brought back to vibrant life; a new age was dawning, of honour, chivalry and victory.

He resolved to rebuild the Great Castle at Windsor, according to Geoffrey of Monmouth the seat of Arthur's power and the place where the Round Table had been originally set up. The first work to be undertaken was most mythologically significant; the great mound, a conical flat-topped artificial hill of unknown age, had traditionally been the place of power, specifically pointed out by Chaucer as the spot where 'Arthur built his castle'. It was the place where Arthur and his knights had gathered for their Whitsuntide ceremonies at the Summer Solstice (White-Sun-tide).

In 1344 work began, and Edward of Windsor ordained that the Knights of the Garter assemble on April 23rd, (the feast of St George), to inaugurate the new era. He felt that St George exemplified all he wished to achieve, and was the perfect model for his Knights, an illustrious heroic figure who had already exerted a profound influence on the history of Britain. Stories of Arthur's times also claimed that the fabled King had personally chosen St George as his own protective saint, and gone into battle flying the red cross which had become his emblem. In surely what was an inspired masterstroke of visionary brilliance, Edward had brought together two myths and made them one. In future the nation would be united under the banners of both the red cross of St George and the dragon of Edward's ancestral heritage. The Pendragon bloodline of Arthur had merged with the Templars and Crusader knights of Jerusalem to found a new dynasty.

The King had a special standard made of red silk with a gold and vermilion image of a 'burning dragon' which was raised first at the battle of Crécy when, signalling the attack, he shouted Richard the Lionheart's battle cry 'By the help of God and St George'. The same ensign was raised at the naval battle of Sluys, the first time the English defeated the French on the high seas. As they went into this battle the King reminded his knights that it was Richard who had originally caused the 'blue thongs' to be tied around their legs, symbolising, like the Sufic orders, a bond of brotherhood and mystic power. He promised that if the day were theirs he would fulfil Richard's intention of fully restoring King Arthur's fraternity and adopt the blue garter as the badge of the New Order. Victory was to be theirs in both battles, and Edward naturally attributed this to the miraculous and ineffable power of St George.[3]

In 1347, as the campaign against France drew to a close, the triumphant Warrior-King and his Queen celebrated the victories of Crécy and Calais amidst great public rejoicing, first at Winchester, (another of Arthur's Round Table sites), and then at Edward's birth-place at Windsor Castle. It must have seemed as though the new Arthurian era was blessed by God. In future the Round Table of Arthur and the Knights of the Garter were to be forever indissolubly linked.

For the next twenty years, Edward, assisted by the High Sheriff and

St George's Chapel at Windsor

Constable of the Castle, William of Wykeham, devoted himself to the establishment of the Order, completing the Round Tower on the ancient mound and building an upper ward to the existing castle. The completion of the magnificent St George's Chapel, the spiritual home of the Order of the Garter, symbolised something more than a desire to commemorate such a seminal moment in England's history; it was also a powerful statement of independence. In 1348 he obtained from Pope Clement VI a papal bull declaring it a free chapel, outside the jurisdiction of the Roman Catholic Church. In future any officers, clergy or even choristers were duty bound to sever any connections with their former religious communities. Henceforth their allegiance was to be solely to the Monarch and the Knights of St George. Such was the care taken to make the Chapel completely autonomous that it survived unscathed the terrible destruction of the Reformation, with its power, and its treasury, intact. In fact it became the model for the post-Reformation cathedrals and churches which were to become such a feature of the English ideal, remaining free and independent of all foreign powers, just like the golden age of King Arthur.[4]

St George, who took on the mythic mantle of Arthur, naturally became very popular during this time, especially in liberty-loving Britain. The country was renowned for its universal welcome to foreigners, a legacy from its long seafaring tradition which had encouraged a libertarian attitude of freedom and openness since Druidic times. Throughout the ancient world Britain was known for its individual freedoms and absorption of other cultures. As such St George, the hero of many other lands, was the perfect figure to rally around.

In fact Edward largely succeeded in achieving what he set out to do when he conceived of his kingdom as a new version of the Golden Age of Arthur. He reintroduced the magnificent spectacle of medieval tournaments and restored harmony amongst the barons and aristocratic nobles of England, who had previously been in disarray. He also restored the shattered dignity of the monarchy after the disastrous reign of his father Edward II, and freed the country from anarchy by bringing a new sense of liberation and tolerance. He was a great leader and a re-incarnation of the old spirit of Albion, famed for his extravagant parties and celebrations as much as his success in battle.

The entire ethos of his reign, drawn from the original Round Table with its chivalry and codes of honour, had inspired the country to one of its greatest times of stability, for it was one of the few times of the later Middle Ages that saw no civil war. There seems little doubt that Edward's success for the greater part of his reign was achieved almost exclusively through the promotion of the archetypal myth enshrined in the cults of St George and King Arthur. Both these heroic figures had as their iconic emblem the dragon, as if it somehow represented a universal truth to which humanity naturally aspires.

Footsteps of History

Visitors to St George's Chapel today who have an empathy and a sense of history can hardly fail to be aware of the atmosphere that exudes from the glowing, highly-polished English oak and the finely-wrought stone within. The colourful banners hanging above the knights' stalls speak of old battles, moments in time when the fate of the nation rested upon split-second decisions in the heat of conflict. They also remind us of the noble aspirations which guided this elite brotherhood. The lofty fan-vaulting is reminiscent of a great stone forest, its roof interlacing like the fingers of a thousand delicate branches frozen into stars and geometric patterns. It is one of the finest examples of the unique 'English' style of medieval architecture in Britain.

It was in 1240 that Henry III first ordered a chapel to be built in the lower ward at Windsor Castle, but it was his grandson Edward III who rebuilt it and made it one of the greatest in England by inaugurating the Most Noble Order of the Garter as 'a society, fellowship and college of knights'. The 26 knights, including Edward himself, pledged 'to show fidelity and friendliness one towards the other', with the famous blue garter as a symbol of amity.

The founding members included the Black Prince, the Earl of Warwick and the Earl of Salisbury, whose beautiful wife was to be remembered by generations of schoolboys as being the inspiration behind the Order, when the garter slipped from her leg during a dance. The tale is patently apocryphal, designed to impress itself upon the popular mind, but symbolically it alludes to the chivalric ideal and the Sufic bond of mystic brotherhood which the knights aspired to. The dances also became legendary, along with the colourful tournaments and feasts that were such an important feature of the rebirth of Arthur's realm.

If we could hear the mute stones speak, the whispering voices of many centuries would echo through the vast cathedral-like interior. If only we could tap into their memory we would see history parading before us; the Emperor Sigismund bringing the arms of St George into a building full of vibrancy and colour; Charles the Bold of Burgundy placing his shield behind his stall;

the King of Spain kneeling in front of the altar to swear an oath of allegiance. Perhaps we might still hear the prayers said by Henry VIII as he asked God to deliver his realm from the deadening grip of the Roman Catholic Church.[5]

Can we imagine Shakespeare (who was himself born on St George's Day) sauntering through the aisles and musing about an idea for a new play, *The Merry Wives of Windsor*, which the chapel's choirboys were to act before Queen Elizabeth? Or George III making his way to communion at 8 o'clock in the morning, inspecting the restoration work he commissioned as he went. Edward's sword—his *excalibur*—still hangs there to immortalise the ideals that were to become enshrined here. We may forgive ourselves for allowing a fleeting moment of romanticism to overtake us in such a place, amidst the ornate and monumental architecture of one of the most famous buildings in Britain. Its status as a 'peculiar' or royal free chapel promotes a feeling that somehow it exists beyond the restrictive boundaries of any creed or religion, true to its own philosophy. In its heyday the chapel was crammed with a profusion of glittering vestments, copes and altar hangings, and all manner of jewel-encrusted chalices, crosses and censers whose gold reflected the glow of a myriad flickering candles.

Of course it had its sacred relics too, including a piece of the 'True Cross' captured by Edward I in 1283. Another great relic was the 'Heart of St George' given by Sigismund when he attended the feast of the Garter in 1416 and became a companion of the Order. Every service was accompanied by the heavenly sound of the chapel's choristers, noted as being among the finest in Europe. The choir, the energetic centre of the whole building, has resonated with such sacred music daily since 1348. Centuries later, even Samuel Pepys after his visit in 1666 commented on the excellence of the 'sacred art'.

As a place of pilgrimage St George's Chapel became one of the great centres, and its reputation for cures of all kinds spread afar. The pilgrims prayed among the ornate tombs of former kings and nobles, including that of Henry VIII, Jane Seymour, Henry VI, Edward IV, George VI and Charles I, as well as a constellation of other famous and notable people whose spirits hover over the place. They were also particularly attracted to the miraculous and mortal remains of one John Shorne, the rector of North Marston towards the end of the 13th century, who had been renowned as a healer during his life. His reputation continued after his death, with his tomb drawing large numbers from all corners of the land.[6]

One of the most memorable things about this great building is the collection of plates fixed to the stalls of each knight; 'a heraldic storehouse of the highest artistic excellence, unequalled in Europe.' They tell, in symbolic form, the history of each knight, and emphasise that the beginnings of the Order were built upon a blending of the myths of Arthur and St George, when the 'nine poor knights' who founded the Knights Templar went to live on the Temple Mount in Jerusalem.

It was not until 1833 that William IV changed the name of the Knights of the Order, used since its inception, the 'Poor Knights', to the 'Military Knights'. The unspoken connections between the Order of the Garter and the Templars could hardly be more explicit.

Like the families behind the founding of the Templars, the legends of the Grail and the entire cult of medieval chivalry, they shared the same ideals, and after the war against Templarism it appears that many of its aims were absorbed into the new Order. As one chronicler noted: 'No Order in Europe is so ancient, none so illustrious, for it exceeds in Majesty, honour and fame all Chivalrous Fraternities in the world.'

The Sacrifice of the Green King

The mystical lore of kingship runs like a green thread through the traditions of the British monarchy. It comes from a way of thinking extending to all pre-Christian religions, and forms the basis of much that is mysterious in the historical record. Quintessentially, the King or Queen embodies the qualities of the Sun God, bringing fertility and good fortune to the people. In Egypt this is especially well documented. Each Pharaoh had a 'Horus-name' that typified their relationship to the divine power of the solar principle. Many European monarchs also followed this immemorial custom, the most well-known being Louis XIV, the Sun King of France. Yet this deeply held religious principle of divine kingship is often ignored by those who view mythology as mere meaningless superstition. However, to the common people of past ages the King was the living personification of the dying and resurrecting God of Nature. Great celebrations accompanied the coronation (a word linked to the corona, or halo of light surrounding the Sun, and the symbolic ritual of drawing down the power of the Sun into the royal head). From that moment the populace anticipated a reign of bounteous plenty, ruled by someone who brought to Earth the truth and justice of the heavenly realms. The rulers literally became, during their lives, Gods on Earth.

This concept can be traced through many epochs, and the manner in which Edward III focused on the myth of Arthur and successfully recreated the Golden Age, even if only for a while, shows how powerful the idea can be. Of course there comes a time when the King is ailing, either in health or his divine duty to bring order and stability to his subjects. It then becomes necessary for rulers to accept the other side of their responsibilities, and sacrifice themselves for the good of the land. They become living, and dying, embodiments of the principles of nature, that must die to be reborn every year. Frazer's *The Golden Bough* explores this concept in great detail, and traces the idea back to deep antiquity, as one of the most crucial beliefs of the human race.[7] It is the essence behind the basis of Christianity, where Jesus dies, the Holy Blood being absorbed by the Earth to renew humanity.

Other aspects of the old religion often feature strongly in the histories of monarchy, and the beheading of Charles I (who was buried in the choir at St George's Chapel) may well be a distant echo of the Cult of the Head, albeit perverted by the harshness and expediency of the times. It seems beheading was reserved only for Kings and Queens; lesser folk were hanged. One reign in particular has a strong claim to be connected with the timeless rituals of kingship as the spirit of the Green Man, whose death fertilises the beginnings of a new cycle of growth and plenty. The great majority of the British populace, who still

King Charles II, the 'Merrie King', in the Oak Tree, from St Kew Church, Cornwall.

lived in the countryside and followed the old pagan rites associated with this cycle, understood and instinctively knew that the King was in some indefinable way responsible for the continued bounty of the natural world. Thus when Charles II (who was crowned on St George's Day, April 23rd 1661) allegedly hid in an oak tree whilst escaping from soldiers after the Battle of Worcester in 1651, he adopted this personification of the Green Man perfectly. It became the most famous popular exploit of his career in the common mind, although the 'Merrie King' as he was called, was also well known for his own personal fertility and famous sexual appetite. The image of the King peering from within the branches and leaves of a Druidic oak became a widespread theme in the folk art of his day. He had struck a chord in the collective consciousness of his subjects, and become the Green King of the Woodlands. A series of new festivals was inaugurated, including Oak Apple Day on 29th May (which is still celebrated today and involves an oak branch being hoisted up church towers and left until the following year). In 1660 Charles also proclaimed 'Arbor Day' when trees were 'dressed', and this is still practised in Shropshire. The 29th May is also Garland King Day in Castleton, Derbyshire, when the King proceeds through the town on horseback, carrying a garland, stopping at pubs and ending up at the Maypole in the town square. A statue of the Merrie King is then decorated with oak leaves.

It is possible to hear echoes of this strong association of kingship with the customs of the Green Man when visiting certain cathedrals, where king's heads are shown with greenery and leaves issuing from their mouths just like the classic image of the Green Man. But of course he must be sacrificed to continue the sacred cycle. The most intriguing example of the sacrificed god in this context is that of Rufus 'The Red', son of William the Conqueror, who came from a background powerfully immersed in the esoteric beliefs of kingship. In her classic study of the survival of pre-Christian worship into the medieval period *The God of the Witches*, Margaret Murray interprets the death of Rufus as the archetypal 'dying god', the priest-king who was ritually killed to ensure the continuity of his realm. Just like the Corn King and the Green Man, who both must die to create the circumstances for the land's future fertility, so the King must die to rescue his country from the ravages of disorder.[8]

When Rufus was killed in the New Forest on 2nd August 1100, England was, according to the chronicler Peter of Blois, in the grip of a host of pestilences and natural disasters, with plagues ravaging both man and beast, and the land rent by storms and earthquakes. Famine was rife, and the natural order had broken down. Rufus, it is said, experienced visions of his fate and submitted willingly to it. His hunting companion Sir Walter Tyrrel, shooting an arrow at a stag deep in the forest, became his executioner as the arrow was deflected by a stag's antlers (or in some versions, a tree), to bury itself in Rufus' heart. The symbolism of the stag, as the horned god, the Cernunnos of the Celts, and the tree, as spirit of the wildwood, alerts us even further to the mystical nature of these events.

As the country lamented, the dead king's body was placed on a cart and drawn in sombre procession to Winchester, the great Round Table site of Arthur, a former sacrificial victim himself. The most vivid account is that of William of Malmsbury: 'The sun was now declining, when the king, drawing his bow and letting fly an arrow, slightly wounded a stag; and keenly gazing following it, still running, a long time with his eyes, holding up his hand to keep off the power of the sun's rays…' Sir Walter then let his fatal arrow fly, which glanced off the antlers of another stag and pierced the king. 'On receiving the wound the king uttered not a word; but breaking off the shaft of the weapon where it projected

from his body fell upon the wound by which he accelerated his death.' The chronicler continues with a dramatic account that is perfectly in keeping with what we know of ritual sacrifice.

*The Rufus Stone in
the New Forest, marking
the spot where the king was killed.*

As the body is born to Winchester in sombre procession, with great crowds lining the route, it bleeds profusely all the way, with many people smearing the blood upon themselves and gathering it for its miraculous healing properties. The bleeding king thus fulfilled the timeless rite of royal sacrifice, with his blood soaking into the Earth, Jesus-like, to restore the wasteland. Rufus the Red had become the mythic hero so that the land could replenish itself in the time-honoured way.

There seems little doubt that Rufus was unashamedly pagan and followed the traditions of his Viking ancestors. His red hair marked him out as an inheritor of the old rites of kingship, for his father William was a Norman or Norse-man. Rufus openly jeered at Christianity for claiming to be the one true religion and plundered churches and monasteries, ridiculing the saints and the power of the Christian god. Right from the beginning he had been popular with his subjects, who may have sensed his beliefs that chimed so well with the ingrained ways of English folklore.

This is all the stranger as his father had recently savagely conquered the country. Despite this, Rufus was to be cast as a devil by the monks of the established Church who chronicled his reign. The propaganda after his death is powerful testimony to how much he was hated. When he was buried in the choir of Winchester Cathedral there was evidently no funeral service, not a prayer was uttered, nor a bell tolled. He was even blamed for part of the cathedral's roof collapsing after his interment. As Margaret Murray concludes, 'The whole story of Rufus has been presented to the modern reader from the records of his bitter enemies'.

Rufus' end was attended by many miraculous events, and his behaviour indicated that he knew precisely what was about to happen, even encouraging Tyrrel to choose the sharpest arrows and let them fly with true aim. Warning dreams from across the kingdom and even further afield foretold of his death, yet he ignored them. Within a few hours of his death news of it had travelled throughout his realm, including Devon, Cornwall and even as far as Italy.

The date of Rufus' death, August 2nd, is significant in the old rituals, and was called 'the morrow of Lammas'. Lammas, or Lughnasad, August 1st, marked the point in the annual cycle of harvest-time, when the Earth offers its bounty to sustain the population until the following spring. the Corn King is dead—Long Live the King! It was the time of ritual sacrifice to synchronise events on Earth with those in the heavens, and bring peace and plenty back to the Earth. Thus Rufus became the sacrificed god of immemorial tradition, the kingly equivalent of the Spirit of the Land immortalised in the English folk song *John Barleycorn*.

The following version is one of many variants, sung in Oxfordshire by Shepherd Haden to the musicologist Cecil Sharp:

> *There were three men came out of the west, their fortunes for to try,*
> *And these three men made a solemn vow John Barleycorn should die.*
> *They ploughed, they sowed, they harrowed him in, threw clods upon his head,*
> *Then these three men made a solemn vow John Barleycorn was dead.*

But the dead god grows stronger through his contact with the Earth:

> *They let him lay for a very long time till the rain from heaven did fall,*
> *Then little Sir John he raised up his head and he soon amazed them all.*
> *They let him lay till midsummer, till he looked both pale and wan,*
> *Then little Sir John grew a long long beard and so became a man.*

Yet our hero knows the cycles of life and death, and realises that he will be sacrificed:

> *They hired man with scythes so sharp to cut him down by the knee,*
> *They rolled him and tied him around by the waist, served him most barbarously.*
> *They hired men with the sharp pitchforks who pricked him to the heart,*
> *But the loader he served him worse than that, for he bound him to the cart.*

Worse is to come: 'Sir' John suffers such treatment like a true hero, but then he is mutilated, his body crushed between stones, very like the martyrdom of St George in the Coptic texts:

> *They rolled him around and around the field till they came into a barn,*
> *And there they made a solemn mow of poor John Barleycorn.*
> *They hired men with the crabtree sticks who cut him to the bone,*
> *But the miller he served him worse than that,*
> *for he ground him between two stones.*

John Barleycorn is dead! Long Live John Barleycorn! His funeral rites are celebrated with the eating of his body and the drinking of his blood.

> *Here's little Sir John in the nut brown bowl and brandy in the glass,*
> *And little Sir John in the nut brown bowl proved a stronger man at last.*
> *For the hunter he can't hunt the fox nor so loudly blow his horn,*
> *And the tinker he can't mend our kettles without a little bit of*
> *John Barleycorn.*[9]

7

The Assembly of the Wondrous Head

'The Human Head is the image of the world'

Plato
The Timaeus

The old Welsh tales collectively known as the Mabinogion are the earliest stories of pre-literate Britain that we possess. No-one knows where their beginnings lie, but they are likely to have been heard around the blazing fires of prehistory and endlessly revamped by the bards and storytellers of Celtic, Bronze Age or even Neolithic times. They are mainly drawn from 13th and 14th century manuscripts such as the *Red Book of Hergest* or the *White Book of Rhydderch*, thought to have been composed about 1325, just a few years before Edward III's succession. As the word *Og* appears quite prominently in the name, as well as Mabin or Mabon, (the Druidic Sun God), we can conclude that elements of the stories are certainly of considerable antiquity. Scholars are united in believing that they were passed on for many centuries, or even millennia as we have observed, before they were finally written down in the distinctive long and rambling style of the bardic tradition.

Although their origins are lost in time, some of the elements—however garbled they may appear due to endless retellings, changes due to transient fashions or the whim of chroniclers—are of great interest. The tales include the first mention of King Arthur in Celtic prose, with the main characters easily recognisable. Guinevere is Gwenhwyvar, Bedivere is Bedwyr, Gawain is Gwalchmai, Perceval is Peredur and Bran the Fisher King is Bron. It is very likely that this collection of stories is the original version of the Grail mythos from which all others are derived, since the earliest European manuscript of Chrétien de Troyes, *Le Conte du Graal*, says unequivocally that Perceval was a Welshman like Edward.

The theme held much significance for its time, for it explores the spiritual element of knighthood, as the hero (much like The Fool of the Tarot) starts with a childish innocence, and through his experiences achieves spiritual grace. He shares the limelight in his quest for the Grail with Gawain of Green Knight fame, who seeks a magic lance that drips blood. This is said to be the 'Spear of Destiny' that pierced Christ's side during the crucifixion, but how far the Christian myth overlaid an older idea we can only guess. If Chrétien had survived to finish the story it seems clear that Perceval would have eventually found his way back to the Grail castle and asked the question that eluded him, 'Whom does the Grail serve?' The answer always lies in knowing the right question.

It seems clear that the influence of the continental writers is inextricably entwined with the old British traditions at a time when the Knights Templar had been largely destroyed or driven underground by Philip le Bel of France and the Pope. Many, however, had escaped the cataclysm and sought refuge in other lands, especially Britain where they were incorporated into the Knights Hospitallers, Portugal, where they became the Knights of Christ, and Scotland, where they were to establish Scottish Rite Freemasonry.

It seems reasonable to assume that much of the esoteric wisdom that had made the mystical brotherhood so powerful therefore became absorbed into these legendary histories, while they in turn added a certain home-grown flavour to the mix of influences from the Holy Land that had fired the Templars' imaginations. What themes from the old tales might add to the mystical power they already possessed? What stories from their own past would strike a chord in their hearts and blend with all they had learnt from the sages of the East? Were there any common links between the different cultural traditions?

At a time when they were being persecuted and horribly tortured for their beliefs on the Continent, they must have looked upon these events, and the fact that the Roman Church sought to dominate human thought in such a brutal manner, as the nadir of their age. They had rediscovered the mystical sciences during their sojourn in the Middle East and reintroduced an entire body of knowledge which had created vast wealth and power. Yet almost all had been lost. The treasures had vanished, often spirited away at the last moment, but the spiritual treasures could never be destroyed, if only they could incorporate them into the customs of their own lands.

They must have seen in the old stories poignant echoes of their own predicament. In the *Mabinogion*, Bran the Blessed, King of the 'Isle of the Mighty', is wounded in the foot by a poisoned arrow, whereupon the fertility of both Britain and Ireland declines and they become wastelands. This may well have seemed a metaphor for what had happened to the Templars, as their attempts to bring religious truths to Europe had come to nothing, as if they had become lame themselves. The same story is told of Perceval's uncle, the Fisher King, whose wound is the cause of strife and battle throughout the land. It is because Perceval is rather naïve that he blindly obeys his uncle and fails to ask that crucial question which could restore the ailing realm.

Bran is the owner of a magic cauldron, which, like the Grail, has the power to perform miracles. If a slain man were to be cast into it he would emerge reborn, although unable to speak. The cauldron came originally from a lake near a magic mound in Ireland. Bran gives his sister Branwen to the King of Ireland, and gives him the cauldron too. But soon they come into conflict with one another over insults that question their honour as warriors, and Branwen suffers punishment from her husband. Hearing of this Bran sets sail for Ireland to do battle, but because the Irish immerse their slain warriors in the cauldron their army is continually replenished, until the magic vessel is finally broken into four pieces and becomes useless. In the end the British are triumphant, but at a heavy price. Only seven warriors remain and Bran is wounded by the poisoned arrow.

The King commands his men to cut off Bran's head and take it to London where they must bury it at the 'White Mount' (thought to be where the Tower of London now stands) looking towards France. Bran tells them that the 'wonderful head' will talk to them on their journey, which will take forty years. They set out and arrive in Anglesey, Bran's homeland (and the last great bastion of the Druids in Britain, where Caesar finally exterminated them in 59 AD). The place they land is *Holyhead*, a name that speaks of this episode in the mythological annals of Albion, and still one of the main routes to and from Ireland. Branwen, however, dies of grief at a place still called Ynys Branwen. Curiously, a funeral urn with cremated ash and bone was excavated in 1813 at the place long believed to be her grave.

'And notwithstanding that they themselves had suffered there came no remembrance either of that, or of any sorrow in the world. And then they passed the fourscore years so that they were not aware of ever having spent a time more joyous and delightful than that. It was not more irksome, nor could any tell of his fellow that he was older during that time, than when they came there. Nor was it more irksome having the head with them when Bran the Blessed had been with them alive. And because of those fourscore years it was called The Assembly of the Wondrous Head.'[1]

The protectors of Bran's Head, which is as lively and fresh as when alive and ceaselessly utters poetry and prophecies, enter a strange and enchanted timeless zone, as if they had somehow stepped into the Otherworld. They spend seven years at Harlech, and then find themselves at a great hall overlooking the Severn Sea, which had been foretold by the wondrous head. But they look through a doorway towards Cornwall in defiance of a warning from the head. From that moment on the head begins to decay. It is finally buried at London, where it becomes a protective spirit over the land. A later story has the spirit of Bran in the form of ravens (still to be found at the Tower). This legend says that if they ever die out then the country will be no more, and to this day the ravens are bred on Anglesey to maintain the population. The miraculous head remained as guardian until the arrival of Arthur, who dug it up, apparently insisting that he should rule by the might of the sword alone. However, could there be an unwritten reason for Arthur's strange defiance of Bran's prophecy? Could it be that he wanted to possess the wondrous head himself?

In Celtic mythology Bran is associated with the fading power of the latter half of the year, as the strength of the Sun diminishes. His death occurs at the Midwinter Solstice when the Sun King of the old year gives up his mantle of glory to Mabon, the Celtic Apollo, who is the virile young new god reborn again. Thus Mabon represents the fertility of the coming spring with its burgeoning growth and sprouting seeds, his power gathering towards the Summer Solstice, when he himself becomes his father Bran as the year turns, in the endless cycle of life on Earth. Bran was the evergreen Holly God of the Druids, remembered in the Christmas carol 'The Holly and the Ivy':

'Of all the trees that are in the wood the Holly bears the crown.'

It is from this that we get our holidays, holy-days or holly-days. Can we see in the myth of Bran a memory of the essential cycle of fertility that 'guards' the country against becoming a wasteland? The final act of harvesting used to be when the last sheaf (or head) was triumphantly cut, in the ceremony known as 'Crying the Neck'. This was then preserved, usually above the hearth, in order to pass

on the spirit of the dead Corn King to the following year. These pre-Christian rites of fertility appear to be interwoven in the legends in such a way that people close to the natural cycles would have instinctively understood. The Christian saints who took over from the old gods frequently have the same holy-days as their precursors, marking the moments in the Sun's progress that determine prosperity and plenty.

18th century Oak Carving of 'Crying the Neck'

It seems that these old indigenous stories were merged with the imported myths from the Holy Land (which may not have been difficult, as they all derive from the same observations of nature) to create a mix of the new and old, reinvigorating the life of the countryside. In this way, the wondrous head of Bran became practically synonymous with the head of the Templars' iconic saint John the Baptist, the one who comes before Jesus (or Mabon, who is to die himself and yet be reborn again at the Midwinter Solstice). John is beheaded at Midsummer, for his day on June 24th marks the transition between the two halves of the life of the Sun. In mythic terms the Sun is decapitated and starts to decay. In the Templars' new mythology Bran becomes John the Baptist in a masterly blend of the myths of East and West.

The tale of Bran's head might strike us as rather quaint and confusing superstition unless we can see the connections, and realise the central role of the miracle-working head in the Templar tradition. The Mabinogion was being written down in manuscript form at the same time as new ideas from Eastern mysticism were flooding into Europe. The suppression that the Templars suffered on the Continent was never enforced in Britain, other than as a token persecution. Edward II was very reluctant to arrest them, and when he did he treated them with a certain respect.[2] It appears this created a particularly fertile background for a fusion of the old myths. Bran's wondrous head which continues to prophesy, uttering words of great power and wisdom, strikes a remarkable parallel with the famous 'Baphomet' head of the Templars, which was said to speak to them in a similar way.

Talking Heads

'O, no man knows, through what wild centuries roves back the Mabinogion'.
Walter de la Mare

Throughout the Celtic world the cult of head worship was central to religion. The head was believed to be the seat of the soul, and sacred relics, as well as stone representations, were believed to perform a powerful oracular function, communicating directly with the living.[3] In the earliest times warriors collected the heads of their slain enemies and hung them on poles outside their houses as a protective influence, the distant origins of the architectural practice of having carved heads over doorways and entrances today.

Heads of particularly powerful people were preserved as relics so that spiritual communication with the Gods could take place. Especially holy or wise people often had their heads removed after death, and the skulls cleaned and used as receptacles for imbibing sacred water from holy wells. The place where the water poured forth from the Earth was strongly associated with such rituals, so closely linked to the fertility of the land, and so they became known as the 'Head of the Spring'. Often these cranial goblets were mounted, covered in silver or gold, and inlaid with special jewels. This was a practice so steeped in antiquity, and so central to the old religious practices, that it quite naturally carried over into Christian times; the vaults of cathedrals and churches throughout Christendom are stuffed with lavish reliquaries containing the skulls of saints. Head worship is thus one of the most potent aspects of both Christian and pre-Christian belief.

The many stories of Celtic saints who lost their heads, however, contain a deeper esoteric meaning beyond the head being the seat of the soul and a source of some mystical energy. For these saints do not die when beheaded. They frequently pick their own heads up and carry them around, prophesying and preaching as they go, like Bran. The stories, as ever, are symbolic, and refer to the achievement of a higher form of consciousness centred in the spiritual organs of perception within the head. When this is reached, one 'loses the body' and goes beyond the physical limitations of corporeal existence. The head thus becomes the symbol and the vehicle of becoming at one with God.

To the Templars, as the inheritors of Druidic customs, this aspect was paramount. The head of John the Baptist became one of their prime mystical symbols. One only has to wander about places with a strong Templar influence to realise exactly how prominently the image was employed.

A classic example of this can be found at Penzance in Cornwall, situated near the furthermost western tip of Britain, a place long associated with the legends of Jesus and Joseph of Arimathea, and hence the Grail. The town looks across to St Michael's Mount, perhaps the fabled Ictis, where the Phoenicians came to trade for tin. The Templars guarded the old route to the west (now the main A30 road) and had a church and pilgrims' hostel at Temple on Bodmin Moor. In their day they were the great maritime merchants, the 'new Phoenicians' who controlled the Cornish tin trade with the rest of the world. Examples of Templar tin-stamps can still be seen in the church at Madron (the name of the Celtic mother-goddess), with their insignia of the Agnus Dei, or Lamb of God, to identify the ingots to be shipped out. Nearby, a farm now occupies the site of their preceptory, or headquarters. A short stroll around the town reveals dozens of heads of the Baptist on display, demonstrating the enormous power and longevity of the head cult. Penzance, in old Cornish, is *Pen-sans*, meaning Holy Headland.

So it is no surprise that one of the main charges levelled against the Templars by their persecutors was one of head-worship (conveniently neglecting the fact that the Catholic Church itself also indulged in prayer and worship directed at the skulls of their saints). Whilst there can be no doubt that under torture they would probably have admitted to the most heinous and unbelievable acts, all the evidence points to the fact that this was indeed one of the most fundamental rites performed in the chapels and lodges of the Templar knights.

Without repeating the many references to support this view, there are a few especially interesting facets that must engage our attention. Some of the heads that survived into the secretive lodges of later centuries were said to have been those of former Templars, like that of Hugh de Payens who was burnt at the stake during the persecutions. According to the Church's interrogators some were female, some apparently bisexual, while others possessed often curious and sometimes alarming characteristics, if we can believe the confessions wrested from the hapless victims of the Church's torturers. Some were apparently terrible to behold, having a demonic appearance, different faces at the front and back, or even feet (which may mean they were mounted on some type of stand). The name most commonly associated with such heads, many of which were described as being mummified and probably of great antiquity, was *Baphomet*.

This word is usually explained as a corruption of the Arabic term *Abufihamat*, meaning 'Father of Wisdom or Understanding'; furthermore in Greek the words *Baph* and *Metis* mean 'Baptism of Wisdom'. The translator of the Dead Sea Scrolls Hugh Schonfield also felt the name referred to Wisdom, for when he applied the ancient Hebrew Atbash Cipher, a Biblical code employed by the Templars, the result spelt ***Sophia***, the Greek word for Wisdom.[4] In the latter half of the 19th century the French occultist and ritual magician Eliphas Levi depicted Baphomet as the horned 'Goat of Mendes', an androgynous winged composite figure with a bearded goat's head and female breasts, bearing the serpent-entwined staff in his lap. This image derives from the ancient Egyptian and Greek Mystery traditions, and equates with the transcendental form of the great god of nature, Pan.

If Levi felt that Baphomet was Pan, and it appears from his books he was no armchair theorist but a practising magician (who once scared himself badly by conjuring up the spirit of the magus Apollonius of Tyana) then perhaps we should pay attention. For a missing element in the midst of all the intellectual and theoretical forays is that of practical application, the use of real magical techniques to access different levels of reality. Modern occultists, magicians and witches make no excuses for their rituals which focus on the figure of Pan, the all-god of nature who possesses the power over all earthly life. He represents the uncultivated side of nature, and the innate principle in every seed and flower. The hermaphroditic qualities of Baphomet also indicate the true nature of the initiate into the Mysteries; symbolising the balancing of the male and female polarities in each of us.

Baphomet, by Eliphas Levi

So behind the Cult of the Head lies one of the oldest and most universal features of human experience, and one that continues as a powerful thread, from Bran's chattering miraculous head through to the Templars and the jewelled reliquaries of the Christian Church. The head cult takes us right back to the beginnings of human civilisation, and extends to all ages and parts of the world. In Jericho, one of the oldest cities on earth, archaeologists during the 1950s found skulls that had been sculpted and decorated with clay, with shells inserted into the eye sockets. They were estimated to be some 9000 years old, and apparently designed to stand on the floor of the homes of the city's early inhabitants.

The list of charges against the Templars includes some revealing elements. Amongst the specific charges, we find included:

Item: That in each province they had idols, namely heads, of which some had three faces, and some one, and others had a human skull.

Item: That they adore these idols or that idol, and especially in their chapter and assemblies.

Item: That they venerated them as God.

Item: That they venerated them as their saviour.

Item: That they said that the head could save them.

Item: That it could make riches.

Item: That it gave them all the riches of the Order.

Item: That it made trees flower.

Item: That it made the land germinate.

It appears that the legendary voyage of Bran's Head, which sang and prophesied to his assembled warriors, has a direct link to the head-worship of the Templars. Bran, who was the original Grail-keeper, also bequeathed this role to the Templars as well, for they were known as the keepers of the Grail in their time, just as John the Baptist was said to have had charge of the miraculous vessel before Christ. The oracular heads, the vessels of Wisdom, are thus 'founts of knowledge' directly providing contact with the spiritual worlds. Just as significant in our quest for the spirit of the Green Man, alias Green George, are the last two observations mentioned above; that the wondrous heads personify the fertile principle in nature.

8

Message from the Templars

The main reason there is so much speculation about the Knights Templar is because, as a heretical mystical society as well as a military force, hardly anything was written down. Just as with Freemasonry, which many say derives from Templarism, (and indeed Druidism, with which it shares much common ground) initiates were required to take oaths of secrecy, the breaking of which could have serious consequences, even death. The popular impression of modern Freemasonry is, however, somewhat different from that gleaned from history. It seems to many to have become denatured and somewhat distant from its roots, perhaps now only a shadow of the old brotherhood which was once dedicated to the highest ideals of raising human consciousness. On the local level there is no doubt such groups do much that would resonate with the intention behind the ideals of their precursors, raising money for charities and doing all manner of good work. But at the higher levels, apparently so submerged in secrecy, the impression today often appears to point to a misuse of power due to vested interests.

Books written about the Templars can consequently be at either end of two extremes, and anything in between. One end of the spectrum is the classic official history, full of battles, dates and the political intrigues of the day, with little mention of their esoteric interests. The other is often of the wild-eyed speculative type where just about anything goes, from conspiracies involving the Vatican to sinister plots to take over the world. In between is a burgeoning and ever-growing collection of works that explore various aspects of the secretive brotherhood, some of which offer genuine insights into various levels of the mystery. For if one thing can be certain it is that the existence, history and demise of the Templars constitutes one of the greatest enigmas of the last thousand years.

Exactly why the Crusades were first undertaken is itself a baffling conundrum. Why the Cistercian Abbot Bernard of Clairvaux and a close-knit group of aristocratic families, under the protection of the Count of Champagne, hatched a plot to create a Holy War and invade Jerusalem is a deeply tantalising question. How they managed to persuade the populace to take up arms and set off to war against the Muslim world, noted for their skills in battle, will probably forever remain one of history's great mysteries. Yet, conducted in an atmosphere of secrecy and intrigue, this was to transform the medieval world. Here is not the place to delve into an investigation of the true reasons; our quest is to discover why the knights adopted, and then spread, a particular god/saint/prophet figure who became their guide and inspiration. There are many books that attempt to draw the veils back to reveal why, when Jerusalem was taken and Godfroi de Bouillon's brother Baldwin was crowned King on Christmas Day, 1100, a select group of knights soon established themselves at the heart of the city. It was to be some years before the official record told of the 'nine poor knights', the first Templars, who made their headquarters in what is now the al-Aqsa mosque and spent a number of years excavating beneath the site of Solomon's fabled temple.

According to Hebrew tradition Jerusalem was the very centre of the world. Interestingly Jerusalem was often spelt **Gerusalem** in old manuscripts, and contains within it the ancient word for the Earth. The Dome of the Rock, the highest point of the mountain on which the city is built, was believed to be the navel of the world, a sort of umbilical cord to the cosmos. It was here that Abraham tried to sacrifice his son Isaac, and the prophet Mohammed, the founder of Islam, later ascended to heaven. It was the priest Melchizedek who was said to have first named it *Salem*, derived from *'shalom'* meaning peace. Jerusalem thus means Great Peace, or perhaps because of its prefix, 'Peace on Earth'.

An even older form of the name is Solyma, derived from Sol, the Sun. The name Solomon is thought by many to come from Sol-o-Moon, which combines both solar and lunar principles, focused on a point at the mystical centre of the earthly globe. There is certainly a deep mystery here; even more so when we realise that the word Saracen (Jerusalem was often called *Sarras* in the Grail literature) means something other than 'pagan', although it came to represent that in the medieval Christian world. As the etymologist David Elkington discovered whilst researching the word:

> 'Saracen' probably derives from the Arabian sharq, 'sunrise'. Sunrise… is symbolic of the hero, the dying and rising god. The Templars celebrated their rituals at sunrise, which, in keeping with the tradition of dying and rising gods, is symbolic of the resurrection of Christ. Sunrise is also symbolic of fertility, especially of the crops… in French sarrazin is buckwheat. 'Saracen corn' and 'Sarrasin wheat' are terms common in both English and French… 'sarsen' as in a boulder is a variation on the theme of Saracen.'[1]

Here we can see that the holy site of Jerusalem was originally connected with the fertility of the Earth and the cycles of Sun and Moon. In fact before it became a centre of the patriarchal Hebrew tradition it was a shrine to the Earth Goddess. The derivation of 'sarsen' is also significant, for it is the name of the great stones from which both Avebury and Stonehenge are constructed, and indicates that the stones themselves were once connected to fertility, as tradition says.

Both these temples are dedicated, through their positioning, layout and geometry, to the Sun and Moon. Because of its serpentine avenues and its central importance in Neolithic times, Avebury could claim to be the navel, or umbilicus, of ancient Britain.

The facts concerning the rise of the Templars are, however, clear. They were a small group of knights engaged upon a mystical quest, just like Arthur's knights of the Round Table. The object of the quest, like that of their Arthurian counterparts, was of enormous significance to them, yet veiled in allegory, understood only by those taking part. Mystery was an essential feature of this quest, but it had strong ties with the paganism of both pre-Christian Europe and the oriental religions. In this respect it is interesting that the father of the first Grand Master of the Templars, Hugues de Payens, Hugh of the *Pagans*, (1070-1131), was of Moorish origins.

Whatever they may have eventually found, the same group of families commissioned writers to merge their own quest with the older Arthurian material and the legend of the Holy Grail, as if they were one and the same. This had an extraordinary effect on society at large. The bards and troubadours who travelled across Europe spread their stories throughout the royal courts and the tales soon became absorbed into common culture, with echoes of the native myths blending seamlessly with the ethos of the time.

There is, though, one very significant aspect to this time of religious and cultural renewal that everyone can access. The Templars and their compatriots may not have written anything down about their secret rites and beliefs (or if they did, which seems very doubtful, any remaining records were destroyed during their persecution), but nevertheless they left a legacy every bit as enlightening.

This legacy is their most striking achievement; the construction of the Gothic cathedrals and the great wave of church-building that exploded throughout Europe during the 12th and 13th centuries. No one knows where the truly vast amounts of money came from for such a grandiose project, or who originally inspired a vision of such ambitious scale, but we do know where the skills originated, in the Islamic universities of the Moorish world.

We are above idle speculation here; we know from the introduction of the Gothic, or Byzantine, arch, as well as other architectural features, that these ideas were taken directly from Islamic temple building.[2] The sacred geometry of the cathedrals' design and the form of the buildings themselves reflect preoccupations with space, form and function that are part of a perennial tradition extending back to Solomon's Temple and the extraordinary structures of ancient Egypt. In this way the Gothic revival was the flowering of an entirely fresh religious impulse across Europe, yet rooted in both the practical and mystical sciences of a truly ancient system derived from the natural world.

We may not be able to read the writings of the Templars, but we can read the symbols and clues they left behind. It is said that the carvings in churches are 'stories in stone' and this is indisputably true, for ordinary folk in medieval times had no access to formal education or literature. The teachings of their cultural heritage were encoded in stone and wood. The familiarity of the spoken traditions and the images in churches were all they needed to tease their imaginations and remind them of the themes of their ancestral past.

But symbols are like parables. They operate on different levels, depending on the understanding of the observer. To the man in the street, or the aisle, a particular image may convey one thing; to an initiate into the Mystery Wisdom it can indicate a far deeper truth, something more esoteric, accessible only to those who have undergone certain types of training.

These are the messages left for us to discern, so exquisitely carved, and carefully placed within the buildings in order to add to their innate power. Created by masons and guilds of craftsmen, the forerunners of modern Freemasonry, the images that can still be found, as often in a remote country church as a soaring Gothic cathedral, have the power to illuminate our understanding in a way that perhaps words never can.

Although much of this vast library of symbolism has been lost during wars and religious upheavals there is still a wonderful richness, a treasure-house of great wealth, in these surviving carvings. Their message could never be edited or completely eradicated, as would be the case with an old manuscript. They speak of a world where the religious impulse was central to existence, and also of the myriad faces of God, as perceived by those who created them.

At this stage of our investigation we are about to embark on a journey to try and understand these words written in symbol and allegory. Our pilgrimage will reveal some surprising results, making us question much of the received wisdom of the official histories. For, concealed in the midst of the richness of these images adorning old churches we will find recurring themes that possessed a great power in the minds of both those who carved and gazed upon them. One thing we should realise at the outset is that very little ecclesiastical 'decoration' was purely for decorative purposes. This was a concept that was virtually unknown in the religious atmosphere of the Middle Ages. Everything meant something. And everything was a celebration of the cycle of Life in all its complexity and multitudinous forms. The theory we have come across before, that images of the Green Man vastly outnumber those of Jesus Christ throughout European churches and cathedrals, seems so intriguing at face value that it cries out to be investigated. The results of these researches will leave us in little doubt that behind the image of the Green Man there is an important story that we, perhaps as the Templar-inspired creators of these buildings intended, should heed.

The Awakening

The modern revival of interest in the image of the disembodied head with sprouting foliage that we call the Green Man began at the remote Welsh church at Llangwm, situated at the end of a farm track close to the River Usk in Monmouthshire. It is attributed to the inquisitiveness of Lady Raglan, who lived not far away. As she explored the small church, once part of a monastery, she came across a number of stone heads built into the walls of the choir.

One in particular grabbed her attention; fronds of oak leaves curled out of its mouth to surround the head, blackened with age, and its staring eyes gave it a formidable appearance. The vicar, the Revd J Griffiths, said he believed them to represent the spirit of inspiration, but Lady Raglan took a different view. She thought they represented the Green Man of British folklore, and harked back to the rites and beliefs of a lost world. In an article published in the magazine *Folklore* in 1939, after studying numerous examples on her travels, she concluded that they were remnants of the archaic religion that preceded Christianity, but had been absorbed by it. She thought them to be real portraits of men who once took the main role in the old celebrations of fertility:

> 'The question is whether there was any figure in real life from which it could have been taken. The answer, I think, is that there is only one of sufficient importance, the figure variously known as the Green Man, Jack in the Green, Robin Hood, The King of May, and the Garland, who is the central figure in the May-Day celebrations throughout Northern and Central Europe.'[3]

Lady Raglan thought that the image was also connected to the idea of ritual sacrifice to ensure the fertility of the land, once so widespread in the ancient world, as argued by Sir James Frazer in *The Golden Bough.*

From this moment on an amazing thing happened; people began to see Green Men everywhere. It is very curious indeed that until Lady Raglan's article appeared no-one seemed to have ever noticed them before, almost as if they had become completely invisible. Despite the fact that they were in great abundance throughout Britain and Europe, they never previously appeared to draw comment.

Perhaps it was due to the preoccupations of the age, with the Great War decimating the old traditions and leaving too few menfolk to carry on the old fertility and folk rituals of the pre-industrial era. Or a hangover from the prim sensibilities of the Victorian age, when anything remotely sensuous that might remind people of licentiousness was discretely ignored. The straight-laced religion of the time may simply have been too embarrassed to notice them.

The Green Men of Llangwm thus possess a fond place in the history of our investigation. They are remarkable too for the fact that one of them has a number of small holes drilled into it. This is rare, and probably means that at certain times real foliage was inserted into the head, bringing it alive with living greenery. Thus we can see that it was not meant to be merely decorative, or even some dead vestige of an old religion, but a spiritual presence, a shrine to nature that was honoured and worshipped like a God.

Another thing that Lady Raglan seems to have missed, or perhaps not noticed, gives an important clue to the beliefs of the Church in the medieval period. The other great treasure of Llangwm is a remarkable early Tudor rood screen that erupts into a riot of greenery, flowers and fruits. It is a breathtaking celebration of vibrant nature. So exuberant and full of vitality is it that in 1817 a Revd Cook of Gloucestershire tried to bribe the parishioners with a peal of bells if they would let him remove it and install it in his own church. They declined, and in the end he had to make do with an inferior copy.

But the most significant thing of all about this screen is not that it is full of the natural vivacity of growing plants that spill out in every direction. It is that the lush tendrils of the plants forming the screen are issuing out of the mouths of dragons. These are clearly not the dragons of Biblical hell and torment. They are Green Dragons, symbolising the Dragon force of nature.

The rood screen at Llangwm gives a clue to how much medieval woodcarving was preoccupied with the fertile draconic aspect of the natural world. Many screens were ripped out during the wave of Victorian 'restorations', stripping our churches of so much of their ancient heritage. When the Vicar of Morwenstow, R.S. Hawker, turned up at his new parish on the North Cornish coast, he found the local farmer burning the rood screen from the Norman church on a bonfire outside. He managed to rescue fragments of it, and cursed the farmer roundly. A similar thing happened throughout the land. Very few remain today, and where they do they are justly treasured as outstanding works of art reflecting the beliefs of the time.

One that escaped these depredations, to our great good fortune, is that of Norton Fitzwarren in Somerset. Here is a local legend that a dragon had spontaneously come into being and taken up residence at the nearby Iron Age hill fort, before being slain by the Norman knight Fulke Fitzwarren. The 15th century Rood Screen shows a number of people, including one unfortunate naked man being swallowed by a strange, almost panther-like dragon. The carvings are so lively and unusual they suggest that an entire story was once depicted, which may have become garbled by the dismantling and subsequent resurrection of the screen. Nevertheless it is one of the finest of its type in Britain, a reminder that such ritualistic tales were right at the heart of local tradition.

Another example of this is in the church at St Buryan in the Land's End area of Cornwall, where one of the most outstanding screens in the Westcountry can be found. Painted in vivid azurite, gold, green and red, this was also torn down in the 19th century but was fortunately re-erected in 1909. This Green Rood Screen is indicative of the early Church's roots in the natural world, with its knotted vines and fantastic beasts, including Green Men and Dragons peering out from the twining foliage. It may have held a special significance at this location, for St Buryan takes its name from its use as the burial ground for many of the surrounding villages. The symbolism of fresh green growth may well also refer to the idea of rebirth and resurrection, the great renewal of the natural cycle.

Churches throughout Europe and beyond contain within their twilit interiors countless examples of this anthropomorphised spirit of nature. Many have strong Templar associations, such as Lostwithiel, once the capital of Cornwall and a centre of the Templar tin trade, with the royal residence of Edward III's son the Black Prince, Restormel Castle, close by. The most remarkable feature within the church is an octagonal Norman font carved from a block of porphry set upon five pillars. The numbers eight and five had special significance in Templar lore, as they indicated the feminine principle in nature and were especially connected with the rite of baptism. Carved upon it are what must be one of the weirdest collections of images in the country. A hunting scene depicts a mounted man blowing a horn, with a falcon on his arm and a dog at the feet of his horse. His spurs are in the style of the mid-13th century. But two other images demand our attention. One is of a quite alarming grotesque head, certainly not of this world, with a prominent spiral carved into his forehead, just where the spiritual organ of perception, the 'third eye', is found. This is always associated in mystical lore with visions and prophecy. It bears the marks of having been especially revered in the past, for it is worn smooth and discoloured by the touch of generations of hands. Around its head twine two serpents. This head looks at us from another world, and we may well wonder what it is doing on a Christian font. The serpents on its head, and the spiral (one of the earliest symbols for the dragon), may lead us to conclude that it may represent some otherworldly aspect of the Dragon Force.

On the side directly opposite to this strange image is the head of a Green Bishop. His head has been damaged (probably by Cromwell's troops who used the font as a trough for their horses), but here is another image of a Church official as a Green Man, complete with sprouting foliage. With its Templar history (and, as noted before, the royal residence of Edward III's son the Black Prince at Restormel close by) this speaks eloquently of the prominence of the 'Green Man' principle in the Church of the 12th and 13th centuries.

In the church of St Materiana on the cliffs of Tintagel, overlooking Arthur's legendary birthplace, is another example of a 'Green Bishop'. This time it is carved on the back of a Jacobean chair, with the figure wearing a Celtic-style bishop's hat, his body transforming into fronds of foliage. Did those old bishops consider themselves the direct descendants in a long line of nature-priests responsible for the fertility of their parishes?

Woodbury is a small village in East Devon that takes its name from an Iron-Age hillfort close by. The church stands on a raised enclosure typical of Celtic foundations, and it is thought that some sort of building has stood there since at least the 7th century. The place exudes a curious power that is almost tangible. Inside the church is a rare example of the object of our quest, or rather four of them. Carved into the top of a column on the north side of the nave are four heads that the

Tintagel's Green Bishop

church guide bewilderingly describes as 'parishioners'. One can only think there must have been some very strange characters hereabouts in the old days. They are Green Men, with each one oriented to one of the cardinal directions. One has foliage issuing from his ears, which intertwines with leaves flowing from the mouths of the others. Giant flowers likewise grow from mouths and ears, with huge Alice-in-Wonderland stamens. One in particular leaps out from his lofty position atop the column. Out of his mouth spills not the usual foliage, but a very lively winged dragon. This dragon is not at all menacing. His tail curls out of the head's lips and his open mouth is nibbling the stamens of a flower which issues from the adjacent head.

The pamphlet ascribes a moralistic interpretation to this unique series of foliate heads, with this one meant to signify that he is 'expelling evil influences'. Yet this statement ignores the more obvious idea that this was never meant to be a group of ordinary people at all. It is more likely that the idea attached itself to the dragon simply because of the Church's association of it with the dark powers.

Yet no-one looking at this rather tame and attractive creature could possibly consider it so. Surely it represents something very different, the vital life force of the natural world?

The image at Woodbury is something of a talisman in our quest to discover the link between the Green Man and the Dragon. As we journey onwards we will come to realise that the idea of the dragon as a symbol of satanic power, as the Church propaganda would have us believe, is simply untenable. The most powerful evidence for this is the occurrence of very fine dragons in the architecture of churches and cathedrals across Europe. Their extensive use apparently has nothing to do with evil. It seems on many occasions to indicate exactly the opposite, as we will presently discover. It simply became expedient at a certain stage for the Christian Church to seize upon the image and attempt to change its meaning in the minds of ordinary folk in an effort to destroy the last vestiges of the old pagan religions.

If dragons were thought to represent dark forces, then we should perhaps ask ourselves why are they so prominently displayed on many of the great cathedrals, including Lincoln, Bristol and Manchester? On these and many others throughout the Christian world they are to be found guarding the entrances as if they were protective spirits. At Lincoln the size and positioning of two large dragons over the west door surely cannot mean the devil inhabits this place. In reality it implies a potent mystical truth, that dragons represent natural forces, a truth that was twisted by the Church as a propaganda tool to wipe out the remnants of the old ways through fear.

The Demon Dragon

It may initially seem strange to admit that dragons are not the creatures of evil that the medieval Church encouraged people to believe in. But if we take them as the universal symbols that they are, existing throughout the ancient world as representations of the forces of the natural world, we can see that they have often been misrepresented and demonised almost beyond recognition. One Victorian clergyman, the Rev James King, summed up this attitude in a particularly nationalistic manner that leaves no doubt as to the Church's position on the matter:

'The Dragon is the personification of the Evil Principle, while St George represents the Good Principle, so that this emblematic device typifies the conflict of good and evil, of light and darkness; and as the Valiant Knight is triumphing over the Dragon, so this National religious device of England foreshadows the final triumph of Virtue over Vice, and the ultimate victory of Christ over the Devil'.[4]

We can see that this makes a sort of simplistic sense, yet it barely scrapes the surface of the mystery. The concept of the Light and the Dark is tied to Good and Evil, although this was never the meaning in pre-Christian times. The statement also fails to recognise that the Devil, as the medieval mind understood it, was largely an invention of the Church. In fact it could be said that the Devil is the best friend the Church has ever had, for without him it would probably have gone out of business centuries ago.

The Dragon, as a symbol of beneficent power, royalty and the highest human aspirations, has been in existence since the earliest times. In ancient Sumeria the great Dragon Lord Ningizzida had as his emblem the serpent-entwined Caduceus, the ultimate symbol of healing and transformation. In Egypt, China and South America, Dragons or winged serpents signified spiritual enlightenment and the power of gods and kings, and are frequently shown accompanying the Sun-Disk above the entrances to temples in a manner reminiscent of the later designs on medieval cathedrals. In India the Buddha is commonly depicted sitting on a nest of Nagas or serpent gods, and has an enormous hooded, or 'winged', cobra as a canopy over his head. One of the names of the Druids was the *Nadder'*, meaning serpents of wisdom. The Romans, Vikings and Anglo-Saxons all used the Dragon as a power symbol as they went into battle, as did the Pendragon kings of Britain whose champion, Arthur, bore the symbol on his shield. The Dragon was re-introduced into the Royal Coat of Arms during the reign of Henry VIII, who sought to restore the power of the monarchy, and used it as a glyph of freedom and independence. It was also extensively used in Elizabethan times, when it became the symbol of an esoteric 'Dragon Society' to which many of the notable movers and shakers of the period belonged.

Soon we will realise that there are even greater depths to the mystery of the Dragon, a mystery that lies at the very foundation of human existence. But for now the quest must proceed, for only by coming face to face with our quarry can we determine how much the Church really knew about its real power. We have already begun to see that there seems to be a unique empathy between the Green Man and the Dragon. The true extent of this seems to have hitherto passed us by, so now let the scales fall from our eyes as we continue to decode the remarkable images that still exist throughout the cities, towns and villages we inhabit.

To test the theory that the Green Men vastly outnumber the image of Christ, and to see what part the Dragon plays in all this, I undertook a tour of churches and cathedrals in the company of author and fellow enthusiast David Elkington. Church-crawling is one of those occupations that has many delights for the unsuspecting pilgrim, for you can never know what lies beyond the door. These buildings are time-capsules, museums of the spiritual lives of our ancestors that preserve our whole history, while everything around them changes relentlessly. They are repositories of the lore and wisdom of former times in a way that nothing else can quite match.

We may be at first surprised to come across such an extraordinary collection of Dragons, especially allowing for their removal and destruction as they fell out of favour and became associated with the 'Devil'. Wandering about the cathedrals of southern Britain confirmed the claim that a truly extraordinary number of Green Men inhabit their interiors. Every day we kept a tally; in one day alone we reached a count of over 50 (admittedly we included foliate heads along with the classic heads sprouting greenery). At Ely Cathedral there was a bewildering variety, each one beautifully carved, gilded and painted, which helped us realise how deeply the Green Man was embedded in the psyche of the 13th century. The staring eyes and strange faces peering from their surrounding foliage seemed to emphasise that the Green Man was an integral part of life—and death. An impressive collection clustered together in the Lady Chapel, and one whose face was bursting with joy, sparkling eyes full of laughter, lifted our spirits greatly. This was complemented by another that looked caught in a storm, the leaves thrust back from his face by the force of the wind. This time his wild eyes seemed to allude to the tempests that come and go in human existence. There was also a Saracen version with an unmistakable Turkish or Persian moustache. The sheer quantity of Green  Men in the Lady Chapel was something that stood out and indicated a certain empathy between these faces of nature and the feminine principle in nature. It was an observation that was to become even more intriguing later when we discovered that Green Men frequently appear at famous European 'Black Madonna' sites.

Yet there was more; close examination of the roof-bosses that made up most of the examples revealed another amazing fact—that dragons were almost as abundant as their foliage-sprouting counterparts.

In the cloisters of Norwich Cathedral, one of the most heavily infested places, dragons appeared more prominently than we could have ever imagined. The main roof boss at the entrance was a whole nest of Green Dragons, as if guarding the place protectively. Dragons were repeated throughout, many together with those close cousins of the Green Man known as Jacks-in-the-Green, or alongside the many foliate heads peering from brightly-painted undergrowth.

They were in such profusion as to cause a degree of astonishment. On examining the misericords inside the cathedral we were approached by a helpful lady who explained she had been there for years and knew the place intimately. What were we looking for? She seemed somewhat taken aback to hear we were dragon-hunting. Whilst she showed us one in the choir stalls, we mentioned the admirable collection in the cloisters, as well as the large number of figures depicted fighting with dragons, including many hairy wild men, and she thought it a joke. We had to accompany her and point out the virtual bestiary that lived amongst the tracery; she was dumbfounded. She had never noticed this amazing collection before. Just like Lady Raglan's interest that made the Green Men appear to those who had never seen them before, the dragons had suddenly come to life. Previously they had evidently vanished, probably for the same reason the Green Men had once escaped the attention of observers; they did not fit in with the prevailing ethos, and so became invisible.

It was in Gloucester Cathedral that we realised why cloisters provided the ideal home for both Green Men and Dragons. The tracery and fan-vaulting creates what in is essence a forest of stone. The resonance of the woodland is everywhere, with dappled light from the stained glass flickering like sunshine through leaves. Cloisters, as places of meditation and contemplation, are the natural successors of the Druid groves that probably once stood at this very spot before anyone had ever laid a stone. The worship of nature is thus perpetuated in a stylised form, tamed but still honouring its vital powers. The interior of the building is also designed as if it were somehow organic, with columns like great tree trunks that fan out into branches supporting the roof. At Gloucester too, another common feature of the Green Men was noted; that the greatest profusion was concentrated around the North Door, at the entrance to the cloisters. In the porch was a riot of nature in stone, with faces appearing from flowers as well as foliage. Also present was a true Green Dragon, with its body transmuting into leaves.

We considered that the 'bosses' were just that; the topmost and most critical part of the whole structure. It is where our modern term 'boss' comes from. The message seems clear. The Dragons and Green Men are central to these structures. If one were to remove them the entire edifice would come crashing down. This is surely a profound statement of their innate power, for the craft of the masons conceals many secrets. Both these images speak of magic; a strange and imaginative world, full of invisible intelligence. This has haunted the human psyche since the beginning of time, and is still deeply lodged within our subconscious. This is the power of the Green Man and the Dragon, to shatter the illusion of a spiritless society and awaken us to the intelligence which is within nature itself. They are indeed talismans into the Otherworld of our spiritual heritage.

9

The Dragon Power

'At one time it was recognised that every hilltop and sacred centre stands on the path of a line of current and at certain seasons this line is animated by the flow of those fertilising influences which derive from one or other of the heavenly bodies'

John Michell
The View over Atlantis[1]

ne of the great secrets of the mystical sciences is that of the forces of nature symbolised by the Dragon. In one of its most powerful manifestations it is the raw energy in the Earth, concentrated at certain places that have always been understood to possess a special power. In the midst of nature, in a grove of trees, at a holy well or sacred hill, these sanctified spots became a focus of rituals that honoured the creative essence of life itself. Places where subterranean streams of water create a strong energetic field were also in the past often marked by standing stones or shrines to focus the effect.

These places frequently have such a powerful energy that they can be sensed directly by both the human mind and body. It is quite common to see energy rising from standing stones when the conditions are right; it appears like heat rising on a hot summer's day, causing the background to waiver. Dowsers can detect it with rods or pendulum, and even mark on the ground the patterns formed by the invisible force. Ancient fonts often mark the crossing of underground streams, as the pioneer dowser Guy Underwood found in ***The Pattern of the Past.[2]*** The energetic structure of such places invariably creates a spiral effect, for the energy reflects all natural systems, from the DNA within the creative heart of living cells to the growth sequence of shells and plants and the spiralling movement of the Earth through space. The spiral is the basic form of the universe, and is the earliest form of what later became the serpentine coils of the dragon.

In those who have developed sufficient sensitivity this energy can have a physical effect, running up the spine and making it tingle. The hairs at the back of the neck may also react, as can other parts of the body, especially those most sensitive instruments, the fingertips. The more sensitised one becomes, the stronger the experience; the organs of spiritual perception which have largely become dormant in modern times through disuse are nevertheless lying latent. They can re-awaken at any time and bring a different level of consciousness flooding into one's being.

Many people report that, even today, they can feel the energy of megaliths. The dowser Tom Lethbridge wrote of how, when he and his wife touched a stone at the Merry Maidens circle in Cornwall, they received 'electric' shocks. Lethbridge ended up on the ground. He believed that the stones had become so charged with a type of energy he called 'bio-electricity' that the result was quite alarming. He also thought that this energy could be greatly increased by the ring-dances of witches, who are known to use such places, turning them into a sort of megalithic dynamo for building up and storing energy, like a capacitor.

In former times the Dragon energy was stronger because honouring the Earth through rituals at these sites was conducted in accordance with the natural cycles, and this caused a reaction in the Earth's field. Dowsers report that such ritual activity increases the level of earth energies significantly, especially when movement, in the form of procession or dancing, is involved. In those times people were also more attuned to the natural world about them, their psychic senses uncluttered by the denaturing effects of continuous noise and debilitating vibrations. It is well said that the last fairies in Ireland fled when television came; peoples' perceptions shifted and they could no longer *feel* the powers inherent in nature. For this is a feeling thing, you cannot see it (unless gifted with clairvoyance) but one can *feel* it. This is the reason why everyone loves to stand in the midst of nature, listening to the wind in the trees or watching a sunset reflected on the sea. For a moment the brain stops its endless chatter and the sense of being one with nature takes over.

Across the world, the Dragon power is known by many names. In China, that famous land of Dragons, it is called *ch'i* (Japanese *ki*), a word that denotes the vital breath which animates the cosmos. Modern quantum physics speaks of a concept that bears a notable similarity to this idea, where 'the quantum field, waving and vibrating, rhythmically alternating like the yin and yang, forms things and dissolves them.'[3] Ch'i, as the principle of change, is the basic energy of life, which never stands still. The Chinese philosophy of Taoism, especially in its earlier forms, is a way of life based on rhythm and flux and the natural harmony of nature, or as we might say today, 'going with the flow'. Since men and women have always sought good fortune they naturally aspire to create a harmony between themselves and the flow of ch'i, especially in relation to their habitations, temples and tombs.

Consequently nothing can be built unless a 'Dragon-man' has first surveyed the site to ensure that the vital flow of life-force is not interrupted. The science of feng-shui, before it became a fashionable lifestyle accessory in the West, was drawn from a system that originated in the observation of natural forces and strove to co-operate with them for the greater good. Feng-shui (literally Wind and Water) is based on the concept of the Earth as a single living breathing organism, through which the ch'i flows in meridians in the same way that blood or the energy channels of acupuncture course through the human body. The ch'i energy, like earthly magnetism, changes and pulses according to the cosmic tides, and runs along serpentine paths called 'Dragon's Veins'.

The lay of the land is an important aspect of how the invisible currents of ch'i flow. In a flat, 'yin' landscape they move slowly; in more 'yang' country, with mountains or hills, the Breath of the Dragon becomes more active. The ideal situation, where a balance is created and there is an interaction with the heavenly realms, is when a hill projects from an otherwise undulating female surface. A good example of this in Britain is Glastonbury Tor, rising steeply from the Somerset levels, a place noted for its spiritual properties as well as other strange phenomena. The greatest generation of ch'i occurs at the point where the male and female energies cross, or 'mate', forming a point of creation.

Conversely, under certain circumstances the energy can become disharmonious, even injurious to human and animal health if the Yin and Yang aspects are not balanced. The Rev E.J. Eitel, who wrote the first English account of feng-shui whilst living in China in the 19th century, spoke of a 'poisonous deadly exhalation of nature's breath' called *sha ch'i* or negative ch'i.[4]

This can affect the land and its creatures causing ill-health and even a wasting death. Sometimes this cannot be harmonised and so the places affected are shunned by both humans and animals, which have a natural sensitivity to such things. In other cases it can be rectified by certain techniques, such as the use of a grove of trees or pool of water, strategically placed to absorb the noxious emanations.

In ancient times mirrors played an important role in the feng-shui geomancer's armoury. They were worn on a breastplate, or a polished shield was used to deflect the bad ch'i away from the practitioner whilst work was being undertaken. Nowadays mirrors still form an important part of the discipline, hung on doors or in stagnant areas to quicken the flow of energy, the classic type being an octagonal shape with the I Ching trigrams inscribed around it. This responsibility, trying to achieve a harmonious situation, is the basis of the art and science of feng-shui. As Eitel wrote, 'Man's place in all things is to carry out the will of heaven by maintaining the balance and harmony between the yin and the yang.'

According to feng-shui practitioner Michael Page, 'All forms of Taoist-inspired art and science are aimed at being the outward and visible expression of ch'i.[5] All creation should be in yin/yang accord, whether it be in painting, poetry, music, the creation of a garden, a landscape or townscape.' Here the Dragon energies of feng-shui are beginning to sound remarkably similar to *baraka*, the mystical force of the Sufi mystics that so fascinated Robert Graves and Idries Shah.

Considering the all-encompassing nature of the Chinese Dragon tradition it is not surprising that the inspirational power of the Dragon became fabulous; the eight mystic trigrams of the I Ching were said to have been brought to the Emperor by a Dragon. The Dragon was particularly associated with ancestor worship and fertility, and became the royal symbol for the Emperor, appearing on the Chinese flag. Dragon lore divided them into five families representing aspects of nature, including Spirit Dragons which rise to heaven, and Earth Dragons who are hidden in the landscape and protect treasure. This type is especially linked to lakes and pools.

In the western world the Dragon energy exists too, although the scientific knowledge of its characteristics has become largely forgotten or corrupted. The neglect of our sacred sites, both Christian and pre-Christian, can often cause them to fall into a state of entropy. For the Dragon is *energy*. If it is not used or channelled in some purposeful way it can stagnate or twist itself into a knot in the Earth and cause singular disharmony, just as a pool of water can become fetid if there is no flow. It can also become blocked because of unsympathetic building or a spiritual malaise with the Earth. This can often be felt as a tangible reaction at old churches that are unloved, unused or neglected. Instead of a tingle up the spine, there is a shiver. The natural response is usually to leave as soon as possible to avoid one's own subtle energies becoming contaminated. A similar effect can be noticed at places such as 'haunted houses', battlefields or accident blackspots which have become the focus for negative emotions.

The problem is that as the network of sacred sites linked by this energy fall into disuse (many churches are now firmly locked and rarely used), the entire spiritual atmosphere of the land changes. This is exacerbated by the destruction of the natural features of the landscape that are the crucial sources of the Earth's spirit. The feeling of connection with nature, and the sharing of it with each other that human beings crave, is no longer there. The values of society, the finer feelings that have always motivated the human spirit, decay. The patterns of life begin to break down. We become fragmented from our true natures and start to suffer from a terrible collective insanity that imagines humans are separate from their environment, both physical and spiritual.

That the science of the Dragon was once well understood in the West we cannot deny, even though it is the Oriental traditions which preserve what are probably the best-known examples today. The Chinese discipline of feng-shui resulted in a harmony that is evident in much of the Chinese landscape. The

Indian tradition, derived from the Vedas, amongst the oldest sacred books in the world, is specific about the energies inherent in nature.

It speaks of the *Prana* and the *Kundalini*, very similar to the 'Wind' and 'Water' of the Chinese system. The serpent power of the Kundalini rises up from the Earth, through the feet, and continues to the base of the spine. This, according to the mystical science of the Indian sages, is where the serpent lies sleeping, ready to awaken when the time is right. When that time comes and the body, mind and spirit are properly prepared, the awakening centres of consciousness known as the chakras, seen clairvoyantly as iridescent wheels of light or spinning lotus flowers, become increasingly empowered and start to function on a higher level. As the Dragon power ascends the spine, the person begins to feel different states of consciousness. When it reaches the heart an energetic balancing of the qualities of the lower regions takes place; as it moves higher, a great flowering of love for all fellow beings and creatures is felt. Nature itself becomes sentient; the Earth's intelligence becomes apparent; you become one with it.[6]

As it continues to rise the Dragon awakens the spiritual centres within the head, and normal vision is transformed into something beyond the physical sense; one becomes clairvoyant, or 'clear-seeing'. When it reaches the topmost part, known as the 'Crown' chakra, a state of consciousness is achieved that gives a connection with the wider Cosmos, total illumination. This is when the halo of light can become visible to others, and when the individual discovers their own personal kingship. Is it any wonder that the Dragon is a symbol of royalty, or that Egyptian Pharaohs have the Ureaus, or King Cobra on their foreheads?

For evidence that all this was understood by those of former ages we only have to look at the legends of the Dragon slayers. This concept is something that goes back to very remote times and has been immortalised in widespread mythology, especially the early Creation myths. But as ever, there are hidden depths to the mystery. When the Church decided that the Dragon was a Devil, it was natural to ensure that the hero figure, archetypally depicted as St George or St Michael, was shown in the act of killing the Dragon, thereby destroying the symbol of evil that it had come to represent.

Yet there is evidence that this may not have been the original meaning. Many representations show them not killing the Dragon, but 'fixing' it with their spears, in many cases quite playfully (as depicted on the font at Avebury, the Serpent Temple of ancient Britain, where the 'bishop' looks as though he is 'teasing' the serpents while they nibble his feet). This is the initiated way of looking at the phenomenon, and not the more aggressive manner of the late medieval Church. It alludes to the true function of the priest—to draw the primal energy of nature from the Earth through spiritual techniques involving higher energies, and channelling it into human consciousness.

This is the real root of all religions, an understanding of how the forces of nature can help human beings to achieve godhood. These powers are freely available to every living being so that we can elevate ourselves to become one with the soul of Nature, the essence of the Dragon.

Further evidence that all this was known in antiquity, and continued into later times through various religious and mystical sects like the Templars, can still be seen today. As well as the cults of the Dragon slayers, of which St George as the Lord of the Earth became the patron, these sects left indisputable evidence in the form and function of their sacred buildings.

Now we continue our journey through the centuries to discover how this knowledge was encoded into architecture. As we proceed we will realise that the Dragon is not an embodiment of the darker side of life that has so often been projected into our minds. Such an idea fulfilled the Church's agenda perfectly as it reversed the Dragon's original role and induced fear where the opposite might have been the case. We will come to know that the Dragon, in a real and powerful sense, is one of the ultimate symbols of transformation.

The Dragon's Tail

As we proceed with our quest we find ourselves briefly at one of the most intriguing stained-glass windows in Britain. Now hidden amongst the houses of suburbia, where once trees and meadows stood, is the parish church of All Saints at Trull in Somerset. Like many places, a Dragon legend hovers around it, and Castleman's Hill, not far away, is remembered as the site of the Dragon's demise. But what claims our attention is the 15th century window, which remarkably features no less than three Dragon-slayers. There is St George and St Michael, as we might expect. But they are also accompanied by St Margaret, who according to the legend

*One of the 26 Green Men
in Trull's Dragon Window*

did not use a spear to despatch her foe but a cross. Swallowed by the Dragon, she held the crucifix aloft and burst from its body. Could the swallowing, another theme in the old Dragon-lore, be drawn from the former use of caves and underground chambers for initiation? The Dragon is the Earth, and having undergone the initiation the candidate emerges triumphant. Here though we appear to be dealing with a story where the feminine principle of the Earth is released through the use of a weapon of light; not a spear this time but something more overtly Christian. A Cross of Light. The window is a remarkable surviving example, but what makes it even more interesting is that the three Dragon slayers are ringed by no less than 26 Green Men. This emphasises the symbiotic relationship between the Green Man and the Dragon we have noted before.

We have already come across other examples of how the Church understood the use of the Dragon power, and evidence abounds of this esoteric side of religion when our eyes become accustomed to seeing beyond a preconceived horizon. Early bishops who conducted the ceremonies and rites were continuing a tradition that their precursors had inherited from pre-Christian times. A notable example of this can be seen at the Bishop's Palace in Wells, Somerset, which was originally created by Bishop Jocelyn in the 13th century. Here, as one ascends the main staircase, are four magnificent Green Dragons, standing so proudly that one simply cannot ignore them. They seem to be the presiding spirits of the place, once the centre of ecclesiastical power. How could we ever explain this if we accept that the Dragon is in any way demonic? Are we to imagine that every day as the Bishop walked past them he doffed his mitre to an image of Satan? The only explanation surely can be that the Bishop of Wells knew that the Church's power was based squarely on another, that of nature itself. And, perhaps unsurprisingly, there is a

Bishop Jocelyn's Dragon crozier

local Dragon legend associated with the foundation of both Palace and Cathedral. Jocelyn became Bishop in 1206, but was exiled in France when the Pope closed the churches because King John refused to allow Rome's appointed Archbishop of Canterbury to land in England. He returned bearing a gilt and enamelled Dragon crozier featuring St Michael, and very soon gained a reputation for Dragon slaying himself. The earliest account is found in a manuscript by a monk from Chester named Ranulf Higden, who died in 1364. He tells how Jocelyn killed a human-headed winged serpent in the park near Wells (perhaps the nearby Tor, a wooded hill with an ancient enclosure at its summit). Every 50 years a re-enactment of this event is performed by local people to prevent the re-appearance of the 'Worminster Worm' or Dragon, which was also said to have a particular liking for small children.

Another version of Jocelyn's encounter tells how the Bishop borrowed a magical sword called Meribah from the Abbot of Glastonbury which, it was said, had actually been used by St George himself. It had originally been brought to England by Joseph of Arimathea, along with the Holy Grail and the staff that he had plunged into the Earth at Wearyall Hill, instantly taking root and flowering into the famous Glastonbury Thorn. George had been given a 'blank' shield by an enchantress so he could never know his true lineage, and three shields are depicted on the front of the George and Pilgrim Hotel in the high street, with one left blank as though unfinished, to commemorate this local legend.

Since Dragons love pools of water it may also be significant that the famous wells or springs, from which the city of Wells derives its name, rise within a short distance of the Palace. These give a very large flow of water from the depths of the Earth, bubbling up from four springs to create a pool in which the cathedral is reflected, one of the memorable sights of Wells.

Another aspect of how the Dragon power was acknowledged, and an important part of the mystery behind the rituals, is the enigma of the bishops' crooks, of which Jocelyn's is a good example. Few seem to have been able to convincingly explain why this mystical tool of the foremost priests of the Church so often has the form of a Dragon. One could argue that the bishop is re-enacting the myth of St Michael and St George, and this may partly be true, but is by no means the whole story. The earlier the example the more likely it is to show that these magical staffs of power were dedicated solely to the Dragon. Those from the Coptic Church especially are stunning works of art, often showing two Dragons instead of one, referring to the male-female polarity of the Dragon energies. Anglo-Saxon crooks are similarly decorated with carved Dragons, and many from this and later ages can be seen in museums worldwide. This is an enlightening avenue of investigation, and we will see later that these magical rods of power have a very ancient pedigree, originally used by those performing rites long before being adopted by Christianity. The basic spiral form of bishops' crooks is a reminder that their power derives from Nature itself.

The Dragon in the Earth

Pausing briefly at the village church of Sampford Courteney in Devon, drawn there by its collection of Green Men lurking somewhat menacingly in the blackened oak roof, we come across a very fine Green Dragon. It is an excellent example of how country folk even as late as the 15th century understood the meaning of the Dragon. The oak carving around the Chancel features a rather cuddly winged creature, from whose open mouth spills serpentine foliage. In this case it is a vine, with large leaves and bunches of grapes hanging from it. The Dragon's body too *becomes* the vine. This is a clue to the curious overlays of different myths that were blended together in the minds of folk who were still largely pagan. The vine was associated with Christ, who said 'I am the vine', having a strong resonance with Dionysus, Pan and Bacchus, the Green Men who preceded him.

The earliest mention of Kilpeck, on the Welsh borders, is in the **Book of Llandaff**, the oldest British document extant (c. 650). On approaching this tiny church it seems obvious that it is on a site of even greater antiquity, for it is raised on an egg-shaped mound, and it is thought that megalithic stones may lie beneath the building. The present vicar and his parishioners seem to sense that there is a mystery about its existence. Various alignments to other nearby sites are drawn to the visitor's attention and there is mention that a number of these create ley lines, or leys, as discovered by Alfred Watkins in the 1930s, who frequently roamed this area on horseback. He was to bring this intriguing facet of our past to a wide audience in his book **The Old Straight Track** where he outlined his discovery that old churches, holy wells, mounds, standing stones and other notable features of the landscape formed straight lines often leading to points on the horizon where a significant sunrise or sunset occurred.[7]

This fascination with the layout of ancient sites has obviously transferred itself to the parishioners of Kilpeck today, for they commissioned a dowsing survey of the church, intrigued as to why it does not align on an East-West axis. They found that running directly underneath the centre of the apse, chancel and nave, was a stream of very pure water. This orientation is continued along the route of an ancient road through the site of a medieval village to the east of the church.

The Domesday Book records that Kilpeck was given to William fitz Norman in 1086 by William the Conqueror. William fitz Norman went on to build a priory and castle which attracted royal favour and were visited by King John three times in the early years of the 13th century. The story of Kilpeck during the following century reflects the parlous state of Britain at the time the power of the Templars was being dismantled. A famine in the early part of the century reduced the population drastically and then in 1349 the Black Death arrived and continued the decline. The priory was eventually dissolved in 1428, leaving only the church that still stands today.

The reason Kilpeck is so well-known and draws large numbers of visitors is its truly extraordinary collection of carvings, created by the famous Herefordshire School of sculptors during the 12th and 13th centuries. There is much here to dwell upon and to make us wonder what its creators wished to convey; four heads above the altar in the round apse have streams of energetic chevrons, almost like lightning, issuing from their mouths. Is this a reference to the cult of head worship, or to the streams of water that run directly beneath? An ancient font, apparently found in a chapel in woodland nearby, has hands clasped around its belly and possesses serpentine legs. A corbel on the outside depicts a Sheela-na-gig, surely the ultimate image of female fertility, holding her vagina wide open, personifying the ever-fruitful nature of the Earth Goddess.

The south doorway, carved from richly-coloured red sandstone that glows in the sunlight, is the greatest treasure, and takes one's breath away at first sight. The arch is alive with a bestiary of grotesque beasts and astrological symbols. The columns supporting it are writhing with serpents that interlace with figures, foliage and curious creatures in the style of Celtic art. The church guide exhibits a very open-minded attitude to these images: 'The snakes on the outer columns of the door, tail of one in the mouth of the other… might illustrate the defeat of the dragon of evil. But it is as likely that, true to Celtic belief in the spirits of nature and the importance of new life in the spring… they illustrate the continuous cycle of life.'[8] On the capital of the right-hand column is one of the best-known Green Men in Britain. Opposite is a Basilisk, a curious mythological creature supposed to be 'born from the egg of a cock, hatched by a toad or serpent, and, by its very glance, lethal if it saw you before you saw it. The only way to counter this was to carry a mirror to reflect back its deadly glance.' A further mystery for us as we contemplate the possible cosmological nature of these images must be

Detail of serpentine imagery on Kilpeck porch

the fact that the columns terminate in two rows of 'diagonal designs' which we recognise as crosses of St Andrew, the ancient sign of the Solstice.

The figures on the left-hand column are unique. They wear 'Phrygian' caps, closely associated with the mystery schools of antiquity, and quilted jackets, with trousers and soft shoes that look distinctly oriental. The lower one, encircled by serpentine coils, carries a lance or spear, whilst the upper one holds what looks like a club (although the guide insists it is a cross or a double-headed axe) and grasps the tail of the serpent.

The wonders of Kilpeck are only just beginning for those who see in the carvings what must surely be encoded teachings from a school of artisans who felt it their duty to pass this knowledge on to future generations. Right at the very centre of the arch is a Green Man, upside down this time as if staring heavenwards, with a Dragon enclosed in the abstract foliage spilling from his mouth. Close by is the insignia of the Knights Templar, the Agnus Dei, stamping this work with their indelible fingerprints. Other Green Men can be seen at the heads of columns that writhe with serpentine forms at the west window. These, as well as being strikingly beautiful, give a further clue to the mystery encoded in the carvings. The columns rest on foundation stones cut with Dragon spirals.

A Green Man looks down on a Dragon's head at Kilpeck

The Serpent Stone at Kilpeck

Above them are the most prominent carvings of the entire building, great finely-cut Dragon's heads, their tongues curling into a bishop's-crook-like shape, protrude from the stonework. They are surely making a very profound statement.

Yet for the most extraordinary example of the secret knowledge of the Dragon power at Kilpeck we must return to the magnificent doorway. Beneath the two Phrygian-capped figures, holding their weapons as if 'teasing' the serpentine coils that envelop them, is an exquisite Serpent's or Dragon's head. This is carved from a block of stone which is a completely different colour to the rest of the doorway, and must have been specially selected by the builders to stand out. It gives the impression of having been the original foundation stone. The head faces downwards towards the Earth, and its forked tongue darts forth as if feeding from the soil of the ancient mound itself. As its body merges into the column it supports the arch of the heavens, with its astrological designs, above. It is an unmistakable image of the knowledge of those who built this place, that the power energising the sacred building comes from the Earth. It may not surprise us to learn that at nearby Wormelow Tump an old legend tells how a Dragon once coiled about its earthen banks.

The Dragon Power of the Earth is also shown on countless Celtic and other crosses, the old megalithic standing stones that were adapted during the early years of Christianity. The swirling designs typify the spiral energies that issue from the ground and encircle the stones, charging them with vital energy and imbuing them with a reputation for healing and fertility.

The Viennese artist and architect Friedensreich Hundertwasser (1928-2000) incorporated the spiral in his organic designs, for without it he considered them devoid of life.

Dragon spirals on a megalithic cross at Lanivet, Cornwall.

He said, 'The spiral lies at that very point where inanimate matter is transformed into life... I am convinced that the act of creation took place in the form of a spiral. Our whole life proceeds in spirals. Our Earth describes a spiral course... it

is characteristic of a spiral that it seems to be a circle, but is not closed.' He was also aware of the spiral nature of Time, and commented, 'If we do not honour our past we lose our future. If we destroy our roots we cannot grow.'[9]

Egyptian stele of Paneb worshipping a serpent, 1195 BC, from Deir el-Medina

10

Heavenly Treasures

Rosslyn Chapel, a few miles south of Edinburgh, has in recent years become almost as famous as the Temple of Solomon amongst those who quest for the Holy Grail of enlightenment. In fact its ground-plan is, according to a number of researchers, a scaled-down copy of the Jerusalem temple. Some believe the reason for this is that secret scrolls, dug up from beneath the Temple Mount, were reburied at Rosslyn and the site marked by a replica of the original Temple. Others are convinced that the Holy Grail itself is hidden in the exquisitely carved 'Apprentice Pillar', or that the mummified Head of Christ is located beneath it. Still others claim the Ark of the Covenant resides there along with other biblical relics including a piece of the ubiquitous 'True Cross'.

Nazi conspiracy theorists even think that Rudolf Hess, Hitler's second-in-command, who parachuted into Scotland towards the end of World War II, was searching for the Holy Grail. The wife of author Trevor Ravenscroft believed the Grail was at Rosslyn too, and rode on horseback from Cintra in Portugal, where there is a similar pillar, to Rosslyn and chained herself to the Apprentice Pillar until the claim was taken seriously. However, despite modern scanning techniques and the attempted desecration of it by at least one committed believer armed with power tools, nothing has yet been found, much to their chagrin.

Today, Rosslyn has become a focus and amplifier of some of the strangest theories that can be conceived. It has become a legend in its own right, and one that attracts other legends to it, creating a veritable industry that has gathered around its mythical aura. Yet it deserves its reputation. It is certainly one of the most fantastical religious buildings in Britain, and has been called 'an enigmatic, arcane library of secrets, sculpted in stone and shrouded in mystery'.[1]

The reasons for this are twofold. On the one hand, it was built by William St Clair, one of the richest and most influential figures of his day, often called the second King of Scotland, and reputed by some to be a hereditary Grand Master of the Knights Templar. Hughes de Payens, the first-ever Grand Master, is said to have married Catherine Sinclair (the spelling of the family name varies over time) a century or so before, although this is disputed by some historians. Carved into the masonry is the date of the chapel's foundation, 1450, and this is borne out by other records showing it was dedicated on the Autumn Equinox of that year. William's ancestor was Henri St Clare, who had accompanied Godfroi de Bouillon on the First Crusade in 1096 when Godfroi refused to be crowned King of Jerusalem because he thought Jesus Christ the only true King. Ironically, their first success in battle had been at Nicea in Turkey, the very place where Constantine had laid the foundations for his new state religion.

Some years later, around 1119, the Order of the Knights of the Temple was officially founded, their brief being to guard the pilgrim routes to and from the Holy Land. Yet they were to live as a monastic community, and on Christmas Day they were given the al-Aqsa Mosque on the Temple Mount as their headquarters. Henri was supposed to have taken his name from a religious hermit, William St Clare, who lived near Paris and became one of the long tradition of saints who were famous for losing their heads. He is depicted, like countless others throughout the Celtic-Christian world, as holding his severed head in his hands, like the Green Knight of Arthurian legend. His name is derived from the Latin *Sanctus Clarus*, meaning 'Holy Light'.

His 15th century namesake, William St Clair, was buried in the chapel, and inherited a legacy somehow at the very heart of the mystery. It is no wonder that for this reason Rosslyn has become such a magnet for those who seek to discover the truth behind the rise of the Templars and their ultimate secret. Although of moderate size compared to some larger chapels it is a rich store-house of the arcane wisdom that helped the Templars to achieve their position of power during the 12th and 13th centuries. The interior is smothered with a visual cacophony of carvings, each one executed in a masterly display of the finest craftsmanship. One shows St George standing on a board decorated with stylised roses, probably a reference to his title as 'The Rose of Sharon'.

The Green Chapel

The bewildering array of sculptures within the building are a veritable repository of esoteric beliefs. They convey many Biblical scenes, yet they are not necessarily the Bible stories we are accustomed to. They seem to speak of a secret history that somehow lies beneath the commonly accepted versions we are familiar with. A 'fallen angel', said to be Shemhazai, one of the 'Watchers' who descended to Earth mentioned in the Book of Enoch, is depicted hanging upside-down and bound with a rope, very much like the Hanged Man of the Tarot. He is reputed to have instructed humanity in the heavenly arts and sciences, and because of this there seem to be parallels with Osiris, another great teacher of mankind, the Egyptian version of the Green Man. Robert Graves thought Shemhazai strongly connected with the constellation of Orion, which is also often linked with Osiris.

The pagan imagery is especially intriguing and makes Rosslyn unique; an amazing fact is that there are more Green Men in evidence here than in any other existing building. It is relatively easy to count over a hundred both inside and out; persistent and eagle-eyed Green Man afficionados claim many more. A number of observers have noted it does not give the impression of being a Christian chapel at all. It is certainly true that upon passing through the entrance one becomes immediately 'entranced', as if in a strange faery-like world.

The craftsmen who carved these images were 'Free Masons', the specialist artisans whose brief it was to encode information in a way that would withstand the ravages of time. By contrast, the 'Rough Masons' handled the stone blocks that gave the building its solidity. It is known that each carving was specially commissioned by William Sinclair, and created in wood first before being cut into stone, so we can be sure that every image and its placing had special significance, as if to convey a particular message.

Amongst this singular collection are many angels, some making music with a variety of instruments and others holding scrolls as if privy to some arcane secrets. A macabre but curiously lively 'Dance of Death' scene reminds everyone that in the end bodily flesh must perish, and that we should prepare. A series of decorated cubes are a strange and unusual addition, which many feel represent some sort of mysterious musical code.

However, the overwhelming number of Green Men marks the place as one of his greatest lairs. They are literally everywhere. One observer, Peter Hill, has noted that there seems to be a progression, marked by the main entrance, from birth to old age, as the Green Man in his youthful aspect gradually ages to become the 'dying god' of the old year.[2] In stark contrast just one image of Jesus Christ exists, hidden away in a corner of the barrel-vaulted roof. Nobody knows if there were once others, for many statues and sculptures were defaced or destroyed completely during the Reformation and other occasions when angry mobs, who thought the place idolatrous, caused more damage.

The most prominent Green Man, who has the curious face of a wrinkled new-born child, or some impish, otherworldly character, protrudes from the eastern end. This is the most sacred part of the chapel, and the carving is very exposed as it juts out from the stone. Why was this image, which could have easily been knocked off without hardly a thought, spared by the destroyers? Could it be that they held it in special veneration whilst the statues of saints were being smashed? For some unknown reason this Green Man was quite deliberately left untouched. The decorative panels exude a great variety of green things, for the spirit of nature is everywhere in this garden of stone. Flowers include roses and lilies, while sunflowers blossom forth from the walls, with hart's tongue ferns, curly kale, trefoil and oak leaves cascading around them.

Maize is also depicted, evidently supporting a theory that the Sinclairs discovered the New World before Columbus.

It is impossible to absorb the magnitude of this vast array of subjects within Rosslyn; many visits are required to even begin to penetrate its mysteries. Volumes have been written describing and decoding the many images. But few have apparently noticed or commented upon something that immediately

appears obvious to anyone on this particular quest. The place is teeming with Green Dragons.

As soon as we recognise the fact they begin to appear before our eyes in a very striking manner. Leaves and vines issue from their mouths, and all manner of foliage, fruits and flowers are created from the Dragon's heads, frequently in the close company of Green Men. Rosslyn is the most stunning example of a chapel that, judging by the prevalence of these images, is dedicated overwhelmingly to the Green Man and his seemingly ever-present companion the Dragon.

What must vie for our attention most of all amongst this riot of arcane imagery is the famous Apprentice Pillar. Eight Dragons encircle the foundation stone on which the Pillar rests. From the mouths of four of them grow vines that spiral around the column. The message seems clear. The Dragons in the Earth create the fertility which supports the Green Chapel, an edifice of nature's mysteries.

In Philip Coppens' *The Stone Puzzle of Rosslyn Chapel* he refers to the fact that numerous observers have seen in this imagery the pillar of the Yggdrasil, or 'World-Tree' of Norse mythology.[3] This is analogous to the Qabalistic Tree of Life of Hebrew mysticism, with its 'path of the serpent' leading up to the highest level. In the Norse legends the great serpent Nidhogg lives beneath the tree, gnawing continually at its roots. Another possibility is that the Dragons represent the rock-splitting serpent Shamir which helped Solomon build the Temple at Jerusalem by shaping its stones. Either way it seems that the Dragons are crucial to the message of Rosslyn; that they are one of the foundations of earthly life. The streams of greenery issuing from their mouths form a rising spiral, just like the energies of the Kundalini that, when activated, bring higher knowledge of the all-encompassing consciousness of nature, and may be a further clue to the intention behind the pillar.

The serpent Nidhogg again represents a primal form of energy, later vilified by official Christianity, wishing to control human religious experience rather than encourage the self-initiation of the gnostic and pagan systems. So Nidhogg is the Kundalini that in human terms lies at the base of the 'Tree of Life', the spine. The exact spot in human physiology is said to be the perineum, where the earth energies are collected from the ground and flow up the legs to bring life, and (in the developing initiate) spiritual enlightenment. Intriguingly the perineum is a muscle formation in the shape of a figure of 8, symbolising infinity, or two serpents biting their own tails.

This stone on which the Pillar stands represents the foundation stone of the world, like the rock in the Jerusalem Temple that was said to hold back the waters of the Abyss which caused the biblical Flood. The myth is common to many places in the world that have been at the core of ancient religion and mythology; such points mark the 'navel' of the Earth.

The concept of the 'World Tree' also has its roots deep within the heart of all ancient traditions, and signifies the pole that joins Heaven to Earth. For Christians, the centre of the world is at Golgotha, the place where Jesus Christ was crucified on a cross that symbolically manifests the idea of a tree marking the axis between spirit and matter. This tree, a tree of suffering, just like the one on which the Norse God Odin hung upside-down for nine days, was erected over the 'Place of the Skull' or Golgotha, where the head of Adam, the First Man, was buried. Here the Cult of the Head and that of the World Tree merge together. The Church of the Holy Sepulchre which now marks the spot has thus become the spiritual axis of the Christian world.

The World Tree is also the ladder on which one can ascend to heaven. In the Qabalistic system the evolving soul moves from Malkuth, the earthly kingdom, up through various spheres of manifestation called Sephira, becoming progressively refined until reaching Kether, the crown, or the heavenly kingdom. This ladder is very like the ladder of Jacob, who saw angels climbing up and down between Heaven and Earth. The metaphysical World Tree also has its parallel in the physical reality of the Earth, whose axis runs through the north and south poles and provides the stability of the spinning planet. According to ancient custom every locality once had its central tree or mound which fixed the centre of the microcosm of the cosmological landscape, and provided an immovable feature where kings were crowned and laws proclaimed.

Just as the magnetic flux between the north and south poles of the planet affects all life, so the terrestrial magnetism that brings health and fertility, the *lung mei*, or 'dragon's veins' of Chinese tradition, were believed to influence the material and spiritual well-being of the land. Is the Apprentice Pillar an image in stone of Rosslyn's World Tree, symbolising the polar axis?

It stands at the entrance to the underworld, the subterranean crypt, just as we would expect if it was intended to fulfil a geomantic function as a link between the upper and lower worlds. It was in this crypt that the ancestors of the Sinclairs were laid in full armour, like sleeping Knights of the Round Table, before being interred in the vault. Was this too a ritualistic act to do with death and rebirth, echoing the dying and rising Green Man and the Dragon energies of transformation?

The Dragon of Time

Rosslyn, built according to the plan of Solomon's Temple, is a classic example of ancient temple design. This tradition is preserved in the layout of all Masonic temples, for its basic elements reflect the patterns created between the heavenly bodies and the Earth. The first thing when constructing such a place is to mark out the area with a double square to create a boundary, and then, as we have seen before, to determine the central point and overlay a cross, the cross of St George, with reference to the four cardinal directions. This is of critical importance, for, just like the pyramids of Egypt, from which Freemasonry claims to have sprung, every sacred structure must be aligned to correspond to the Earth's magnetic field and the positions of the equinoctial sunrise and sunset. Thus this simple act creates a microcosm of the greater earthly and heavenly environment.

As we have observed, the next stage is to draw the cross of St Andrew over this; both together form the Union Flag of Britain. The axes formed by the diagonal lines indicate the positions of the Sun's extreme points at the Summer and Winter Solstice. In Templarism and Freemasonry these axes are encoded by assigning them to two Christian saints, both called John. John the Baptist is linked to the Summer Solstice, and his feast day falls on Midsummer's Day, June 24th. This is associated with the Cult of the Head, when the Sun God 'loses' his head to mark the declining half of the annual cycle. The Winter Solstice comes under the jurisdiction of St John the Evangelist, the author of the Book of Revelation, written whilst he was exiled on the Greek island of Patmos.

These solsticial axes are essential features not only of the Temple layout but of Masonic ritual too. Initiates undertaking the ritual of the First Degree stand in the North-West corner of the Summer Solstice line; in the Second Degree the candidate moves to the South-East marking the Winter Solstice, the moment of rebirth. When he aspires to become a Master Mason he is placed on the East-West axis indicating the Equinoxes, the times of balance between dark and light. This is where he is symbolically sacrificed in darkness, wrapped in a shroud and then resurrected, as the light of a five-pointed star shines in the East. In Rosslyn these three positions are marked by three pillars, including the Apprentice Pillar that links the underworld crypt with the upper chapel.

A true Temple does not only fulfil the ritual purpose of allowing would-be initiates to harmonise themselves with the rhythms of the cosmos so that they may become part of the greater whole. To ensure that the building itself is a model of the universe is essential, but it must also be located in accordance with the landscape that, too, reflects the movements of the heavenly bodies. This is an area that is rarely investigated by historians or archaeologists, who tend to view ancient sites in isolation from their surroundings. Yet by doing this we misunderstand the real reason behind the location of such places. To discover the macrocosmic aspect beyond the microcosm of a 'heavenly' temple it should be recognised that each structure is specifically positioned as if the Earth itself is a living temple. So the site of Rosslyn was not chosen arbitrarily; its position was defined by cosmological considerations.

Megalithic sites and later temples, including Gothic cathedrals and ancient churches, are part of a wider pattern that mirror the heavens. This line of enquiry is currently being pursued by a number of researchers, and future developments in this area promise to make us begin to realise the extent to which this was employed in the past.

It is relatively easy to discover that such sites conform to a wider pattern. We could choose Stonehenge as a good example, where the axis of the Summer Solstice sunrise/Winter Solstice sunset can be extended for many miles through a series of barrows and other prehistoric features, all of whose siting seems to have been determined according to some principle that has largely been forgotten. We can glimpse an even greater pattern showing that Stonehenge, like the centre of a terrestrial Round Table, is the focus of a number of alignments. As Sir Norman Lockyer, one-time Astronomer Royal[4], the surveyor Alexander Thom[5] and the Ley Hunter Alfred Watkins found, practically every ancient structure was sited as part of a greater system of alignments related to solar and stellar patterns.

As well as the Midsummer Sunrise/Midwinter Sunset line that runs through the main axis of Stonehenge, which can be extended to include the prehistoric sites of Sidbury, Winterbourne Camp, Grovelly Castle and Cerne Abbas, there are others that emphasise its greater significance. Stonehenge, the prehistoric earthworks of Old Sarum and the site of Salisbury Cathedral all fall on a dead straight line and indicate an evolution from megalithic temple to medieval cathedral. Directly due East is another line from Stonehenge that runs across St Michael's Church on Gare Hill, a local landmark and centre for other alignments (including one linking Wells Cathedral and Brent Knoll, the highest hill around and studded with ancient earthworks). As John Michell has pointed out, this East-West alignment from Stonehenge next leads through the site of an old priory and then directly to Glastonbury where it joins with the main axis of the Abbey.[6]

The meaning seems clear; Glastonbury, the greatest ecclesiastical centre of medieval Britain, a former Druidic College, is linked by this easterly alignment to the place where the Sun rises at the Equinox, and Stonehenge, the most sophisticated megalithic Sun-Temple of its kind. Both are an integral part of the Arthurian mythos which conceals much of the wisdom of the ancient astrological and solar traditions, and both are connected by the East-West line, the very axis that in Masonic temples signifies rebirth.

We can begin to see that the patterns of the heavens are reflected by those laid out on the surface of the Earth. At one time the whole planet was considered to be a Temple and every sacred site played its role in the greater scheme of things. Apart from solsticial alignments there are others that are crucial to the heavenly cycle; the old Celtic cross-quarter days of Imbolc, Beltane, Lughnasad and Samhain are also frequently important. Lockyer was convinced that stellar alignments too were significant, such as the rising of Sirius or star groups like the Plaiedes at certain times of the year.

Over a number of years of travel and investigation into these matters it became apparent that there was yet another significant aspect to the siting of ancient temples, and one that is far easier to determine than many of the previous examples. Indeed, it may even be more significant in its way. For just as the orientation of the groundplan of temples must be set according to the cardinal directions and the solsticial axes, it seems that they often have a North-South axis connecting them with other sites. These axes, pointing to True North, that is the Pole Star, can be easily read off on any map (although magnetic North currently varies by about 5 degrees which must be taken into account). Over relatively short distances, though, the grid lines on a map are accurate enough to demonstrate that this was an important consideration in the positioning of sacred sites.

So it became evident that Rosslyn Chapel was built where it was by reference to another significant factor; directly due North is the site known as Arthur's Seat, high on a rocky crag overlooking Edinburgh. Although it seems somewhat curiously to have only acquired this name since the 15th century, at about the time the Chapel was built, it appears the spot has always been associated with the power of Kingship. It is no accident that Holyrood Abbey, where many Sinclairs have memorial stones, lies at its foot. The earliest mention of Arthur in Scotland occurs in a 13th century manuscript by the bard Aneirin, but is believed to be based on earlier records from the 6th century. It describes the exploits of a tribe known as the Gododdin, and is firmly anchored in Din Eidyn, or Edinburgh.

A curious thing about these matters is how an idea can hover in the ether, to be picked up by a number of people at the same time. Soon after noticing this North/South alignment other researchers began to mention it in their writings. Before long this was to become one of the best-known examples of landscape orientation ever; the novelist Dan Brown seized upon it and popularised the idea in the bestseller *The Da Vinci Code*.

Yet whatever the imagination of a novelist may weave, the fact remains that Rosslyn Chapel is oriented to the North Pole, the Pole Star or the World Tree, however it is conceived. From the Chapel the Pole Star can be seen rising between the saddle of the two rocky hills known as Arthur's Seat, and it would appear to be the perfect location to observe the circumpolar constellations, the 'everlasting stars' that endlessly revolve around the Axis Mundi. Today the Pole Star is Polaris, at the end of the tail of the 'Little Bear'; at about 3000 BC it was the star Thuban in the constellation of Draco, the Dragon.

Could one of the functions of Rosslyn Chapel, built on 'College Hill', have been that of an astronomical observatory specifically dedicated to viewing the rising and setting of the circumpolar constellations beyond Arthur's Seat? Arthur, as the central figure in this endlessly spinning round table, in this way represents the hub of the universe, the Pole that connects Earth with the eternal stars.

Two of these constellations may give us insights into how mythology was first written in the stars. The first is the Great Bear, the most recognisable of them all. Previously it was known as Arthur's Wain, or Chariot (interestingly it was also known as Charles's Wain during the reign of the 'Green King' Charles II). Much more difficult to see with the naked eye is the constellation of Draco, whose long body composed of lesser-magnitude stars revolves timelessly around the Pole.

The star-lore of Draco is of great antiquity. Mesopotamian astronomy depicted it as a much larger constellation than we now see it, and considerably more serpentine. It coiled around the universal axis and was the guardian of cosmic order. Before the Greeks adopted the Little Bear, Ursa Minor, as a separate constellation, Draco had wings as well. It also spits fire, for meteor showers known as the Draconids can be seen occasionally, sometimes reaching the rate of several hundred a minute (as in 1933 and 1946), creating celestial fiery breath issuing from the Dragon's head.

So what conclusions can we draw from all this? One may be that the legend of Arthur Pendragon, the Dragon's Head, is a metaphor to describe cosmic order at a time when humanity, through its rituals and understanding of nature, felt itself at one with the heavens: *a Golden Age*. Another is that Draco is symbolic of the guardian of the ages of Man. The reason is that the Pole Star gradually shifts due to the Earth's 'wobble', rather like a spinning top that has begun to run down. It is this effect that causes the phenomenon of precession, whereby every 2000 or so years the Spring Equinox sunrise moves into a different astrological sign. According to esoteric wisdom this determines the nature of life on Earth, for the characteristics of each sign become the dominant influence upon all earthly life.

It is the shifting of the Pole that creates a spiralling motion as the planet dances through space and is responsible for the different ages of human evolution. It is probably this celestial phenomenon that gave rise to the ancient understanding of the Earth encircled by a great serpent, illustrated in the Orphic creation myth. In this, the serpent Ophion coiled seven times about an egg laid by Eurynome the Goddess of all things, which gave birth to the Sun, Moon, planets and stars.[7]

Some of the connections between King Arthur and St George have already been explored, but here we can see they represent the same spiritual principle. Perhaps one of the most profound aspects of the meaning behind the story of St George and the Dragon is that his spear symbolises the Pole, around which the starry Dragon eternally revolves. In this context, he could be thought of as the presiding god of the evolving planet, and every human being. George, in Greek, means *Earth-worker*. Are we here to work on and with the Earth and thereby raise our consciousness to the heavens?

On a more mundane level, the symbolism (for it is in the nature of symbols to have many different layers of meaning) refers to the field of terrestrial magnetism that courses through the planet. This is not mysticism, but a scientific fact, and there are stations around the planet that measure the flux of the Earth's local field on a daily basis. Arthur's Seat overlooking Edinburgh is the core of an extinct volcano that now rises 800 feet above sea level, and is therefore a conduit for the energies emanating from the magnetic core of the planet. Such places can cause compasses to go haywire, as the localised magnetic field can fluctuate wildly. It is a natural source of that power we call the Kundalini or Earth Dragon, drawn from the lines of force that sweep between the North and South Poles. In this way the two sites are linked energetically as well as by line of sight, and share the same magnetic resonance. Are the great profusion of Green Men and Dragons in Rosslyn keys to this understanding; that the Dragon guards the Pole, the Tree of Life, thereby determining the natural cycles of fertility, the birth, death and rebirth of the Green Man?

There are many other examples of how North-South alignments link ancient sites. Here is not the place to explore them, but a couple may be relevant to the current investigation. In South Wales near Carmarthen, the legendary birthplace of Merlin, is a town called *St Clears* (Welsh Sancleer). This is directly due North of the Cornish village of *St Cleer* across the Severn Sea, located in the middle of Bodmin Moor with its many Arthurian sites. Both places were occupied at one time by the Knights Templar, and both too are presumably named after the Sinclair family or the root words that gave them their name—Sanctus Clarus, or *Holy Light.*

Another example of the strong links between Wales and Cornwall, which have so many Celtic saints in common, is *Lansteffan*, a Norman stronghold a few miles to the South-West of Carmarthen. This is directly due North of the Cornish town of Launceston, the capital of Cornwall for 700 years after being claimed by Robert de Mortain, William the Conqueror's half-brother. The old name for Launceston was *Lanstephan* (the sacred place of Stephen). St Stephen was the founder of the Cistercian Order in 1098, only a few months before Godfroi de Bouillon and his fellow Crusaders stormed Jerusalem. This monastic order grew to become one of the great movements of its time, but started to decline after Stephen's death. It was however to be totally transformed into a dynamic force by Bernard of Clairvaux, the great churchman and visionary linked to the formation of the Templars. The correspondences between the two organisations are apparent, and after the persecution of the Templars many former knights sought the haven of Cistercian monasteries to end their days.

Many more places in the Celtic regions of Scotland, Wales and Cornwall share similar characteristics, indicating that this was once a common feature of the pre-industrial landscape, where power centres were located according to some Polar function, which was often encoded in the similarity of their names. Such a grand plan gives us a tentative glimpse of the breadth of vision of antiquity, and its transmission through the Templars.

Rosslyn Chapel by Samuel Dukinfield Swarbreck, 1837

11

The Dragon of Revelation

ne of the greatest mysteries surrounding the Green Man is who fulfils the role of his consort? The Green God of the Earth cannot endlessly recreate the fruitfulness of nature simply through his own energy; everything needs its opposite polarity to bring forth new life. In what guise might she appear? Green Women are so rare as to be virtually non-existent, although there is a 'Green Family' of man, woman and child on display at Tewkesbury Abbey.

There have been suggestions that his consort may have been the Sheela-na-gig, that startlingly erotic figure pulling open her vulva in an act of apparent bountiful fecundity. If it is something of a shock to behold such an image in an old church we can only wonder what previous generations must have thought, especially during times of religious prurience. Overt female sexual imagery such as this is, however, exceedingly rare, while the Green Man occurs in great profusion. Many may have been destroyed during successive waves of intolerance, as were a great number of Green Men, yet even allowing for this they are sufficiently rare to retain their air of mystery, a distant misty glimpse of the prehistoric mother goddess transposed to the cloistered atmosphere of medieval sculpture. The Sheela-na-gig may be part of the answer to the mystery, yet her very rarity argues against anything more.

Others have suggested, more prosaically, various female Christian saints, many of whom took on the mantle of former pagan goddesses. These include St Anne, the 'Mother of Mary', St Catherine, favourite of the Templars, who holds the Sun-wheel of the seasonal cycle, and St Mary the Virgin. Whilst many female saints might offer themselves as candidates for the Green Man's affections (and there may be some truth in this as they all represent aspects of the universal goddess) it is the latter that may, on examination, reveal herself as a possible partner in the role of mother of the continuous creation fertilised by the Green Man. The cult of Mary extends far back beyond the beginnings of Christianity, long before she became the orthodox vehicle for the goddess principle within the medieval Church.

Our Lady, who gives birth to the Divine Child, is one of the principles at the very core of human experience, gathering to her many of the attributes associated with deities of pre-Christian times. She is often shown with a ring of 12 stars as a halo around her head, symbol of the zodiacal realms (as described in the Revelation of St John), for in one of her earliest incarnations she was Virgo, the sky goddess. In her hand she holds the brilliant star Spica, one of the brightest in the night sky, known as the *Ear of Wheat*. This suggests she may indeed be the perfect partner for the Green Man. In Sumerian-Chaldean astrology Virgo was the supreme goddess of Creation (and procreation) *Ishtar*, the Queen of Heaven. Her name gives us a whole group of words, including the Babylonian *Astarte* or *Ashtoreth*, the Hebrew version, as well as the Latin *Aster* from which the word Star is derived. It was about the 12th century when Virgo became associated with the Virgin Mary in the common mind. In Islamic astronomy she was called *Al Athra Al Nathifah*, or the Wheatsheaf.

The Islamic astronomer al-Biruni called Spica *Al Halbah*, the Bristle, on account of the fact that the ear of wheat usually shown in illustrations is of the spiky kind, like barley, just as the name Spica suggests. It is the star of the grain harvest and the great staple provider of nourishment. It is also the root word of the Hebrew 'Shibboleth', which is the old Jewish name for Spica, and also means an ear of corn. Spica is also significant astrologically for its religious and spiritual properties, and people having it prominently placed in their horoscopes are often drawn into these fields; their psychic awareness too is often markedly pronounced.

Mary is also depicted with her feet resting on a crescent moon, for she represents the feminine lunar principle, and its influence on the psychic and physical ebb and flow of tides and menstruation. In former times when navigation and seamanship depended on a finely-tuned knowledge of both the stars and the tidal patterns governed by the Moon it is therefore not surprising that she was worshipped as the 'Star of the Sea'.

Thus the modern cult of the Virgin has its roots in a far more ancient tradition of worship. It is surely no accident that the enormous popularity of the Green Man in the centuries following the Crusades was complemented by another equally powerful and balancing impulse, the widespread acknowledgement of the quintessential female spirit in the guise of the Black Madonna, the Virgin in her dark, earthy aspect.

These became the twin forces of renewal firing the engine of the spiritual revolution of the 12th century. St Bernard himself spoke of how he had undergone a transforming revelation whilst as a boy he prayed in front of an image of the Black Madonna near his home at Châtillon-sur-Seine. She appeared to him in a vision, and from her breast three drops of milk miraculously formed, which she let fall on to Bernard's lips. From that moment on he was possessed by an unquenchable thirst to bring about a renaissance of the human spirit. The event stamped his character with an indelible imprint that guided all his future actions, and he dedicated himself uncompromisingly to the worship of the Black Madonna. The hundreds of

Cistercian abbeys that flowered after his reforms were all dedicated to Our Lady, Notre Dame. Another statue of the Black Madonna at Affligen responded to his devotions by advising him to continue with his writings, inspiring him to produce many of his Madonna-worshipping hymns. He wrote hundreds of hymns and sermons to her, and reworked the biblical 'Song of Songs' of Solomon and the Queen of Sheba; 'I am black but I am comely, o ye daughters of Jerusalem'.

The Christian image of the Divine Mother suckling her child bears a strong resemblance to the Egyptian goddess Isis and her Sun God infant Horus.[1] The cult of the Madonna seems to reflect the worship of Isis which was at the core of religion right across Egypt and its protectorates including the Holy Land. This area was intermittently ruled by Egypt for many centuries, and religious activity throughout the region was deeply influenced by this pervading ethos. Interestingly, *Meri* was the Egyptians' name for their own land, Egypt being a later Greek word. It is quite possible then that the cult of Marian worship was actually called after Egypt itself.

The worship of *Black Isis* had its focus directed in particular to the Earth itself, for her

12th century Black Madonna from Moulins, France, carved from dark wood to signify her role as presiding goddess of the underworld.

dark colour reflected the black soil of the Nile floods that gave the land its fertility and produced the wheat and barley Egyptian civilisation depended on. It was also symbolic of the caves and subterranean chambers, the entrances to the underworld, and the precursors of the underground initiation rooms in the Temples. Yet in the Egyptian Mystery tradition, Black Isis is not Isis at all, but her sister Nepthys. She was the dark female power of the Earth, the goddess of initiation into the mysteries of the underworld. She was married to Set, the god of the night sky, and carried a receptacle on her head, perhaps a container for unguent with which to anoint those being initiated. It was she who, in the esoteric teachings, became the Black Madonna who was later to inhabit the crypts and grottoes beneath churches and cathedrals.

At such places the natural energy issuing from subterranean cavities intoxicated her devotees, in the same way that the priestesses of Delphi were entranced by the vapours pouring from a crack in the rocks beneath the Temple of Apollo. It seems this dedication to the Dark Goddess of the Earth stems from some very deep-rooted memory, yet there are further levels to the mystery, for the Black Madonna is often identified specifically with Mary Magdalene. The Templars venerated her above Mary the Virgin, and she was the one who was thought to be closest to Jesus Christ, anointing him with spikenard from an alabaster jar, (with which she is frequently shown), in a kingship ritual very like that from Pharaonic times. She is also sometimes shown with a skull, as in a painting at Rennes-le-Château, implying a connection with head worship. It was the Magdalene who was believed to be the High Priestess of the Mysteries, and this heresy was communicated to initiates through the art and sculpture of the day. Throughout Europe and Russia, ancient mounds as well as churches are dedicated to her, indicating the Magdalene's special links with the traditions of the earthier side of religion. Allowing for the eventual attempt of the Church to blend the two Marys into one all-encompassing female deity, thereby absorbing the heresy and making it orthodoxy, it seems that the Magdalene and the Black Madonna both represented mystical initiation, hence their connection with the secret openings within the Earth.

It is clear that the power of the Black Madonna over human hearts was revivified by the returning Crusaders, many of whom are known to have brought back images of her, carved from dark wood, to their homelands. They were enthroned in caves, grottoes, crypts and churches, and complemented the Green Man whose likeness began to appear at the same time. These images are a recognition of the dual aspect of the natural world and the fact that nature itself is a sentient being possessing an intelligence beyond our understanding, but which can be nevertheless symbolised by anthropomorphic images.

We can sense these forces of nature when we visit shrines of the Black Madonna, for pilgrimages can be transformational experiences. Especially after a long journey, the act of approaching a shrine where the dark mother of the Earth has been worshipped for countless years, often stretching back to the deepest antiquity, is enlightening on many levels. To walk into a towering cathedral or dimly-lit church and sense the deliberately contrived cave-like atmosphere is to be enfolded in the dark shadows of a deeper and perhaps hitherto suppressed element of our psyche.

Many of the other images that loom out of the darkness, like the tortured saints or the sight of the suffering Christ, may instil sadness or even fear, such was the Church's preoccupation with sin and misery at certain stages of its history. But there, away from the main altar, a flickering pool of light beckons; hundreds of glowing candles surround the image of a Black Madonna, dressed in jewel-spangled tapestry. Flowers scent the air with a sweet perfume, that incense of the Earth whose smell reminds us of her ever-renewing beauty. Worshippers sit lost in meditation before her, just as their ancestors did almost a thousand years ago.

Shrines to the Black Madonna are spread across Europe and beyond, and indeed they were also once common in Britain and Ireland before being transformed into more formal images of the Virgin Mary. Hunting them, like the quest for the Green Man, would take many lifetimes. France is by far the greatest repository of Black Madonnas, and there are also many lining the pilgrim route to Compostela in northern Spain, patrolled in its heyday by the Templars. But there is an interesting collection in Holland, Belgium and Germany which can be visited in just a few days. Such a pilgrimage reveals a number of connections with the Green Man, confirming our suspicion of strong links between the two.

One of the oldest surviving Black Madonnas in Europe can still be seen at Walcourt, Namur, in Belgium, and is reputed to date from the late 10th or early 11th century. Tradition has it that the Bishops of Cologne and Tongeren were responsible for its installation, placing it on the altar of a pagan oratory where an earlier goddess had been worshipped. Carved from dark wood it is clad in silver which has now turned an appropriately dark colour, befitting the attributes of a true Black Madonna.

The living cult of this Madonna is evident. Even early in the day, dozens of candles illuminate the altar and bouquets of bright flowers provide a vivid contrast to the dark interior. It is still a great centre of pilgrimage, and the miraculous healing powers of the Madonna have their own testimonials; numerous ancient crutches and wooden limbs hang from the walls of the shrine, left by those who believed in her power to make them whole again, and whose dreams were fulfilled.

High above, easily missed by those whose gaze is not directed heavenwards, are two superbly carved Green Men, impassively observing the scene below. They are in such a prominent position it suggests their placing is no accident, but carefully contrived to convey a potent connection between them and the Madonna whose place this is.

The church was built in 992 and the early date certainly indicates that it may have been a former dwelling place of a pagan god and goddess. Above the high altar is a 'green ceiling' of painted foliage surrounding an image of the Madonna, but it is impossible not to notice that a few feet above the Madonna's head is another; that of the Green Man. It is carved on a large roof boss in what must be the most significant spot in the church, and architecturally makes a very profound statement that we have noticed before: if he were removed the entire church would collapse.

Anyone seeking links between the Green Man and the Black Madonna would also be amply rewarded by a visit to the Belgian town of Halle, not far from Brussels. Here an early 13th century statue of the Virgin carved from walnut wood boasts a notable history. Once owned by Elizabeth of Hungary, it was given to her daughter Sophie and then left to Matilda, Countess of Holland, who presented it to the church in 1267. But like so many other sites, the story echoes something far older, and it is likely, so we are told, that a former goddess was honoured at this place.

Many Black Madonna legends speak of her particular connection with sacred oak trees, probably a memory of Druidic rites, and, strikingly, in the crypt beneath the church is the stump of an ancient oak still in the floor. It is quite an extraordinary experience to stand there and ponder that this fragment of an old tree was once the focal point of worship even before a church was built. It is a poignant reminder that Christian places of worship supplanted those of immense antiquity. Among the many miraculous attributes of Our Lady of Halle are the powers to heal sickness and, apparently, to restore the dead to life. She also, according to popular legend, saved the town from attackers in 1580, when she intercepted cannonballs by catching them in her lap. They now rest at her feet.

As far as our quest is concerned, pilgrims cannot even enter the church without being presented with a memorable sight. Over the main entrance is a large statue of the Madonna, below which are two ancient doors. These are completely covered in foliate wrought ironwork, which curls around the hinges and terminates in countless leaves. The hunter of Green Men will be taken aback; each leaf has its own tiny face. Here are literally hundreds of Green Men, before we even set foot inside the church.

Other delights await our gaze within, which strongly echo another of the themes of our quest. A series of stone chambers behind the shrine feature a particularly memorable collection of dragons. Winged dragons are positioned over the doorways, and one chamber is literally a menagerie, with some humorous and others alarming in their features. Why so many dragons in this place, so close to the high altar? Their proximity, in this case, to the Black Madonna— directly behind her shrine—points to a certain empathy between the two. They both inhabit caves and crypts, and both bring forth life from the underworld.

At Maastricht, another Madonna site, the Basilica (the name is derived from basilisk, a type of serpent) is dedicated to Our Lady, 'Star of the Sea'. Adjacent archaeological excavations have revealed the remains of a former Roman Temple on the site, and a number of Green Men adorn the interior of the porch, as well a fine collection inside. Here is most definitely a haunt of dragons: some of the earliest examples of Jurassic fossils, thought by the Victorians to be the physical remains of actual dragons, were excavated nearby in the 19th century.

Outside of church architecture, a wealth of Green Men exist that are not purely decorative, but have been placed over doorways and on buildings as a symbol of boundless prosperity for the homes or businesses they guard and protect. Variants can be seen in any European city at banks, shops and offices, especially in Amsterdam, once a Templar port.

A truly magnificent example exists in the wonderfully grandiose building of the Rathaus in Aachen, situated near the border of Holland and Belgium, better known by its French name of Aix-la-Chapelle. This building occupies the site of Charlemagne's Palace and dates from the 14th century. At the very pinnacle of the building, above the main stairs leading to the Coronation Hall where so many kings have been crowned down the centuries, the face of a very vibrant Green Man looks down. It is in the significant form of a large roof-boss guarding the entrance, flesh-coloured and surrounded by a circle of foliage. Here we have indications of how the Green Man was a protective spirit of royalty, and how the nature of kingship is so closely bound up with the dying and rising god/king.

At Tongeren, which claims to be Belgium's oldest town, the old 12th century Black Madonna now resides in the treasury and can only be viewed by appointment. The statue in the church is a 13th century image carved in dark walnut, but is interesting in that she holds a bunch of grapes from which the Divine Child is carefully plucking one.

This, like a similar statue at Le Puy in France, is sponged with wine as a sacramental act, and shows that the links between Dionysus and Jesus, who called himself 'The Vine', are close indeed. In fact there is a lot of evidence to suggest that Jesus himself was a form of the Green Man, another aspect of this theme that will be revisited later.

To conclude our short pilgrimage to some of the numinous Black Madonna sites, we will return to Rosslyn, and a curious historical incident. This is mentioned in ***The Domestic Annals of Scotland*** of 1623:

'While the Egyptians were everywhere a proscribed race and often the victims of an indiscriminate severity, there is one spot where mercy and even kindness seems to have been extended to them—this was Rosslyn. Sir William Sinclair of Rosslyn, Lord Justice General under Queen Mary riding home from Edinburgh found a poor Egyptian about to be hanged and rescued him.'

In commemoration of this event, we are told, a group of Egyptians (the name by which gypsies were known at that time) gathered every year at Rosslyn, where they acted out a number of plays during springtime. Father Hay, the Sinclair family historian, tells of two towers called Robin Hood and Little John where they lodged. These plays were clearly based on the old Mayday fertility rites associated with Robin Hood, 'Green Robin', an incarnation of the Green Man, and included *Maid Marian*.

They were, according to the authors Lincoln, Baigent and Leigh, 'a handy guise whereby the fertility rites of ancient paganism were introduced back into the bosom of nominally Christian Britain'.[2] The gypsies were also known to venerate the Black Madonna, and it has long been rumoured that one may have been kept in the chapel.

Here are more correspondences between Templarism and the old Egyptian religion, this time preserved and evidently encouraged by William Sinclair, the builder of Rosslyn. It looks increasingly as if the returning Templars brought back to their homelands a living cult of both the Green Man and the Black Madonna, and did everything they could to bring folklore and seasonal celebrations together. In this way they succeeded in blending this cult with the roots of their own native religions to bring about a spiritual renaissance, with the Green Man and the Black Goddess as their iconic deities.

The Dragon in the Earth

One of the greatest centres of worship of the Black Madonna is at Chartres, whose cathedral is built to create an appropriately dark, cave-like atmosphere. Before the cathedral, there was a sacred mound on the site, which was the focus for Druidic worship of a statue of the Dark Virgin called *'Virgini pariturae'*, 'The Virgin who will give birth to a Child'. Carved from the hollowed-out trunk of a pear tree, it had a miraculous reputation. It is said that when the first Christians came to Chartres they found the statue in the Druid grotto next to a well and were amazed. Generation upon generation had made pilgrimages there for healing and spiritual nourishment from at least the time of the Celtic tribe of the Carnutes. Yet Chartres is dedicated to both the Virgin Mary and Mary Magdalene, with a statue of the Virgin above ground and one of the Magdalene below in the crypt.

In *The Mysteries of Chartres Cathedral*, the writer and initiate into Templarism and Freemasonry Louis Charpentier explains why the Druidic crypt, directly under the cathedral, was believed to possess such power. This power, he insists, is nothing less than the Spirit of the Earth: 'The prime mystery of Chartres is its situation, which conceals one of nature's most extraordinary secrets, one that affects the very life of men.' He notes that the act of pilgrimage dates from long before Christianity, and adds 'one goes in search of something one cannot have by staying at home. One seeks the Gift of Earth; something Earth gives like a Mother.'[3]

What is this gift? According to Charpentier it is the natural energy of the site, the 'Breath of Nature' or 'Earth Spirit', to which he gives the old Gaulish name 'Vouivre' or 'Wouivre' (Welsh *Nwyvre*). The word means a snake or dragon, and is a poetic description of a force he believes is responsible for creating such an intense energetic atmosphere at places like Chartres. It signifies a spiritual power that glides in serpentine currents through the Earth, and the essence of the word has evolved into many that we still use today; including the French *Vivre*, 'To Live', and English words like *vivacious*, both signifying the vitality of the universal Life Force. It is also the root of *weave*, giving another clue to its nature. This force is an entirely natural phenomenon, springing from the movement of subterranean waters and the magnetic flux created by different types of rocks and crystalline structures beneath the surface. It is also enhanced by differences in electrical potential and temperature caused by the molten magma within the planet:

'These currents are a manifestation of a life that goes on deep in the Earth herself and where they fail to reach, the soil is dead, without fecundity, as a part of the human body would be were it no longer irrigated by the bloodstream'.[4]

There are different types of the Wouivre or Dragon energy, just as in the Chinese tradition of feng-shui. The beneficent force attracts human habitation on account of its fertility and health-giving properties, for there vegetation thrives and animals prosper. Standing stones were erected 'where the telluric current exercises a spiritual action on man, a spot where 'the Spirit breathes'.' Even today, in certain remote areas, these places are resorted to by those who seek healing, or wish to bear children. They perform a simple ritual according to local folklore, the reputation of the sites undimmed by the passage of time. The curses attached to many such stones are not superstition, for they are functional objects and their removal can radically affect the fertile potential of the surrounding country. Many are the legends that tell of a farmer who ignores the warning and removes the old stones; soon his crops are seen to wither and die and he or his animals grow sick. This is not the gross superstition of countryfolk, for it is firmly based on the mystical science of the Wouivre or Dragon power that vitalises the Earth.

The crypt below Chartres Cathedral, once a megalithic dolmen, contains a well from Celtic times uncovered in 1904 which has always been thought to have magical powers. Drinking its water becomes a sacramental act, for it is impregnated with the Dragon energy coming from deep within the Earth. These currents—the planetary meridians analogous to the acupuncture channels of the human body—fluctuate according to the seasonal pulse, which coincides with the times of pilgrimage in the Church calendar. Charpentier emphasises that the experience of the pilgrim is not determined by any accumulated knowledge or religious instruction, but by true initiation. This is a form of gnosis, what Christians refer to as a 'state of grace', triggered by an actual immersion in the powerful spiritual energies of the place. The dowser Blanche Merz, in *Points of Cosmic Energy*, found that a network of underground streams come together directly under the crypt, creating an unusual effect:

> 'In the centre of the choir where 14 subterranean watercourses curiously converge there is a precise point equidistant between the top of the gothic vault and the underground water which gives the individual an impression of weightlessness'[5]

Charpentier also notes that the symbol of the currents of the Wouivre, and the understanding of the science behind it, gave rise to a common depiction of the Virgin Mary, where she stands with her feet on a serpent:

> 'To make use of an image which the Christian iconographers applied to thousands of examples—not that it is certain they always knew what they were about—the feet of Notre Dame, the Virgin, are on the head of the snake, the Wouivre.'

Just as significant is a statue of Christ on the exterior of the building holding the Book of Life. Here he is standing with each foot on a lion-like draconic creature, representing the twin forces of polarity within the Earth. Like the Green Man 'bosses' within the building, this image makes it clear that the Gothic builders understood where the power of Chartres came from. It comes from the Earth under our feet, and is analogous to the sacred Kundalini of Sanskrit tradition. In that system the serpent or dragon force is always conceived of as female, just like the image of the Black Madonna, known today as Notre-Dame de Sous-Terre, Our Lady under the Earth. Can we be in any doubt they are one and the same?

The Revelation of St John

St John the Divine was, according to Biblical tradition, one of the leading figures in the Jerusalem Church, and, as we have seen, is important in Masonic lore, being associated with the Winter Solstice sunrise and the layout of temples. He is often shown holding a grail-like chalice out of which rises a serpent or dragon. Orthodox Church belief says this is because he was tested by a priest of the Temple who gave him a poisoned chalice to see how powerful his god was. John made the shape of a cross and the poison emerged in the form of a winged serpent. His companions, having already drunk the poison, died instantly, but

John immediately brought them back to life. Concealed beneath this story is another, of how the power of the healing dragon causes a transformation that can be likened to death and rebirth. For in the Masonic and Templar traditions, John was a high priest of the Gnostic Church, the original form of Christianity before it became politicised by Constantine.

John was, in the Bible, the one who witnessed Jesus approaching his namesake, John the Baptist, and uttered the words, 'Behold the Lamb of God, which taketh away the sin of the world'. This was the origin of the 'Lamb of God', or *Agnus Dei*, that was to become the prime talisman of the Templars. John the Divine was the first to offer himself to Jesus as a disciple, and thereafter never left his side, becoming his greatest devotee.

John's career was attended by great success in spreading the word, as well as many miracles. Tertullian says that when John visited Rome he was thrown into a large vat of boiling oil, but emerged unscathed. After this demonstration of the power of his faith he settled in the Turkish city of Ephesus, where he captivated great crowds with his inspired oratory, and became known thereafter as John the Evangelist.

John was a profuse and imaginative author who wrote five books at Ephesus which are included in the New Testament. His Gospel and three epistles are all known for the power of their imagery and expression. In his Gospel he emphasises the divine nature of Christ, in contrast to the others which dwell on his human side.

During the persecution of Domition (81-96 AD) he was exiled to the island of Patmos, where he continued to write profusely. His most famous contribution to the scriptures is ***The Book of Revelation***, a curious and wondrous mix of Creation Myth, cosmology and apparent prophecy. Of St John's other works nothing has survived, and we may but wonder why they vanished.

John's strange visions have given the world some of the most extraordinary images ever, including the famous passage about the 'Mother of God': *A woman clothed with the Sun and the Moon under her feet, and upon her head a crown of 12 stars... and she brought forth a man child...'*. There is one passage in chapter twelve so powerful that it became central to the Church's battle with the religions that preceded it. It is clearly drawn from the Babylonian Creation Myth of Bel (later Marduk) and the Dragon:

'And there was war in heaven: Michael and his angels fought against the dragon; and the dragon fought with his angels... And the great dragon was cast out, that old serpent called the Devil, and Satan, which deceiveth the whole world: he was cast out into the earth, and his angels were cast out with him'.

This powerful passage is uncompromising in its intensity, and also in its identification of the dragon as the ultimate power of evil. Yet we should understand that it was probably chosen for inclusion by Constantine exactly for this reason, for it vilified the force that was at the core of pre-Christian religion. This was a political act, and we do not even have the means to judge whether they are the original words of John, such was the editing and re-writing that took place in the writings deemed appropriate for inclusion in the Bible. It is known from the Dead Sea Scrolls and the Nag Hammadi scripts that much of the Essene and Gnostic scriptures were rejected and destroyed, lest they interfere with Constantine's propaganda.

Mythologists, however, can clearly read into this passage from John's Revelation another story altogether. It comes from the oldest written records known, dating back to the Sumerian and Akkadian civilisations that grew up on the fertile banks of the Tigris and Euphrates. These are over 5000 years old, and form the basis of much of the later belief systems of Egyptian and Hebrew religion. The tablets which record this version were excavated from the library of Ashurbanipal in Ninevah, dated to around 1000 BC, but are based on a far older tradition. In this account, known as the *Enuma Elish*, Tiamat was the primal female principle from the watery Abyss. She was the raw, chaotic power of procreation, a force of nature and the great Mother of all Creation, who challenged any attempt to tame her until Bel/Marduk, the solar god, dismembered her and brought order from the chaos.

Marduk's weapons included a net, with which he snared the dragon, as well as arrows and a lightning trident or thunderbolt with which he stabbed her through the heart. After the battle he split her body into two halves, and, like the Norse dragon slayer Siegfried, ate her flesh. Then he cast one half of her body into the heavens and the other became the Earth. He threw his net and bow into the sky where they became constellations, set the gods in their stations, fixed the stars of the zodiac and measured the year, dividing it into months and determining the times of the sacred festivals. Humans were then seeded upon the planet, followed by the introduction of plants and animals.

So Tiamat, the great Mother Goddess, has a dual character; she is slain but from her death are created both the Heavens and Earth. She becomes both destroyer and creatrix. She appears to be the prototype of all subsequent great mythic dragons, including the biblical Leviathan, the huge aquatic monster in the *Book of Job*. But the fact that Tiamat dies and was resurrected to create Heaven and Earth gives her a dual character that has become associated with the archetypal dragon slaying myth, where the dragon is slain to bring new life.

Thus the Revelation of St John may not be a revelation at all, but merely a restatement of the universal Myth of Creation that was known throughout the ancient world. It seems obvious that Bel (meaning bright or shining) and his successor Marduk are thus the earliest known versions of St George and St Michael. We can also see that the use of the correlation of the dragon (the force of nature) and Satan (the Devil of Christian myth) provided an ideal piece of propaganda for the new state religion, at once demonising the earlier beliefs and creating an archetypal evil force that must be vanquished. It also provided an ideal opportunity to strip the universal female principle of its power, another of the objectives of political Christianity.

The origins of the Babylonian epic are probably cosmological, alluding to the formation of the planets through some cataclysmic cosmic upheaval, which were then drawn into the Sun's orbit and 'organised' by its gravitational and magnetic forces. But the great dragon was divided; half of this primal female power went into the heavens, the other half is the Earth. This is surely a reference to the cosmic energies that animate the upper and lower worlds. *As above, So below.*

If we harbour doubts about this interpretation, we only have to visit the actual place where John received his revelation. The pilgrim who finds himself at the Cave of the Apocalypse on Patmos is shown a very curious feature. Cut into the cave wall is a shallow depression said to have been fashioned by John himself. It is believed by the monks that he did this to attune to the Holy Spirit there, so that he could not only immerse himself in the energy concentrating within the cave itself, but was in direct contact with the cave wall. In this hollow he laid his head, experiencing dreams and visions enhanced by the divine power issuing from the rock, the inspirational and transforming energy of the Earth.

If we are still wondering whether the dragon is a beneficent rather than an evil power, further up the mountain near its summit is the monastery of St John the Divine, an important place of pilgrimage. Directly above the entrance are two golden dragons giving the distinct impression of welcoming those who find themselves at this ancient sanctuary. They can leave no doubt that this too is a place of the Dragon.

The Cave of the Apocalypse on Patmos

12

A Search in Secret Egypt

ny investigation into the mystery behind St George must of necessity explore the roots of Christianity, which were derived indirectly from that ultimate land of religion and magic, Ancient Egypt. Heavily reinterpreted by Hebrew scribes who had no love of Egypt due to the politics of the time, when they were cast out of the land to become wanderers, both the Jewish and Christian ethos is firmly grounded in the thousands of years preceding them.

The traditions and way of thinking that had guided the Egyptians were seminal in all that influenced the Middle Eastern lands, much of which they controlled. The great centres of the Holy Land itself were Egyptian strongholds long before the Hebrew nation arose. The Paul Getty Museum in Jerusalem is replete with Egyptian artefacts from these times, including the massive sculptures of gods and Pharaohs that have come to typify their civilisation.

The quest, then, leads us to the land of the Nile, searching for clues that may shed further light on the mystery. There is much to be discovered, and a hawk's eye is required to discern the patterns and ideas that will illuminate our understanding. Here we find ourselves piecing together the broken fragments of one of the world's greatest civilisations, one that deeply influenced the thought forms of the modern world, even though we may not readily realise it.

The natural place to begin is the Cairo Museum, that extraordinary repository of first-hand evidence, much of it uncatalogued and lying about half unpacked as if in a warehouse awaiting transit. It is literally stuffed with treasures often crammed temporarily into display cabinets into which hardly any light penetrates. One has to squint to discern the pageant of strange images just as if in a dimly-lit tomb. To get to it one has to negotiate a bewildering scene; Cairo people stroll through the dense and chaotic traffic as casually as if they were wandering in a flower-strewn meadow, often passing within inches of the fast-moving cars whose drivers appear utterly oblivious to all around them. Horse-drawn carriages seem just as nonchalant. Strangely, accidents seem rare, although a sizeable proportion of the population do seem to be limping from past encounters.

Cairo is the largest city in Africa, and the most densely-populated, the traffic so frenetic that you take your life in your hands whenever you cross the road. It is also a cacophony of noise, with drivers continually pumping their horns so that it sounds for all the world like a severely demented accordion player with St Vitus' Dance, playing an especially discordant tune.

If we momentarily suspend the conditioning of the last two thousand years as if we were visitors from another world, entering the museum is a most enlightening experience. Amongst the hubbub and the half-hidden sculptures gazing at us is the whole history of the Egyptian world, encrypted in a code that few could claim to properly understand. The sheer quantity of material is overwhelming, from the earliest pre-dynastic times about which little is known, to the golden treasures of Tutankhamun. However, we must keep our eye firmly on matters pertaining to the quest, that of St George and the Dragon.

The thing that immediately strikes us is the great number of serpents in evidence, and the obvious depth of their religious significance. A cursory examination suggests that this one symbol is the most prevalent of all; almost as if Egyptian religion seems fundamentally to have been a cult of the serpent. If we view the artefacts of the distant past without preconceptions, we are left in no doubt that the winged serpent or dragon was a symbol of the utmost importance.

Not only does the prime symbol of Egypt, the winged Sun-disc, occur extensively, flanked by rearing cobras over the entrances to temples and tombs, but serpents are everywhere depicted on the massive sarcophagi. Many of these are very striking indeed, of enormously elongated length, compressed like the image on an oscilloscope screen, as if to signify energy in motion. These, we may assume, are a potent image of the life-force that will resurrect the departed, an image of rebirth and renewal. Some examples, if we were to straighten them out, would probably be in excess of 100 feet. Many have a

Serpent with ankh, both symbols of the Life Force

circle between their wings, as if they are honouring the Sun with wings raised in adoration. One example shows a heavily compressed snake completely encircling a Sun-disc within which is a scarab, the sacred beetle that symbolises the passage of the solar orb across the desert horizon.

Pyramidions, or the capstones of pyramids and obelisks, are the most significant part of the structures that epitomise ancient Egypt, being the topmost section and therefore closest to the heavens. On many, including the pyramidion of King Khendjer of the XIII dynasty, found in fragments at the foot of his pyramid at Saqqara, serpents are shown looped over the Sun-disc with their wings spread downwards, and with ankhs, the symbol of the Life Force, hanging from their necks. Clearly, the symbol of the winged serpent or dragon in Egypt was one of the most sacred icons in religious art, and signified Life, as well as death, in its many manifestations. Its close association with the Sun likewise leaves us in little doubt that besides referring to the darker side of existence, as we in the Western world have come to accept, it signified eternal Life, and the Laws of Nature which sustain everything. This is eloquently demonstrated by many striking works of art, such as a pair of gilded serpents from Tutankhamun's tomb surmounted by the upstanding feathers of Maat, the Goddess of Truth and Justice.

The Rod of Power

One of the greatest symbols of power in Egypt, throughout the 3000 years or so of its civilisation, was the staff or rod held by gods and Pharaohs known as the Uaz Sceptre. It conferred ultimate power upon those who possessed it, yet it is a symbol that very little is known about. It is clear that it was not merely a symbolic device, but an actual physical rod that represented the creative power wielded both by the gods, and by the living being— the King—who was himself of their number.

The first owner of the royal Uaz Sceptre was the original creator god Ptah, he who formed the Heavens and the Earth by uttering the Divine word, the Breath of God. As the Great Architect of the Universe, everything we see living on the face of the Earth, from the tiniest creature to the great forests, as well as the star-fields of the sky, was given life by his command. In heiroglyphic form, he is represented as a seated figure in meditative pose, holding the sceptre before him. This god is the foundation of all Existence, hence Ptah was later Christianised as Peter, the rock on which everything else is built.

The Sceptre itself is of a very distinctive form, and one that did not change or evolve throughout the centuries. At its top was a stylised animal head. No-one has yet discovered exactly what this represents, but those who have explored the earliest stages of Egyptian history feel that it is likely be the god who was at the very root of pre-dynastic religion, Set. This seems both plausible and likely, for the Uaz Sceptre is first seen during very early times when Set was the primeval god par excellence.

There is evidence that the Setian religion was at the root of all subsequent developments. Its cult centre was at Nbt, which means Gold Town, famous for its deposits of the precious metal. Some of the oldest settlements in Upper Egypt have been found in this area and excavated by Flinders Petrie, notably that of Naqada, which has given its name to a pre-dynastic era.

Set was regarded as a beneficent god long before he was vilified by new political and religious fashions. Billie Walker John, in *The Setian*, traces the power of Set from the beginnings of history and notes that:

'Anyone who has read history will have observed how readily the conqueror will demonise, banish, subvert or otherwise coerce the beliefs, deities and religions of the vanquished to serve its needs and purposes. Just as it was with the Setian Mysteries, worship and beliefs. Set, once the chief *neter* of the indigenous people of Egypt, and the guard, friend and psychopompos of the dead had been made into a murdering demon by the Osirian cult.'[1]

The true history of the wild god of the deserts, who famously murdered Osiris and then fought with Horus, the God of Light, shows that he was much more than an adversary and the prototype devil invented by the Church, who called him Satan. He was originally conceived as the source from which all earthly

Set, who was identified with the modern constellation of the Great Bear, or the bull's thigh in Egyptian cosmology, being speared by Horus.

power sprang. One of his titles was 'Son of Nuit', the Egyptian sky goddess. For as Horus was the light of day, Set was the dark of night. But this is not the darkness of chaos, it is the velvet blackness of the night sky when the stars come alive and dance their endless spirals through time. Thus Set, as the Lord of the Night, represents divine order and the star-origins of humanity. All this was before moral judgements were overlaid on the Light and the Dark, and they were understood as dual aspects of Creation, the scales of the Cosmic balance. As perhaps the earliest god of all, it was inevitable that Set would undergo a series of transformations, yet his popularity remained strong. At a certain stage Set and Horus were shown as a single entity with two heads to signify they were different sides of the same power. During the reign of Ramasses II the state god was Amun, but in the Delta Set was of greater importance, and at el-Khargah Oasis in the Western Desert he was worshipped as the deity who would ensure the fertility of the Oasis.

He was also worshipped at Kom Ombo before it became the shrine of the crocodile god Sobek, and so they eventually became merged, much as Set had, by the Late Period, become identified with his former adversary the serpent Apep. In the 5th century BC Temple of Hibis, Set is shown as a winged figure slaying the serpent as if he were an angel.[2]

The Egyptian Gods and Goddesses—the Neteru—were not abstractions or childish representations of animal instincts in the way we might think, but actual living principles of *Nature*—from which our word is derived. This is an important point, for the fact that our word for the natural forces of creation comes from the very roots of Egyptian religion emphasises how the legacy of Egypt lies behind much of Western thought. The animal heads of the gods were keys to

*Set with Uaz sceptre, from
Deir el-Medina, Dynasty XIX*

the particular character of each principle, personified by various totemic creatures manifesting these principles, and without which the world as we know it would cease to exist. The strange long-eared head of Set was from the earliest times associated with the wild desert donkeys that were almost impossible to tame, and so he eventually became the wild god of the desert, who challenged the prevailing order of established civilisation. He was not the personification of evil that later times insisted, but a source of the great and untamed force of Nature. To understand how this primordial god was demonised and changed into a dark and destructive intelligence stalking the Earth as the enemy of the Light, we only have to study the propaganda of the early Church fathers. Just as some politicians today often need demons of a different sort to blame for their own shortcomings, so they invent illusory foes to justify waging war to protect us from imagined evil. In the case of Set, however, the demonisation began even before Christianity, as the politics of the later Osirian dynasties found it useful to mythologise the battle between the religious factions as the attempted murder of Osiris (later miraculously restored by Isis and Nepthys) by the primeval Set. In this way the new order, in the classic and endlessly repeating formula, turns the old gods into devils.

Yet even though later ages reversed his role, Set's power, so firmly established in the popular psyche, could not so easily be vanquished, especially as he was the earliest psychpomp, or guide of souls. His wife Nepthys shared a similar function, that of guiding the initiate through the underworld regions. The mythic memory of Set's place in the cosmic scheme was preserved in everyday religion and he was remembered as the god who tamed the great serpent Apep every day to renew the Light of the Sun. This was a perennial theme in the priestly and royal life of the nation, but it is not one we are often aware of. This is because of the famous story of the battle between Set and Horus, and Set's murder of Osiris, a very late and heavily modified version of the myth, purposely designed to demonise the old god.

To help us understand the true nature of Set, many representations from tomb paintings and papyri show him standing at the prow of Ra's solar barque, the boat of millions of years, with spear poised to tame the serpent that inhabits the deep. For this job he was personally selected by Ra the Sun God himself. Set is thus the specially-chosen one who renews the cycle of Life each night through his taming of the unrefined and chaotic dark energies symbolised by the serpent Apep. To suggest that he kills the serpent is a misunderstanding by the modern mind, for Apep (*Apophis* in Greek) is not slain, otherwise the Sun would not rise again and earthly life would instantly cease. Set was above all a saviour and creator god, and accordingly honoured by his fellow gods and Pharaohs alike. Even as late as the dying days of the Egyptian empire, the military King Seti I followed in the long tradition of *The Companions of Set*, a group of Setian followers, and was named after him, no doubt to identify

himself with the powers of the god in order to subdue the chaotic forces of his rebellious territories. During times when Set fell out of favour, he was depicted in other forms, sometimes as a black pig, sometimes a hippopotamus.

The Egyptian pronunciation of Set was *Shad*—hence our word for the darker aspect of the light, the contrast that creates the shades of the light, the shadow.[3] This gives a glimpse into the original meaning

Set spears Apep, from the Book of Dead, Dynasty XXI

of Set, not as an evil force, but the one that is the natural opposite of the brightness of the Creative Light. He is our shadow side, not our enemy, but another facet of our being and the world we live in, without which existence would cease.

Another curious feature of the Setian Rod of Power is that its lower end terminates in a two-pronged fork. Strange as this might initially appear to our eyes, anyone who has seen a snake charmer in action collecting his quarry would immediately recognise it, for it is the same as the forked stick or rod they use to capture snakes by pinning down their heads. Here then is one of the most significant Egyptian symbols of earthly power, clearly based on the fixing or pinning down of some force symbolised by the head of a serpent. A very interesting collection of these objects from the bottom of Uaz Sceptres, often made of metal and somewhat resembling tuning forks, is displayed in the Cairo Museum, and one is struck by this innate metaphor implied by their shape, as if their function was somehow involved with resonance or vibration.

It becomes apparent that the Uaz Sceptre not only represents the Setian power, but also that of the serpent, Apep, that Set tames so that the Light may return. In this way the Pharaoh identifies himself with Set (like Seti I and others who adopted the name) and takes on the role appointed to Set by Ra the Sun God, transforming darkness into Light. Set's particular time was the evening, when the western hills glowed a vivid red colour, the *Sun-Set*. This was when his power gathered strength as he positioned himself at the helm of Ra's solar barque with his spear which was to ensure the continuing cycle of day and night. In Egyptian, the word Set, or Seti, gives a clue to his true power, for it means literally 'Great in Strength'. The Sceptre may have had a ceremonial function, but it is also likely that it was in reality a truly 'magic' staff associated with the transformation of energy, as the story of Set and Apep indicates. Indeed, other magic rods used by the gods show a serpent coiled around them, notably in the case of Thoth, the God of Magic, the original Egyptian owner of the Caduceus, the serpent-entwined rod that even today is a symbol of healing. Some ceremonial staffs in tomb paintings also take the form of sinuous upstanding serpents, so the symbolism throughout the use of magical rods seems distinctly serpentine. In the Biblical story of Aaron's Rod, Moses' (*Ra-Moses or Ramasses*) brother throws his rod to the ground when challenged by the Egyptian priests, and it is magically changed into a serpent. It could indeed be that these Rods of Power may have been magical tools for the transmutation of certain types of energy. For in myth, as we have seen, serpents, snakes and dragons represent the vital energies of the cosmos which can be transformed through human intervention.

For the moment, though, it is perhaps sufficient to realise that the Uaz Sceptre that signified the power of the gods and Pharaohs and the triumph of Light over Darkness seems to be the original Egyptian prototype of the Spear of St George, through its connection with the taming of the great serpent-dragon Apep.

From Dragon to Crocodile

The mythology of the Egyptians was not some distant and arcane metaphor or remote religious concept, but a living reality that was enacted every day in Nature. Each morning the temple priests gathered at dawn to welcome the return of the Sun with offerings, incense and incantations. There was a threefold pattern of worship, at dawn, noon and dusk, and in this way an entire civilisation was brought into synchrony with the Sun God, sailing in his boat of millions of years across the sky, bringing Light and plenty into the world. Every day the Sun was reborn, shining in his prime at midday, and then grew old as he travelled to the western horizon. Every night he entered the underworld, the Tuat, and was swallowed by the cosmic serpent Apep, to emerge resurrected the next day. Every priest and Pharaoh identified with this eternal principle, for the king brought the solar energies to Earth, manifesting them through magic ritual to maintain the cosmic order and make his kingdom prosper.

The Egyptian Creation Myth referred not to a particular event lost in the primordial past as we might imagine, but a process that was taking place every second and every minute, continuously. The kings embodied in a profoundly mystical sense the Divine principle of the Sun God, and this was reflected in their Horus name, which every Pharaoh was given when he assumed the role of the Sun King. They enacted their rituals on Earth as if they were the gods themselves, fulfilling their duties in the heavens.

Pharaohs and priests invoked the Sun at dawn with certain rites that brought heaven to Earth, and the most significant rite of all was that of ensuring the daily solar cycle continued uninterrupted. From tomb sculptures and paintings we can see how important this was deemed, for the Pharaohs are commonly depicted with their spear poised, aimed skilfully at the head of Apep, the serpent of the inexpressible deep. In the tomb of Ramasses I the King points his spear of Light downwards to the many-coiled serpent, but the spear does not penetrate its head, touching the mouth instead, as if exchanging spiritual energy. The symbolism of breath in Egyptian ritual was crucial, with the ankh, the cross of the Life Force, often shown touching the mouths of gods and Pharaohs. This is not the killing of the great serpent Apep, but an acknowledgement of its power and essential nature. A golden statue of the boy king Tutankhamun shows him standing in his boat, spear poised at the classic angle, which Egyptologists have described as the King 'hunting for fish'. The truth is more likely to be that this is the Pharaoh in his sun-boat hunting something very different, in fact enacting the ritual of taming the serpent; the triumph of the Light over the Darkness.

Such is the wealth of imagery concerning this single ritual act throughout the long period of Egyptian civilisation that we are forced to acknowledge its prime significance. To the Egyptian mind, it was the central core of their cosmology, affecting all life on Earth and essential for its continuity.

When the dynasties fell into decline, invaders and foreign cultures interpreted this symbolic act in their own way, reflecting their particular perspectives. The major influence was that of the Romans and Greeks, who were already familiar with Egyptian ideas. When they came to prominence a

transformation took place. With no Pharaohs to enact the timeless ritual, it became a symbolic myth; yet its power over the human imagination was transformed, rather than diminished. The militaristic attitudes of the invaders changed things radically, and the power of the great serpent Apep was no longer understood in the same way. To Roman centurions the fearsome crocodiles they encountered on the banks of the Nile seemed more appropriate to represent the principle of awesome power that had previously belonged to Apep. The serpent's powers became absorbed with that of the crocodile.

In fact this idea too was to a certain extent an offshoot of the former religion, for crocodiles had a special significance and were often shown being speared like Apep. It was a long-standing tradition that Pharaohs were anointed with crocodile

Horus depicted as a Roman centurion spearing a crocodile

fat, called Messah, from which the word *Messiah* derives. Interestingly the Hindus called the constellation of Draco 'The Crocodile'. During Ptolemaic times, Harpocrates, the Greek version of Horus, is shown standing on two crocodiles, like the sculpture of Christ on Chartres Cathedral with his feet on the twin dragons of the Wouivre. As this idea spread throughout the empire, with legionaries travelling across Europe and the Middle East, the crocodile became a universal symbol for the dragon.

As crocodiles inhabited swamps and riverbanks, legends grew of terrible creatures infesting such regions that would devour unwary humans and animals. In this way a different version of the legend was born, echoing down the centuries from the most remote past, and finding a common acceptance in countries bordering Egypt, where the influence of its mythology was already widespread.

But what of the Divine Hero, the Pharaoh who had previously embodied the principle of the Sun, and Horus the hawk god who triumphantly flew across the daytime sky? Now there were no Pharaohs, he became initially a falcon-headed military hero mounted on his cavalry horse, spear raised to defeat the crocodile/dragon that was being trampled underfoot.

In time, as Egyptian influence waned, this image was replaced by a figure more easily recognisable to us: that of a soldier battling with a dragon. In countries where crocodiles were unknown, local imagination added to the original stories and images that accompanied Roman occupation, and the frightening and terrible legend of the foul-smelling scaly creatures that fed on humans and animals became woven into folklore. The familiar legend of St George and the Dragon as we know it today had been born. The heroic god-like soldier did, though, inherit a significant aspect of his precursors, that of his shining countenance reflected by gleaming armour and—as a direct reference to his incarnation as a Sun God—the solar halo shimmering around his head.

The Sacred Serpent

Centuries of deliberate misinformation have given the serpent a very bad name indeed. Because of its close association with Set, the two images have been combined to create a composite devilish icon, so that Satan often occurs as a demon, this time with a man's head and the body of a snake. The early Church fathers had good reason to make sure the personification of evil took such a form. In pre-Christian ages the serpent was looked upon as one of the great primordial forms of the Creator.

There were many reasons for this. Since the snake sheds its skin to emerge 'reborn' it was a living symbol of the death and rebirth cycle of nature, and of the idea that the human body is an old 'skin' left behind enabling the soul to continue its journey into the afterlife. In this way it is probably the greatest symbol of transformation, especially within a tradition familiar with symbolising natural forces through totemic imagery. Its character is also of mutability; ever-changing, fast-reacting, it can strike sudden fear into the heart of anyone who does not understand how to tame it, and may even cause death to the unwary.

It is also a vibrant metaphor for the energetic nature of the universe. Its writhing movement perfectly encapsulates the idea of primeval energy, that continuous movement behind all life forms. The spiralling, twisting motion of its body, apparently moving effortlessly without visible means, exactly parallels the way energy functions. Today we can observe the frequencies of various types of energy on an oscilloscope screen, and see that the highs and lows create a 'serpent' which changes according to its resonance in the form of a sine wave. It is interesting that the word sine is derived from sinuous, both related to the word Sin, the Babylonian Moon God, who waxes and wanes, sloughing off his skin serpent-like, and the measurer of earthly time. Before the name was corrupted to indicate the Christian concept of evil, Sin was also the god of menstruation (from which we get the word measure) and hence the secret force behind the fertile womb which gives us birth. Here on the oscilloscope screen, we have a modern demonstration of what the ancients instinctively knew; that the universe is created through rhythmic cycles, frequency and resonance, which was first uttered, in the beginning, as the Word of God, the *Uni-verse*.

Throughout the ancient world, serpents were invariably sacred. They still are in countries where religions other than Christianity are predominant. In India the King of Snakes, the Cobra, is both feared and honoured, and many fabulous stories are told of their miraculous interactions with humans. The respect and awe which they are held in is legendary, and they are often said to inspire and guide people in the course of their daily lives, as if gods. Buddha himself is frequently depicted as sitting amidst a nest of serpents, the Nagas, whose heads form a canopy around his own. These are the Serpents of Wisdom that bring spiritual enlightenment.

One of the most striking representations of the serpent divinities of the Middle East is found on a libation goblet from the reign of the Sumerian King Gudea of Lagash, inscribed with a date equivalent to 2025 BC. It was made after Gudea experienced a vision that impressed him so deeply that he ordered it to commemorate the event. The goblet, carved from green steatite and now in the Louvre Museum, is one of the earliest representations of the serpent-entwined staff known as the Caduceus, the symbol of mystic initiation. On either side are positioned two identical images of the winged Dragon Lord Ningizzidda, each holding staffs next to which are the sacred writhing serpents. The scaly winged body of Ningizzidda is one of the earliest images of what we would today definitively describe as a dragon.

The mythologist Joseph Campbell describes the Sumerian Dragon Lord as the consort of the great goddess, called the 'Lord of the Tree of Truth'. A rare account survives of Gudea's dream as he prayed in the temple after the river Tigris failed in its annual inundation, threatening the fertility of his kingdom:

'There was in my dream the figure of a man whose stature filled the sky, whose stature filled the earth. The crown upon his head proclaimed him a god…thereupon the sun rose from the earth before me'

The goddess of the temple interpreted his dream in detail, adding that;

'Now, the sun that rose from the earth before you was your guardian god, Ningizzidda; like a sun, his serpent form rises from the earth…'[4]

This fragmentary glimpse of a profound religious experience over 4000 years ago may seem obscure to us today, yet it will become more significant as we come to discern the process of mystical unfoldment that the St George myth is based upon, a universal tradition that has pervaded the collective mind of humanity for millennia.

Ningizzidda, as the 'Lord of the Tree of Truth', strikes a chord deep within us. He may even be the original serpent of the biblical garden of Eden who guarded the Tree of Knowledge of Good and Evil, a story which was transcribed into the Old Testament by the Hebrews after their enslavement in Babylon. If so, then we can perhaps see how his character was changed from a deity of revelation into a symbol of evil. Depicted as a serpent with its overtly phallic implications, along with the fact that he was the consort of the goddess, this idea linking sexuality with forbidden knowledge may have provided an opportunity for the scribes to demonise him unashamedly, and blame him for that life-denying concept of original sin that was to so permeate Christianity. The Tree was originally the centre of the universe, the Axis Mundi, and a study of Sumerian seals reveals a picture of joyous, worshipping figures, who pluck its fruits with obvious pleasure. There is no sign of wrath or danger

*Horus and Set, the Gods of Light and Dark,
wind up the spiral axis of Creation*

in any of these images, and no indication of the concept of guilt. As Campbell emphasises, the serpent 'had been revered in the Levant for at least seven thousand years before the composition of the Book of Genesis.'

Egyptian paintings and papyri show a similar veneration for serpents. They are full of serpent images, and none of them have any apparent connotations of evil. The walls of tombs are covered in a great variety, including serpents with legs (indicating movement), those with horns (wisdom) and those with wings (which are more draconic). Champollion's **Treatise of Egyptian Grammar**, which decoded the heiroglyphs, is replete with a myriad of them, including the original 'ouroboros' or serpent biting its own tail, which indicated the cycle of day and night, death and rebirth, later adopted by medieval alchemy. This great profusion of serpents is because in the Egyptian cosmology, the serpent represented the many sacred aspects of a living god, including the spiritual vision of the Pharaoh and the all-seeing eye of Horus.

Anyone who has ever seen an image of a Pharaoh will have also noticed the royal Ureaus, the King Cobra, issuing from the forehead. This is one of the most iconic and meaningful representations of serpents. It represents the energy of higher spiritual consciousness, the godlike status of the King. It comes from the Earth, and rises up the spine to bring spiritual vision. This meaning is also apparent in the images of temple priests, who have twin serpents on their aprons signifying the awakening energies, the Kundalini of the Vedic tradition, at the base of their spine. The serpent symbol in hieroglyphics is pronounced as a *D* or *DJ*, and it is noteworthy that the Spine of Osiris, the *Djed* pillar, has the same sound, as does the Egyptian name for Thoth, *Djehudi*, who holds the serpent-entwined Caduceus. Both these root syllables draw attention to the magical function of the serpent power to energise the spine and the centres of the body responsible for spiritual illumination. It is noteworthy that the Djed pillar of Osiris, one of the most common talismans of Egyptian art, is frequently overlaid with the Uaz Sceptre and an ankh (like that shown on a colossal statue of Ptah from the great temple of Ramasses II at Memphis). Furniture found in Tutankhamun's tomb is covered in golden Uaz Sceptres and ankhs in great profusion. The ankh becomes a human figure, arms outstretched, holding a Uaz Sceptre, as on an alabaster vase from the tomb. Can we be in any doubt that the Uaz Sceptre, Set's magic rod with which he tames the serpent, was, in the Egyptian mind, synonymous with the Life Force itself?

13

The Green God of the Nile

At Abydos, the great centre of Osiris worship and one of the most beautiful of the Egyptian temples, there are a number of clues that resonate with our search to find the real St George. Because Osiris was the great fertility god he is often shown with a green or black face. Green is the verdure of the Earth, black, to the Egyptians, meant the rich, dark alluvial silt deposited by the flooding Nile that caused the land to flourish. One of their names for Egypt was the land of Khem, the Black Land. Osiris was the son of Geb, the Earth God, and inherited Geb's characteristics, as well as his earthly throne, to become King. He was also the brother of Set, whom later dynasties turned into a pre-Christian devil when the Egyptian Green Man was murdered by the former spear-wielding god of predynastic times.

In some representations of both St George and St Michael the 'devil' is shown as a green-hued humanoid angel known as a *Hominoida Chlorodraco*, literally, a *Green Man-Dragon*. (A good example of this can be seen in the stained-glass window of St George's Chapel at St John's Church in Glastonbury.) Is this a medieval interpretation of the myth of Set, the god who once preserved the Light by standing in the prow of Ra's solar barque, murdering the Green God Osiris? Such a thought may appear dangerously heretical and reverses the usually accepted roles of the protagonists, yet it may show how multi-faceted these images of the dragon slayer have become. In acquiring universality, the myth has developed such complexity that its true meaning, that of the renewal of the cycle of fertility, has become almost hopelessly obfuscated.

At Abydos, with evidence of habitation extending well back into prehistoric times, there are clues that may beckon to us and point the way. As one of the earliest shrines of Osiris in Egypt and the place where his head was said to have been interred, the spirit of the old god lingers on, even though much of the temple is from the later Ptolemaic period. Wandering through the dusty chambers and halls with their towering papyrus-reed columns, out of the gloom appears an image that stops you in your tracks. It is a massive relief of the Djed column, the stylised Spine of Osiris, the symbol of earthly stability, the Tree linking Heaven and Earth, and, through its association with the serpent energy, the vehicle of spiritual transformation. It is located at the entrance to the Inner Temple, where the sanctuaries of Isis, Osiris and Horus are situated, as if to say 'Abandon all illusions, ye who enter here'.

Only initiates and temple priests were allowed beyond this point, and it provides us with a reminder that the illumination of the adept was the prime motive of all Egyptian religion. In the Hall of Osiris is a wall-painting of Pharaoh Seti I (c.1285 BC) erecting a similarly large Djed column as part of the celebrations of the Osirian Temple calendar. It is thought to have been made of a woven wheatsheaf to indicate that the essence of the soul of Osiris is the cereal god who sustains all human life. In many parts of the world the last sheaf of corn to be cut was believed to contain the spirit of the Corn God, in fact to be nothing less than his actual head. As we have seen, the British folksong John Barleycorn and the 'Crying the Neck' ceremony recall this, and it looks as though a similar ritual was enacted here at Abydos. Harvest time was

Isis and Nepthys
worshipping the Djed pillar

full of joy, but also tinged with regret, for with every stroke of the moon-shaped sickle the body of the god was sacrificed to save the people from hunger and want.

Another unusual feature at Abydos is the 'Osireion', a unique monument thought to have been constructed by Seti I from massive megalithic blocks rising from a pool of green water fed by an underground spring. Its purpose is

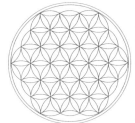

obscure. Some think it a cenotaph or memorial that may have been designed to simulate the original Mound of Creation, surrounded by the waters of the Abyss. Above the entrance that led from this to the Temple was originally a giant image of the head of Osiris. The Cult of the Head looks as though it was one of the most significant features of Osirian worship; inside the Osiris sanctuary a wall-painting shows Seti burning incense before the sacred emblem, the head of Osiris hanging from a pole. At the opposite end of the sacred lake or pool, amongst the jumbled ruins of the Osireion, which some consider to be the remains of one of the oldest structures in all Egypt, is carved the famous 'Flower of Life', a complex geometric design believed to have deep mystical significance concerning the generative force in nature.

Each year at the annual festival of Osiris, a statue of the god in his solar barque was carried from the inner sanctum of the Temple on the shoulders of the priests to the site of his supposed tomb. Everyone wished to be buried at Abydos, but as this was impractical they left enormous quantities of votive offerings in the form of pots inscribed with prayers, giving the place its Arabic name of Umm el-Qaab (Mother of Pots). They still litter the sands today in great profusion. Throughout the greatest part of Egyptian history Abydos was held to be the burial place of the Head of Osiris, the Lord of Life after death. It is almost as if it were the Egyptian equivalent of the Church of the Holy Sepulchre in Jerusalem, where Jesus was crucified at the 'Place of the Skull'. The correspondences between Jesus and Osiris become ever more evident.

Just a short visit to Abydos provides many links pertinent to our quest. The sacred pool (with which serpents and dragons are so often associated), the Head of Osiris (the symbol of higher consciousness), the Djed column (up which the dragon energies rise), the sacred mound of death and rebirth, and— perhaps most striking of all—the amazing Flower of Life, all show that this place was of inestimable importance. From the earliest dynasties of Egyptian civilisation, Osiris was therefore one of the most ancient gods and especially concerned with spiritual cognition. None of this was based on what we might class today as superstition; Abydos was more in the nature of a mystical university, where the science of the unfolding mysteries of nature and human transformation was the motive force. Is this why Abydos was a cult centre for that mysterious group known as the *Shemsu-Hor*, the *'Followers of Horus'*? Were they true initiates into the Mystery Wisdom, studying the patterns of earthly manifestation and the secret meaning of Light, the Sun-God Horus (the central element *'or'* in Ge-or-ge), yet also steeped in the arcane lore of the fertile mysteries of nature (the repeated *Ge* that signifies the old Earth God Geb of which Osiris is the reincarnation)?

When we begin to glean the wheat from the chaff of this old cereal god we begin to suspect more than a shadow of Osiris in St George. The Egyptian god was, for a long period of history, identified with the constellation of Orion the Hunter, the giant celestial figure who comes striding over the horizon in early Spring, signifying the rebirth of the Sun and the beginning of the growth cycle, just like St George in the folk traditions of Europe. Could they both share their powers of fertility with the luminous star-giant of mythological legend?

The Myth of Osiris

The story of Osiris, Isis and their son Horus was the most famous religious myth ever, not only colouring all aspects of Egyptian life but spreading out to encompass the Greek and Roman worlds and even as far as Europe; Paris and other regions of France are still great centres of Isis worship, as well as Nepthys, in her guise as Mary Magdalene. All these elements eventually formed the template for another mythology, that of Christianity.

Schoolchildren today are taught that Osiris was the God of the Dead. This is an eloquent statement of how we have come to view Egyptian civilisation, as if it was death-obsessed simply because most of our information comes from tomb-paintings. Yet on examination, nothing could be further from the truth. The perfect Egyptian afterlife was seen as a continuity of the joys of earthly existence, as the paintings of hunting, fishing, dancing and feasting make clear.

Osiris is the God of Rebirth, of which death is merely one part of the process. His function as God of the Underworld, the *Tuat*, refers as much to the power in the Earth making seeds sprout and shoot as it does to his role as judge of the dead. It is only because we have lost touch with the continuity of birth, death and rebirth of the soul (a central tenet of all ancient religions), as well as that of the cycles of nature, that we see things in this one-sided way. In another of his aspects Osiris was the deity of the flooding Nile that brought stability and plenty to the land, and was in this respect synonymous with Hapi, the God of the Nile, who brought his subjects *happiness*.

It is from the later Greek writers such as Plutarch, in his **De Iside et Osiride**, that we hear of the tales surrounding the Egyptian trinity of Isis, Osiris and Horus, although we must always remember these are in a form which has probably changed considerably over the long ages of Egypt from pre-dynastic times. Here we are told how Nut the Sky Goddess (the wife of Ra) conceived a child by Geb, the Earth God. Discovering her infidelity Ra cursed her, saying her child could not be born in any month or any year. Distressed by this news, Nut called upon Thoth, the God of Magic, to help, and he devised a strategem. He played a game with the Moon God who staked a one-seventieth part of his light, but lost; so the light of the Moon thereafter waned at certain times.

From this light Thoth made five days which he added to the existing year of 360 days to give 365, new days which previously belonged to no month or year. Each day a child was born, Osiris on the first, Horus (known as The Elder) on the Second, Set on the third, Isis on the fourth and Nepthys on the fifth. At Osiris' birth a great cry went up throughout the world; 'The Lord of all the Earth is born!'

Osiris grew up to become a great and wise king, with Egypt flourishing as it had never done before. It was Isis who first discovered wheat and barley growing wild, and Osiris who first picked grapes to make wine. In areas where vines would not grow he taught the people to brew a dark beer from barley instead. He set about civilising the people, giving them a code of laws, teaching them the arts of husbandry, and establishing the correct rituals of worship. When this had been done he travelled the world visiting every country, spreading the knowledge of civilisation and establishing a Golden Age upon Earth.

But Set (who in Plutarch's account has evolved into the Greek Typhon, thus becoming hopelessly entangled with Apep) was jealous, for Isis was made regent instead of him while Osiris was away. Set made a richly decorated chest to fit the King's body, invited him to a great banquet and then suggested some after-dinner entertainment; the chest would belong to whoever fitted perfectly into it. The moment Osiris lay down, Set nailed the lid shut and cast the coffin adrift on the Nile.

Isis, hearing of this treachery, searched the country for her husband's body and eventually found herself at Byblos, where the chest had been flung up into a tamarisk tree by the waves. The tree immediately grew into a magnificent specimen, so impressive that the King, Melcarthus, cut it down to make a pillar to support the roof of his palace. Isis, through magical means, persuaded the Queen to give her the pillar, she then cut it open and removed Osiris' coffin. The tree which had held the body became famous, and was preserved at Byblos where it was worshipped for many centuries. The temple where it was housed can still be seen.

Back in Egypt Isis and her sister Nepthys mourned while Set, hunting by the light of the Moon, discovered the body and hacked it into fourteen pieces, which he scattered throughout the country. The distraught Isis went in search of the fragments of the god's body, and whenever she found one she made a wax model of each member and built a shrine to mark the spot; an effigy of his spine was interred at Busiris on the Nile Delta, of his leg at Elephantine Island in the south, and his head at Abydos. The only member Isis could not find was his phallus which had been swallowed by an Oxyrhynchus fish. So she fashioned a replica carved from wood, changed herself into a kite and, with the help of Nepthys, fanned the breath back into Osiris' body with her wings, reviving the King just enough so that Isis and Osiris could make love. Thus their son Horus (The Younger) was conceived supernaturally after Isis magically resurrected the body of the King. Horus, on reaching manhood, sought to avenge his father's murder, and many battles with Set were to follow. They still fight, it is said— as victory for either one has yet to come. It is the eternal battle between the Light and the Dark.

Even a brief look at this myth (of which there are numerous versions) gives an idea that its themes are concerned with cosmology, and in particular with the mysterious five days marking a shift from the old Babylonian system of 360. The birth of Osiris on the first day of this new sequence (probably equivalent to the 'nameless day' of the Druids) seems to indicate this was connected with the Winter Solstice, when so many of the old gods were born. The hacking of Osiris' body into fourteen parts is probably a reference to the Moon, whose body is gradually diminished by the powers of darkness during the last fourteen days of its cycle.

J.G.Frazer believed that Osiris was 'One of those personifications of vegetation whose annual death and resurrection have been celebrated in so many lands, the same as Tammuz, Adonis and Attis.' They do indeed appear to be one and the same, a primeval Green Man; the 'God of Many Names'. The Babylonian Tammuz was the lover of Ishtar. The Phrygians called him Attis, and the Greeks Adonis, from the Semitic word Adon, meaning Lord. In Babylonian myth

Ishtar followed Tammuz into the underworld. As a result nothing would procreate or grow, so they were sprinkled with the waters of Life and allowed to return to the surface to make the Earth fertile again. The Greek myth of Persephone is a variant on the same theme. There is also a strong similarity of myth and ritual throughout these examples. In all cases we have a god whose untimely death is mourned by a goddess and commemorated in seasonal rites by his worshippers. The legend of Osiris tells how he was the first to teach humanity the use of cultivated cereals, and so his annual festival began with the tillage of the Earth. The Greek year is still divided into two, with summer beginning on St George's Day (for he is the old patron saint of the country), when animals are taken from their winter pastures to graze on the fresh spring grass of the hills.

How much the Greeks took Osiris to their hearts can be seen in their adoption of the Egyptian Mysteries at the great Mystery Temple of Eleusis, where wheat and fruits were of singular symbolic importance. This time it was Triptolemus who travelled the world (in a dragon-chariot according to the myth) holding an ear of wheat given to him by Demeter, teaching every country agriculture.[2] We should also note that Osiris was said to have introduced the cultivation of the vine, showing that he was also a precursor of Pan, Dionysus and Bacchus. Pan especially was known, like Osiris, as the great civiliser of the world. Whenever we look at the old Egyptian myths we can see that the Greeks borrowed heavily from them, adapting them as they went, and so the old stories continued, although clothed in different garb.

Osiris The Corn God

In the Cairo Museum are some particularly poignant reminders of how Osiris, the Lord of Life after death, was manifested as the spirit of new life sprouting from seed. A number of near life-size wooden figures of the god are on display, which have been found in a great many tombs, including that of Tutankhamun. However, they are not the usual sculptures. These are seed-trays taking the form of the god himself. They were hollowed out and filled with black Nile soil, with seed sown in them that was then allowed to sprout. The plants often grew to a height of 10 inches before the images were wrapped in linen, to signify the rebirth of Osiris as the original mummy. This was an essential part of the funeral rites, the creation of a true 'Green Man', with Osiris becoming a living bed of germinating seeds. It is intensely evocative to examine them closely, the dried sprouts and blackened linen, remains of a ritual performed so long ago.

This theme is continued in many tombs and temples, with

different varieties of seeds placed within these 'Corn-Osiris' figures, to link both the dead and the living with the regeneration of the growing seeds. The concept behind this is symbolically pregnant with a powerful idea; the god Osiris becomes a tiny cornfield himself, created from grain and the black earth, both of which appear to be dead but harbour the potential for the continuity of life. In a chamber dedicated to Osiris at the island Temple of Philae, the dead body of Osiris is represented with stalks of corn springing from it whilst a priest waters them from a pitcher. The identification of Osiris with wheat and barley goes further than simply indicating that he is a Fertility God. It represents the kernel of the Mysteries which only initiates might understand, where the sowing of seed and the winnowing of grain are metaphors for spiritual processes. The scattering of the parts of his body is also a metaphor, for he is Lord of the Earth and therefore the planet *is* his body.

The Ever-Changing God

Osiris is a perfect example of how a god or goddess absorbs the attributes of others as their popularity grows. They roll down the hill of history like a snowball gathering other deities as they go. Thus it is sometimes difficult to disentangle their original character from the accretions of centuries. This is certainly true of Osiris, whose career lasted at least 3000 years, and was then revived as he was yet again reborn as the model for a new religion.

His beginnings are obscure, but the hieroglyphic symbols for his name are the Throne of Egypt (known as the 'Seat of Geb'), symbolising that he was the heir of the first Lord of the Earth, and the Eye of God, who sees all. His name was Asar (or Gasar, Gesu or Giza, all variations incorporating the god-letter *G* to signify his dominion on Earth). By the time he appears in the Pyramid texts, the earliest 'book' of the Egyptians, he has already become a powerful deity, having absorbed the attributes of former gods. Two places in particular became his early cult centres: at Abydos

Geb, the Earth God   he superseded the god Khentyamentui, depicted wearing mummy-bandages (having himself taken over from Upuat, 'The-Opener-of-the-Ways'); and at Djedu (the Greek Busiris), with the familiar root *Dj*, he adopted the Djed column, a previous cult object that was later believed to represent his spine. The Egyptian word Djedu meant both 'pillar' and 'stability', but the shape of the spine of Osiris was probably derived from a stylised form of the last sheaf of corn to be cut. The previous God, Andjety, had held a crook in one hand and a flail in the other, and these were both incorporated into Egyptian culture as symbols of kingship that were to last as long as Egypt itself.

Osiris also took on the attributes of other older gods. He inherited characteristics from his father Geb, the grandson of Atum. Geb is often shown as a goose, which became his sacred totem bird. It is interesting that Geb is an Earth God, often shown with an erect phallus, when many cultures saw the Earth as female, but there is evidence that he was worshipped as a bisexual god at his shrine at Bata in Iunu. Geb, in the form of a Bennu bird, was said to have laid the Great Egg from which the Sun emerged at the dawn of time; he was called the 'Great Cackler' from the sound that attended this cosmic event.[3]

There is, however, another early god that also passed his attributes along the chain of mythic heirs, the fertility god Min. Several fragments of statues of this ancient god were excavated by Flinders Petrie at the city of Gebtu on the Nile. We will notice immediately that this was associated with Geb (the name of the city means 'The Place of Geb'), but its associations run deeper, for it was known as Panopolis by the Greeks and in their time became a famous shrine to Pan. Were Geb, and therefore his son Osiris, the original gods behind the Greek 'All-God', Pan? It seems incontrovertible. The mystery deepens when we realise that Gebtu was also known as Koptos, the home of the earliest form of Christianity known. The Coptic Christians were the link between the last remnants of Pharaonic Egypt, the Greek world and the beginnings of the new religion.

A visit to the Coptic Museum in old Cairo confirms that they worshipped Pan (who is often shown, Osiris-like, with a black face), and that they probably introduced the concept of the pillar heavily carved with intricate greenery at its capital, surely a symbolic form of Osiris within the Tree of Life. A magnificent collection from Saqqara is on display, from the Coptic monastery in the shadow of the Old Kingdom necropolis and the step-pyramid of King Djoser. A collection of crosses is also of interest; one can clearly see the evolution of the Egyptian ankh into a floriated cross carved with greenery, and then into the Christian form. For our investigation, we must also take note of an early Coptic Bishop's crook: it is in the form of a double dragon.

The Coptic connection with the world of Ancient Egypt, from which it sprang, is enlightening in many ways, not least because their patron saint is St George.

To return to the oldest Egyptian fertility god of them all, Min, the colossal figures dug up by Petrie (dated to around 3000 BC) are thought to have stood in the Temple courtyard. One restored figure in the Ashmolean Museum is over 12 feet high and is notable for its missing phallus. The evidence suggests that the Temple was pre-dynastic and dedicated to Isis and Min. The huge size of the colossi, with the attendant quarrying, transport, carving and erection of such large pieces of stone, all imply large scale organisation and expenditure, making such a temple all the more remarkable for such an early date. *The Festival of Min* was one of the most important throughout Egypt, and took the form of a procession where the image of the god was carried aloft. *The Procession of Min* was closely connected with rites of thanksgiving for the harvest, and was intended to impregnate nature with new fertility. Other later statues show him holding a flail, long before it became an emblem of Osiris.[4]

Here we should perhaps draw attention to the question of Min's missing phallus, and suggest there may be some connection between this and the story of the lost member of Osiris. Could this be a distant memory of the fertility rites of Min, who may have had his phallus (perhaps made of wood?) only attached to the statue at certain times?

In later ages Min became Amun, the ithyphallic God of Creation. After Alexander's conquest of Egypt in 332 BC the Greeks identified their own gods with the Egyptian pantheon. Horus was equated with Apollo (both being Sun Gods and dragon slayers), Thoth with Hermes, Amun with Zeus and Hathor with Aphrodite. Pan was equated with Amun-Min, the god of sexual reproduction, who had his sanctuary at Koptos. As the city is at the end of the desert roads leading to the East, Amun-Min became the God of the East, and was often shown with an incense burner symbolising the spices and perfumes of the Orient. From these beginnings, during the Roman period Pan became the God of the Eastern desert, the capricious guardian of desert routes. In this form he is shown not as the Pan of Greek mythology but as the priapic Min, his fertility clearly inherited from his previous life.

In the sanctuary at the Temple of Luxor is a graphic example of how Amun-Min as the Creator God was central to religious life even at this late stage of the Alexandrian conquest. Here he is shown with erect phallus whilst a temple priest burns incense as an offering. Amun was to carry on as the God of Creation even into Christian times, when his worship was absorbed into orthodox ritual. Is this why church-goers say 'Amen' ('Amun') at the conclusion of a prayer? If so, what might they think if they realised they were invoking the ithyphallic god of pre-dynastic Egypt who evolved into Osiris and Pan?

The ithyphallic god Amun being worshipped at Luxor

This association may be taken further, to include al-Khidr. In the Holy Land, Crusaders took the town of Banyas, now situated in a National Park where Mount Hermon meets the Golan Plateau, in 1129. It is a famously beautiful area with springs, caves and waterfalls, and it was here according to the Jewish historian Josephus that Jesus Christ came with his disciples and changed Simon's name to Peter (the rock) saying, 'On this rock I will build my Church'. Pilgrims still come to recall this declaration of the beginnings of Christianity. The place is also famous in Templar legend; a few miles to the Northeast is Castle Nimrod (named after the great-grandson of Noah). The keys to the fortress did not have to be fought for. They were handed over peacefully to King Baldwin II by the Ismai'li sect known as the Hashishim, called after their founder Hassan, 'The Old Man of the Mountain'. But it is of interest here because, besides Templar and early Christian associations, its name was previously Panyas (The Place of Pan). Here there are a number of caves, one of which is dedicated to the Greek Pan, and another to al-Khidr and St George, emphasising again that they appear to be one and the same. Above the latter is a white-domed shrine, once a church but now converted to a mosque. Banyas is one of the places where we can see the masks of 'The Green One' slip to reveal the true beginnings of Christianity, and the innate power the 'Green Man' held with both with the pagan Greeks and the Templars, who could not have failed to recognise that he and St George were the same.

Before we leave the truly old gods there is one further point of interest. R.J.Stewart has pointed out that the cult of St Mena was of immense popularity throughout the early Christian world (Menes was the founder of dynastic Egypt, who had his tomb built at Abydos—but no body was ever found). Although he pre-dated the official St George, the themes and attributes of his exploits are similar. Both had an illustrious military career and were then persecuted by a Roman Emperor (in the Coptic Museum we find an icon of St Mena on horseback exactly like his more famous counterpart). The excavation of a 4th century basilica to St Mena near Alexandria during the last century revealed that the Christian buildings had been erected over a cave-temple containing Egyptian images, including that of Horus, son of Osiris, slaying the dragon.[5]

Osiris the Tree God

Frazer, in **The Golden Bough**, also thought that before he was a corn deity Osiris may have been a tree-spirit, since the worship of trees predates the arts of cultivation. One account suggests this to be true—it includes a description of a ceremony in which a pine tree is cut down, the centre hollowed out, an image of Osiris made and then 'buried' again in the hollow of the tree. It was kept for a year and then burnt, a ritual very much like that performed in the cult of Attis. This is probably a mythical re-enactment of the body of Osiris trapped in the tamarisk tree. It also has elements of the World-Tree and European Maypole rites which are strongly associated with St George as a Spring Fertility god, and the Christmas Tree tradition when the Sun God is reborn anew.

In some temples, as at Denderah, the coffin of Osiris is shown encased in a pine tree, and the pine cone becomes an offering to him. We may recall that in the esoteric tradition this symbolises the pineal gland, the organ awakened to spiritual vision when the serpent energy reaches the head. Pan, Bacchus and Dionysus also carried a mystical wand or spear similar to the Caduceus, entwined with ivy or a snake, called a Thyrsus, which was crowned with a pine cone. In the same chamber at Philae where Osiris is shown with ears of wheat springing from him is a sculpture showing a great tamarisk tree with its branches overhanging his coffin. Here he is referred to as 'The One in the Tree'.

All this leads to one conclusion: that the Green Man so often shown in Church architecture, with his head looking from the top of a pillar or column, is a medieval version of Osiris, the God of Many Names. Here the god is obviously the Spirit of the pillar or tree, his body invisible but his head peering out with its sprouting foliage, bringing verdure to the Earth.

Did the Templars know of the legend of Osiris, the ancestor of the Sufi 'Green One' al-Khidr, and all the other versions of him so prevalent throughout the Middle East? Did they introduce his image into the churches and cathedrals as a potent symbol of how Christianity, mystical Islam and the Egyptian religion shared the same roots?

We can now say with a degree of confidence that they did, as the myth of Isis and Osiris was at the core of the religious beliefs at the time, and the correlation between Osiris, al-Khidr, Pan and St George appear evident. These faces looking down on us from the roof bosses and capitals of pillars may indeed hark back to a time much older that we might have suspected. Of course the tree is also a symbol of Osiris' spine that transmits the dragon force. In many medieval cathedrals the pillars are positioned over streams of water which have been deliberately channelled. It is one of the reasons they can become so damp. But the water is bringing living spirit into the structure, and dowsers report that this energy spirals up through the pillars very much like the rising trails of greenery carved on the Apprentice Pillar at Rosslyn.

The Mysteries of Osiris

An even greater reason to believe that the Green Man of the European spiritual revival is based on Osirian tradition is that the Cult of Osiris was also a mystical system of initiation. These days we might consider the idea of candidates embarking on their own path to salvation or spiritual enlightenment as something of an oddity, understandable in times when magic and superstition were rife, but entirely foreign to modern understanding. We prefer the certainties of science, even though this would appear as magic to other ages.

Yet we should acknowledge that the Mystery Schools of Initiation—the Temples of the ancient world—were the universities of their day. These were not universities in the sense we might currently understand. They were concerned with developing the spiritual awareness of those who studied there. This was the sience of Magic and personal transformation which lies at the foundation of human experience. All the great philosophers and thinkers of the ancient world were initiates, who freely admitted where their insights and information had come from. The Greeks, such as Pythagoras and Plato, made no attempt to deny from where they received their inspiration. It was from the great Mystery Schools of Egypt, the greatest and most long-lived civilisation of them all. Only when it succumbed to its inevitable fate through invasion and civil war did Greece become the new focus, and the Eleusinian mysteries supplant those of the Nile.

Thereafter even the Egyptians travelled to Eleusis, to take part in rituals that derived their inspiration from their own gods, especially Osiris. The Greek initiations were based on the same elemental myth of the God of the Underworld, this time with the name Pluto, who made all things grow. In this myth Persephone is perhaps a feminised version of Osiris (just as they made Geb into a female deity, Gaea). Demeter, her mother, is thought by some to be another version of Isis, who mourns and goes in search of her lost love (this time her daughter).

The reason for the continuing but ever-varying themes is that the growth cycle, the sprouting of grain from the seed and the harvesting, are all spiritual metaphors for the stages of human development. Jesus (the word is a different version of the Egyptian name for Osiris, *Asar-Gasar-Giza-Gesu-Jesus*), continually alluded to this when he spoke of seeds falling on stony ground, the flowering of the vine, and the many other references to plant growth with which his audiences would have been familiar.

They all stem from the understanding of the human soul as a seed that, under the right conditions, can be 'cultivated' to bring forth a new life—the Life of the Spirit. The colour of eternal life is green, and stands for transformation and nature, whose intelligence comes directly from the Creator. The processes of planting the seed in fertile ground, ensuring it is properly nourished, its growth as the Light shines upon it, and its eventual harvesting, are all stages of spiritual development. As the last 'head' of corn is cut, the spirit in it dies, but the soul is ready to be reborn anew. The winnowing of the wheat—the separation of the seed from the chaff—is an allegory of the alchemical process of refinement that takes place within the inner recesses of the Spirit, hence the flail of Osiris with which this is achieved. It is no accident that the Rock at the centre of the Temple of Jerusalem was originally used as a threshing-floor; it was the place where souls could leave behind the physical life, the chaff, and their soul or seed could ascend to heaven.

Thus Christ reveals himself not as a simple carpenter, but as a King in the Osirian tradition, who had been schooled in the Mystery Wisdom of the ages.

Here we come to the crux of the enigma: for each human being *is* Osiris or Jesus. The rituals of the natural cycle of life are those of ourselves, where our seed grows and is nurtured, achieves maturity and is then purified in the winnowing of experience. This is what the Templars knew, and what they were trying to communicate. We *are* the Green Man. That is why he stares at us so piercingly; he is saying I am you, you are me. You and nature are one. All this was incorporated into Templar ritual, for, like the Baphomet head, this knowledge made the Earth flourish and brought wisdom and riches. The inheritors of Templarism, the Freemasons, still identify with Osiris in the form of Hiram, the builder of Solomon's Temple, who was murdered but rose from the dead. Each candidate still undergoes this ritual drama and is resurrected just like the gods of old. The tradition, as they have always claimed, does indeed go back to Ancient Egypt, the land where the barren desert flowered and blossomed into Life.

There are other pointers to how the Osirian Mystery Schools of Egypt influenced and evolved into the Templar, Masonic and occult magical societies springing from them. The soul of Osiris was also thought to reside in a sacred ram worshipped in the western Delta town of Djedet. The Egyptian word for ram was *ba*—a word that also meant *soul*. This place was known to the Greeks as Mendes, and its rituals were notoriously made famous by the writer and poet Pindar, who claimed that the sacred ram was prominent in rites involving intercourse with women. The image known as Baphomet drawn by the masonic magician Eliphas

Levi was also called the 'Ram' or 'Goat of Mendes', and was claimed by Levi to be the 'God of the Templars'. It seems as though this is another side to the worship of Osiris, concerned with the knowledge of the union of the two polar forces for spiritual purposes, long rumoured to be part of Templar lore. On the surface, though, a far more innocent interpretation may be put upon the sacred ram, that it is the animal equivalent of an ear of corn, as indicated by the shepherd's crook held by Osiris. In the Holy Land, and later throughout the Christian world, the sacrifice of the Paschal Lamb at Easter absorbed this earlier cult, and so Jesus instead of Osiris became 'The Lamb of God'. This was adopted by the Templars as their own insignia, and sometimes shown as a lamb holding aloft a cross. In other representations it is a lamb holding the Flag of St George, the God of Rebirth who heralds a new cycle of Life.

Two great serpent and dragon-slayers. *Left:* Hercules wrestles with the serpent at Kew Gardens, London. *Right:* St Michael thrusts his spear through the dragon's head outside Le Mans Cathedral, France.

Dragon Hill at Uffington, Oxfordshire, where according to British legend St George killed the Dragon. The spot where the Dragon's blood is said to have fallen is marked by a white patch, where no grass will grow. High above it, carved into the chalk hillside, is the famous White Horse, a giant prehistoric effigy. Was this once a centre for Druid rites invoking the Dragon Power of the Earth?

Left: the Temple of Luxor, Egypt. The columns represent stylised papyrus reeds, which during later Coptic times changed into ornately carved trees. European churches and cathedrals adopted this style for their own architecture, for the columns symbolise the world-tree connecting Heaven and Earth, up which the dragon energies rise. The Copts preserved much of the old traditions of the worship of Osiris, the Egyptian Green Man. Their patron saint is St George. The great obelisks are conductors of Light and the dragon or serpent force (the word obelisk is derived from basilisk, meaning a type of serpent).

Below: Two serpents depicted on the front of the apron of a Luxor Temple priest, representing the twin polarities of the Life Force. In the esoteric tradition these should be in perfect balance in the aspiring initiate before being awakened to bring higher levels of spiritual awareness.

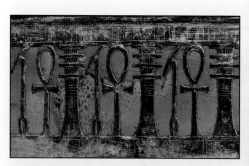

Above: Symbols of the Life Force on a casket from Tutankhamun's tomb. The mysterious Uaz sceptre on the left has a forked end, symbolising the pinning down of a serpent's head. The Ankh is the Life Force itself, and an important magical tool in Egyptian ceremonies of rebirth. The Djed pillar represents the spine of Osiris which conducts the serpent energies.

Left: One of the Green Dragons on the staircase of the Bishop's Palace at Wells, Somerset, referring to the foundation legend of the Cathedral during the 13th century when Bishop Jocelyn is said to have slain a dragon. Its colour shows it to be a true Green Dragon, representing the powers of Nature. *Right:* A giant Wodewose with club and shield, one of two guarding the entrance to Quimper Cathedral in Brittany. Are these primeval figures early shamanic dragon-slayers? *Below:* Stonehenge, Wiltshire, the focus for a number of alignments linking ancient sites in Southern Britain. These all relate to the interaction between Sun and Earth.

Left: The magnificent central column supporting the roof of the Chapter House at Wells Cathedral. This style of architecture is designed to give the impression of a forest in stone, echoing the sacred groves of antiquity. The steps leading up to it are flanked by two dragon-slayers, and the acoustic resonance within the chamber is notable, suggesting a connection between vibration and the science of dragon energies.

Below: The Birth of Taliesin, the Welsh bard and magician, shown with Sun-Wheel and dragon spiral, from an ancient stone built into the church at Llangammaret, Brecon. This emphasises the link between the Sun, the dragon energies of the Earth, and their significance in the Druidic mystical tradition. According to Geoffrey of Monmouth, Taliesin accompanied King Arthur to Avalon, along with the wizard Merlin, after he was wounded at the Battle of Camlann.

Above: Dragon's Head from Kilpeck Church, Herefordshire. Its open mouth and spiral tongue, very similar to the shape of some bishop's croziers, is a symbol for the natural power of the site. The close association of Green Men and Dragons throughout church architecture is a coded reference to the inspirational and spiritual qualities of the pre-Christian sites on which old churches are built.

Two of the most remarkable Irish prehistoric sites, both over 5000 years old. *Above:* the Lios, or enclosure, of Crom Dubh, an ancient God of Fertility. It lies in an area renowned as a centre of Neolithic ritual activity, and its entrance is exactly aligned with the position of the rising Sun at the old pre-Christian Harvest Festival of Lughnasad. *Below:* the entrance stone at Newgrange with its dragon spirals issuing from the Earth. The artificially-constructed chamber within the mound is precision engineered to allow a shaft, or spear, of sunlight to penetrate its length at the moment of the Sun's rebirth at the Midwinter Solstice.

Left: One of two ancient oak trees known as Gog and Magog at Glastonbury, Somerset, believed to be the remnants of a Druid Grove, and named after two legendary giants that may have been the precursors of St George. *Below:* An early Bishop stabs a dragon on the old worn font at Avebury, Britain's prehistoric Serpent Temple, whilst streams of greenery issue from the head of another.

Below: The striking image of a Green Man with a dragon emerging from his mouth at Woodbury, Devon. Both the Green Man and the Dragon symbolise the fertility and intelligence within Nature, and the cycles of Life, Death and Rebirth.

Light manifestations captured on camera. *Above:* A Sphere of Light hovers overhead whilst streams of energy cascade around a pool of water at St Nectan's Kieve in Cornwall, where a waterfall tumbles into a natural stone basin. The place is one of the most numinous in the Westcountry, noted for its spiritual atmosphere and energetic effects. *Below:* A photograph taken close to an altar with Templar symbols inside St John's Cathedral at Trogir, Croatia, which some believe to contain the tomb of St John the Evangelist. The town, built on an island that once had over 30 churches, was an important centre for the Knights Templar. The photograph clearly demonstrates the spiral nature of the energy as it coils up from the Earth.

(Note: None of these photographs have been altered in any way).

Spiral Light manifestations at Chalice Well, Glastonbury, where the waters pour out of the Earth. Such places are invariably associated with dragon energies and spiritual power. Pilgrimages often generate considerable energy which can be almost tangible, and here its effects are captured on camera during a visit to the Well just after Beltane. A group of people had previously gathered for a ritual to honour the Spirit of the place, leaving behind an image of a Green Man decorated with foliage.

14

The Art of Dragon Taming

ne of the best-selling books of all time was ***The Golden Legend***, written by the Bishop of Genoa Jacobus de Voragine. In it he provided the medieval world with a definitive account of the lives of the saints, which everyone at the time believed to be historical facts gleaned by his scholarship from ancient records. In reality, like so many others that were to follow down the centuries, it was a motley mix of fact and, where there were no facts, a liberal dose of fiction. There was also an agenda. But it was a formula that gripped the attention of its readers, who preferred to believe in the fabulous and miraculous exploits of their heroes, just as in Celtic times when people loved to hear of the wondrous world of giants, gods and the Land of Faery. The saints were all these, and more, for they did the work of the one true God.

Printed in English in 1230 it contained a detail of St George's career that had strangely hitherto gone unmentioned in the voluminous annals of the saint's life. Almost a thousand years after his supposed death George was to become famous all over the world for what was his most fabulous exploit of all—the slaying of a dragon.

Jacobus' story is a classic mix of fairytale heroic deeds and propaganda aimed at the conversion of previously pagan believers to the true faith. In it St George came upon the city of Silene in Libya where a terrible dragon 'envenomed all the country'. When the inhabitants set out to rid the land of it they were overcome by its foul breath and fled in terror. To keep the monster satisfied they fed it two sheep every day; if they failed to do this then it devoured a man instead. A local law was proclaimed that children should be selected by lots, and whoever the lot fell upon, whether rich or poor, they were to be sacrificed to the beast. But one day the lot fell upon the King's daughter. He offered the townsfolk gold and silver instead but they would not be moved; it was the King's daughter or they would burn down the palace. Lamenting that he would never see her married he begged for eight days respite, and then, when again approached by the desperate inhabitants who reminded him that the 'city perisheth', dressed her in the finest wedding gown and, blessing her, took her to the dragon's lair.

As it happened, this was the very moment that St George was passing by, and no doubt struck by the sight of an attractive woman dressed for a wedding and hanging around in a swamp, he naturally enquired as to her well-being. She replied that he should go on his way, lest he perish too. But the valiant hero, on learning of the imminent arrival of the dragon, would have none of it; 'Fair daughter, doubt ye no thing hereof for I shall help thee in the name of Jesus Christ.'

At that very moment the dragon appeared and charged towards them. St George made the sign of the cross, struck it with his spear and threw it to the ground. Then he said to the maiden, 'Deliver to me your girdle and bind it about the neck of the dragon and be not afeard'. The dragon, up until that moment a terrible beast that would devour anything, instantly became as meek as a pet. They led him to the city, where the people were aghast and began to flee. But George said that if they would believe in God and Jesus Christ and be baptised into the Christian religion he would slay the dragon and save them all. There was no argument. The King was baptised immediately, the dragon's head was cut off, and all 15,000 men as well as all the women and children became Christian. The King built a church to Our Lady and St George, where the waters of a magic fountain healed the sick. He offered George great wealth, but the saint asked for it to be given to the poor. And so they all (except George who was evidently later to be horribly tortured by Diocletian) lived happily ever after…

The elements of the story are the same as many folk-tales which people would have been familiar with at the time, and this applies to the formula as well: damsel in distress is rescued by brave hero who saves the land from devastation. It is the very stuff of legend as recounted endlessly throughout history. Yet certain parts indicate something else is going on 'behind the scenes', which may help to enlighten us about its real meaning.

To begin with, it is strange that the townsfolk choose to give their children to the dragon when sheep seemed to keep his hunger at bay. Or surely they would have preferred to send one of their more elderly residents to the dragon's lair? This looks as though it refers to some form of ritual sacrifice, where the vitality of the young is an essential feature (the story of Abraham sacrificing his son Isaac on the rock at Jerusalem is another example of a reference to this primitive method of appeasing the gods).

Then we have the King's daughter all dressed up in her wedding finery. This too is reminiscent of ancient ritual. But who is she to be married to? Presumably, as she is about to go into the dragon's cave, she is about to enter the underworld with its monstrous inhabitants. It is very much as though she represents the archetypal maiden of the Earth, an innocent young woman about to confront the hellish denizens of the hidden realms. The word Hell, though, before it came to have Christian associations of torture and retribution, merely meant transformation. In fact after the dragon's death the King builds a church to 'Our Lady and St George'—strongly implying that she does indeed represent the Virgin or Madonna, one of the great themes of early 13th century belief.

The enigma of the dragon is most bewildering. Why, we must ask, does St George not simply kill it outright? The answer is that he must use it to threaten the townsfolk into submitting to become Christians. The choice is clear. Be baptised or the dragon will run free, devour the princess and you as well. So there is in fact no choice. But the method of subduing the dragon is strange, and has deeply magical overtones. The Virgin's girdle is placed around its neck and it is transformed from a deadly and noxious monster into a submissive creature that threatens no-one. It looks as though they could have kept it in a cage and fed it marshmallows for the rest of its life...

As we suspect, the story is full of many-layered symbolism involving the Earth Goddess and the Solar Hero. Here too are correspondences between the divine female principle and the dragon, with the dragon standing for the pagan religions and the princess, with her spotless wedding gown, the unsullied Virgin of Christianity. Most interesting is that the dragon is tamed not by sheer force but by her girdle with which it is led meekly to the city. This has a strong flavour of the legendary beginnings of the Noble Order of the Garter, where the garter slips from the leg of a beautiful woman and becomes the emblem of the mystical brotherhood.

Taming the Dragon

Dragon-slaying, and its more peaceable offshoot dragon-taming, is one of the most widespread mythologies in the world—wherever amateur dracophiles may travel they are likely to come across some version of it. Even in remote areas, especially in Europe, it is often the case that a local cathedral or church was originally founded by, if not a classic dragon-slayer, then one who tames the beast and leads it away to somewhere it can do no harm. Extraordinarily, it is in Genoa, the very place where the St George dragon legend first appeared in print, that there exists a prime example of this. The patron saint of the city is St George, but the basilica, a former cathedral (bombed-out during the war and now looking more like an Art-Deco cinema) is dedicated to San Siro. The earliest foundations of the building are from the 4th century, and in 1006 it became a Benedictine monastery, later to be consecrated by the Patriarch of Jerusalem. Genoa was a crucial port for the Crusaders, with the First Crusade preached in its streets, and the wealthy merchants making their ships available for the coming invasion of the Holy Land. That it was important to the Templars and their compatriots the Hospitallers is evident; amongst the many remains is a commandery of the Knights of St John, standing somewhat neglected, near the waterfront.

*The dragon-tamer
San Siro*

Genoa still seems to resonate to those times. The Bank of St George, first formed in the 14th century by the Templars, the world's first international bankers, still exists. As Italy's largest seaport it has been a trading centre from Phoenician times, but its heyday was during the 12th century, when it became the focus of one of the world's leading maritime empires.

But back to dragons. San Siro himself obviously had a way with them, for his legend tells of a great snake-like monster or basilisk that lived in a well. Unlike St George however he had no need of sword or spear, but coaxed the creature from its lair by the power of eloquence alone. Praying at the well, his virtuous sermons persuaded the serpent to emerge quietly, and he then led it to the edge of the sea where it vanished into the waves, never to trouble the people of Genoa again.

Celtic legend is full of such dragon-taming episodes which go back far beyond the age of the Templars. One of the most famous for his dealings with such fabulous creatures was St Samson of Dol, who was born in Wales towards the end of the 5th century. The *Life of St Samson* is of special interest to those suffering from dracophilia, in that not only was he expert at vanquishing fire-spitting serpents, but the account of his life is one of the earliest and most authentic extant, having been written in the early 7th century not long after his death.[1]

Born in Wales and educated at the famous monastery of Llantwit, the site of an earlier Druid college, he travelled to Ireland, Cornwall and then Brittany, where he established his own monastery at Dol on the north coast. His fame quickly spread throughout Europe, and, because of the unusually early record of his life, he has become one of the great high priests of Celtic Christianity. This gives us a valuable insight into that twilight world where the religion of Druidism merged with that of pre-Roman Christianity.

Samson's prowess was formidable. He could tame wild beasts as well as bring peace to warring factions. When crossing the Hundred of Trigg in Cornwall (Bodmin Moor), he came across the inhabitants worshipping an idol on top of a hill by enacting a mystery play around it. He admonished them, and promised to bring one of their number who had fallen from a horse and died back to life, if they would destroy the idol. He duly performed the miracle and they were amazed. A nearby standing stone was carved with a cross by Samson himself to mark his achievement.

Directly after this incident the chief of the tribe explained their problem: 'We have a certain fair land in occupation by a poisonous and very vicious serpent; in fact this serpent lives in a cave impossible to approach, and it is destroying nearly two villages and allows no man to dwell there'. Samson replied that in the name of the Lord he would help them; 'If indeed thou believest, then thou shalt see with thine eyes in this serpent the wonderful works of God'. They came to the entrance of the cave and Samson went in. The serpent trembled and bit its own tail, whilst the saint seized a linen girdle and slipped it around the serpent's neck. Casting it down from a high place he ordered it to die. But curiously he became strangely enchanted by the serpent's lair, and afterwards spent some years living within the cave (still thought to exist under the church at Golant near Fowey), praying and fasting. This sounds very similar to St John in his cave on Patmos, who carved out a hollow in the rock where he would place his head during sleep or meditation. Were they both inspired by the natural power of these places?

On another occasion a similar situation arises, with 'a vile serpent doing great destruction and making desolate' the surrounding country. Again Samson goes boldly into the mouth of the cave where the serpent dwells, calling out for it to come forth. As it obeys he takes his mantle and binds it around the serpent's neck whilst singing a psalm, ordering it to go to the other side of the river, and commanding it to remain there under a certain stone.

These early legends suggest that the serpents or dragons that were causing havoc in the countryside did not necessarily have to be killed, but rather tamed. And the method, as in the St George story, is not what we perhaps might expect; a girdle or mantle is placed around their necks, when they become docile and harmless. Singing and praying also gives power over them. Other Celtic dragon saints include St Caradoc, who banished a huge and terrible serpent causing devastation in the land of Arthur. He placed his stole around its neck and led it away like a lamb. St Petroc, another famous saint of the early Church, prayed at a venomous serpent and it went harmlessly on its way. On another occasion he healed a wounded dragon by sprinkling it with a magic potion.[2]

So what are these tales trying to tell us? They must have been written to impress the people of the time with the message that Christianity was the only sure way to restore harmony. As propaganda for the new religion this is entirely understandable. There is also a suggestion that the place where the serpent lived had peculiar properties attractive to dragon-tamers like Samson. But these stories must have had something in them that struck a chord in the common mind, otherwise they would have been entirely fabulous and lacked any real power. What might it have been?

Saving the Earth

We have already encountered a living tradition that speaks of how a serpent or dragon can cause villages to be wiped out, crops to fail and the land to slowly wither and die. The only likely explanation for this curious state of affairs is that, as recorded in the science of feng-shui, the dragon energies of the Earth can become, as described by the Rev Eitel, 'noxious emanations' or 'negative ch'i', the 'poisonous breath' of the dragon that can cause all life to be deprived of the vital force that, in a healthy landscape, causes everything to flourish.

According to feng-shui the invisible currents of earthly magnetism coursing through the landscape are constantly in a state of flux, affected by geographical and climatic conditions, especially earthquake activity and heavy rainfall that can overload the subterranean streams of water. Another important factor is the influence of the heavenly bodies, particularly the Sun and Moon which set up tides and currents within the body of the planet. These forces concentrate especially where they issue from the deeper levels of the Earth's crust, in places like caves and springs. In *Science and Civilisation in China*, Joseph Needham writes of the twin polarities of vital force that must be in balance if the dragons are not to have a debilitating effect on the land:

> 'The two currents, Yin and Yang, in the Earth's surface, were identified with the two symbols which apply to the eastern and western quarters of the sky, the Green Dragon of spring in the former case, the White Tiger of autumn in the latter.'[3]

Here Needham identifies the twin polarities in Nature with the times of the Spring and Autumn Equinoxes, the virile 'male' power of Spring and the more secretive, withdrawing female power of Autumn, when the goddess descends into the underworld. Of course she must be rescued the following Spring, otherwise the Earth will become barren. The other early commentator on feng-shui, Eitel, also speaks of this all-pervading polarity, the very essence of the act of Creation, but in the more scientific terms of the Victorian age: 'There are in the earth's crust two different, shall I say magnetic currents, the one male, the other female, the one positive, the other negative...'

This understanding of the Earth as a living being is taken even further in this and many other ancient disciplines, so that the planet is not only alive in the sense that it is reacting continually to cosmic influences, but has an innate intelligence of its own too. The concept of the Earth as a sentient entity stems from the earliest times. In the Mesolithic and Paleolithic ages mankind had no need of settled communities, and people moved around the country according to the seasonal cycle, visiting the traditional sites and shrines of their ancestors. This way of life is still preserved in the 'Songlines' of the Australian Aborigine culture, where the serpentine paths they follow from place to place, the 'Rainbow Serpent', are hallowed in their ancestral memory with localised stories, and were created in the 'Dreamtime' at the beginning of Creation. This was once a universal way of life, as people walked the lines which brought life and spiritual sustenance; these ways became the earliest pilgrim routes, as they, like their ancestors, followed the rainbow paths of the serpent.

As people settled into villages and a more agrarian lifestyle these pilgrimages continued at certain times of the year, but now their lives depended more on the fertility of the land. This is why, during the Neolithic and subsequent eras, standing stones were erected to concentrate the currents that brought harmony and prosperity. If we think these people were savages we do them a great injustice. It is apparent that they were very spiritually attuned to the Earth and its cycles and knew how to make the most of its gifts. As John Michell comments in *The Earth Spirit*:

'The long continuity of Chinese civilisation to which feng-shui has made an important contribution, has in turn preserved the methods of that science up to the present day; and thus has come down to us a legacy from the primeval golden age. Not that early wandering people needed any formal system of feng-shui, because, as they lived and moved under the direct influence of the earth's subtle energies, its principles were naturally integrated into their lives. Like all sciences, feng-shui is an expedient of civilisation, a technique for reconciling human nature to the limitations imposed on it by settlement.'[4]

Here could be a rationale for the otherwise incomprehensible meaning behind the legends of dragons or serpents causing the land to become poisoned. The 'fiery breath' of the creatures, a common feature of such stories, may be a mythic way of saying that the usually harmonious and beneficial forces that make seeds sprout, plants grow, and animals and humans healthy, are in some way out of balance. The Celtic saints such as Samson, who were far more Druidic than the popular image of holy men presented to us by the Church, were well-versed in these matters, having studied the magical sciences at the great Druidic centres of learning (of which Llantwit was a famous example). Samson and his compatriots were not saints in the normal sense of the term, they were shamans who could see into the spiritual worlds and manipulate the unseen forces.

One of the most intriguing things about such dragon tales is how frequently the beast is not 'killed' (for this would have serious consequences for the fertility of the land), but tamed, or moved, by magical techniques of ritual, which include singing, praying, and placing a mantle or a girdle around its neck. If these really were the ferocious creatures we are led to believe, it is most unlikely they could be restrained by such means. These stories speak of spiritual disciplines whereby the noxious and unbalanced energies within the Earth are brought back into balance, much as some dowsers today claim they can correct harmful emanations causing ill-health by a variety of techniques (which may include creating a circle of stones or copper pegs hammered into the ground to isolate and 'earth' the 'negative' energies).

In the St George story (graphically portrayed in the famously futuristic painting by Ucello) it is the girdle of the princess that is used to lead the dragon into the city. This is a metaphor for the dark destructive powers of Nature being brought back into harmony through the use of the opposite force—the White Goddess symbolised by the bride, the Virgin energies of the Earth. In Ucello's painting the maiden is chained to the dragon—a symbol that they are both different aspects of the same thing, the chthonic forces of nature.

The early date of these tales, and the fact they are so widespread across the world, are testimony that they are an inheritance from yet earlier times, when what we might today call magic—in truth a science of natural energies— was well understood, and spiritual techniques involving the transmutation of harmful forces were by no means uncommon. Some authorities believe that the dragon or serpent symbolised the pre-Christian religions, and that is partly the case, for they were certainly steeped in the lore of the natural world. But the taming of these powers suggests that this knowledge was not violently eradicated, but absorbed, like so many other aspects, into the doctrines of the Christian Church.

The actual techniques employed seem to correspond to those often used today by healers to treat the human body. Chinese medicine uses needles inserted under the skin (which standing stones, carefully positioned in the skin of the Earth, may parallel), a process called moxabustion where balls of wax are ignited at certain centres where meridians cross (the old fire-festivals so important in the ancient world are analogues of this), and the freeing up of blocked channels (where the serpent energies have become knotted), all as common ways of restoring balance. All this is based on the science of the bio-magnetic flow of the Life Force. In the human body the acupuncture meridians must flow uninterruptedly for optimum health, and the coursing of the blood (which is heavily impregnated with iron) creates an electromagnetic field in and around the body which sensitives can see as a coloured aura. This can be 'read' to reveal deficiencies or sources of ill-health. The same techniques may also be applied to the body of the Earth, with its own gravitational and magnetic field created by it spinning around the pole, guarded by the constellation of Draco. Thus the terrestrial currents may be regulated or adapted to the prevailing conditions. Those healers of the human body who work through ritual and prayer, two of the most powerful forces in their armoury, can bring about the transformation of inharmonious energies by altering their character, usually by the visualisation of Light flooding into the affected area. It seems apparent that the dragon-tamers of old did likewise. First they would locate the source of the imbalance (a cave, fissure or spring from which the dragon power issued), and then they would ritually 'fix' it (as suggested by the Uaz sceptre of the Egyptians with its forked end, used to pin down the head of the serpent) within a circle, symbolised by a girdle. The word itself means 'to secure' by encircling something with a cord or belt (sometimes made of iron, for it also, in old English, means 'griddle'). This is a classic mystical technique used in many magical traditions. Most modern witches and magicians still mark out their magic circles with a cord to create a boundary that harmful entities or energies may not enter; within the circle only the qualities associated with the purpose of the ritual or invocation can exist.

In summary, the dragon slaying and dragon-taming legends are not fairy tales at all. They are a folk-memory of the magical rituals performed to bring the dark and chaotic aspects of nature back into balance. An earlier method of propitiating the spirits of the land involved both animal and human sacrifice, hence the references to this in the stories. St George rescuing the maiden is yet another mystical metaphor: there is no longer any need to provide sacrificial victims, for the power of faith (understanding) and knowledge (truth) can quell the ferocity of any Dragon.

The Two Dragons

In the *Mabinogion* is a tale called *The Adventure of Llud and Llevelys*. It concerns Llud, King of all Britain, who rebuilt the walls of London and surrounded the city with innumerable towers. Although he had many strongholds he loved London the best. He spent most of the year there, and so it was called Caer Llud, later Caer Lludein, and then Lundein. All this could well hark back to historical fact, for 3000 years ago the people of London spoke Welsh.

After some time three plagues fell upon the island of Britain. The second of these concerned two dragons. There was a scream heard every May Eve over each hearth in the land. It pierced the hearts of the people and terrified them so much that men lost their colour and strength, women suffered miscarriages, children lost their senses, and animals, trees and soil all became barren, and water polluted.

King Llud consulted his brother Llevelys who was the King of France. He told him that the scream was caused by a dragon. A dragon of another race was fighting with it and struggling to overcome it, and therefore Llud's dragon screamed so horribly. He said that Llud must measure the length and breadth of the island, and when he found the exact centre he must have a pit dug. Into this he must place a vat full of the best mead and place a silk sheet over the vat, guarding it himself. This was what would happen, Llevelys said: You will see the dragons fighting, and when they are weary they will sink onto the sheet in the form of two little pigs: they will drag the sheet to the bottom of the vat where they will drink all the mead and fall asleep. When this happens you must wrap the sheet round them and lock them in a stone chest and bury them in the earth within the strongest place on the island. As long as they are within that strong place no plague will come to Britain.[5]

Llud buried the chest at Eryi (Mount Snowdon) and the place was called Dinas Emrys. Years later when King Vortigern wanted to build a fortress, as recounted by Geoffrey of Monmouth, this was the site he chose. But every night the stones disappeared. His Druid advisors told him to find 'a child without a father', kill him and sprinkle his blood around the site. Vortigern sent messengers throughout Britain to look for such a child. After some time they found two children quarrelling in Carmarthen, One was taunted by the other for not having a father. They discovered that the child was the son of a nun, who was herself the daughter of a king. She had been magically impregnated by an angel or supernatural being (a Virgin birth) and the resulting child called Merlin.

Bewildered by this, Vortigern asked his Druids to explain: 'Between the Moon and the Earth live spirits which we call incubus demons. These have partly the nature of men and partly that of angels, and when they wish assume mortal shapes and have intercourse with women.' Merlin, perhaps understandably, questioned the Druids and said that a sacrifice was not necessary, but that they should dig a pit to discover the source of the problem. He prophesies they will discover a pool of water with two hollow stone chambers in which there are sleeping dragons. This they do, but as the dragons awaken, one coloured red and the other white, they begin exhaling fiery breath and fight ferociously. At this, Merlin fell into a trance and prophesies:

> 'Alas for the Red Dragon, for its end is near. Its cavernous dens shall be occupied by the White Dragon, which stands for the Saxons whom you have invited over. The Red Dragon represents the people of Britain, who will be overrun by the White One; for Britain's mountains and valleys shall be levelled, and the streams in its valleys run with blood. The cult of religion shall be destroyed completely and the ruin of the churches shall be clear for all to see. The race that is oppressed shall prevail in the end, for it will resist the savagery of the invaders.'[6]

Merlin continued with a fantastical account of future British history, spoken in allegory and symbol. In Geoffrey of Monmouth's version no-one could understand exactly what he was saying, for he began 'to speke so mystily...' This dragon tale, among the oldest in British literature, is worth briefly dwelling upon, for besides the obvious interpretation of the two dragons symbolising the native British and the invading Anglo-Saxons (who both went into battle flying pennants emblazoned with dragons), it is clear that the dragons preceded the time of Vortigern and the coming Arthurian dynasty. It also seems clear that when Merlin predicts the demise of the churches and religion of the time, he is speaking of Druidism being supplanted by incoming Anglo-Saxon paganism.

The original story in the Mabinogion tells of a 'screaming' dragon whose sound can be heard on May Eve, or Beltane. This was the first day of Summer in the ancient British calendar, and was, as we know, attended by countrywide rituals (as at Padstow) to celebrate the return of fertility. These involved activities in the wildwood as well as Maypole dancing, celebrations, and mystery plays enacting the return of the Sun God and the awakening Dragon energies within the Earth—the very forces of vitality characterising the Beltane rites. The central figure as far as we can tell would have been a dragon-slayer (or dragon-tamer), an earlier version of St George who is still so prominent in the folk rituals today.

A 'screaming' dragon that can be heard at every hearth in the land, terrifying the people, causing illness and a barren, infertile country? What could this possibly mean?

From what we have discovered so far we can only assume that the awakening dragon energies within the Earth, especially at this time when the power of the Sun's radiation is starting to become more intense, affects the planet's magnetic field and the subtle streams of power that course through the strata of its crust. It is a time when they must be in perfect harmony, otherwise the unbalanced forces of nature could cause havoc.

Early Norman font from Luppit, Devon, with a spear-wielding dragon-tamer confronting a double headed dragon. The twin heads symbolise the polarity of the forces of Nature.

Every hearth in the land? 'Hearth' is an interesting word. It contains both 'heart' and 'earth', as if it symbolises the Heart of the Earth in a microcosmic sense. It is the central point of every household where the fire burns at the very heart of the home. Beltane was a time when all over the country great fires were lit on sacred hilltops, purifying the land. Animals were driven through them to protect them from disease and ill-health (very much like the moxabustion techniques of acupuncture, where small fires are lit at the critical energetic points of the body). Can we see here the body of the Earth being purified to balance out the Yin/Yang, Solar/Lunar, Male/Female polarities through the use of magical fire rituals? Is the story of the terrible dragon a warning that if the old rituals are not maintained then the imbalance could affect every plant and living creature, that when the old rituals and understanding die, then civilisation declines? And is the central position of St George in the remaining vestiges of the old folklore festivals a memory of how the Dragons in the Earth were tamed through the use of magical ritual, with his role formerly taken by a High Priest or Druid?

15

Return of the Dragon Slayers

There are two places in British legend that lay particular claim to be the actual site where St George despatched the Dragon. This could, among those who believe he was born in Cappadocia and martyred in Palestine, raise eyebrows. But in one English folk tradition he was born in Coventry and raised by the 'Weird Lady of the Woods'. A medieval ballad by Thomas Percy tells how when born he had a number of birthmarks, including a blood-red cross and a dragon. **Brewer's Dictionary of Phrase and Fable** has him born in Brittany. By now it should come as no surprise that this old god was universal throughout the ancient world, whatever his mask or local legend. Hence he is still patron saint of not only England and Palestine but Aragon, Bavaria, Catalonia, Georgia, Germany, Greece, Lithuania and Portugal, as well as numerous cities including Genoa, Istanbul and Moscow.

The best known of these sites in Britain is Dragon Hill at Uffington in Oxfordshire, situated on the old prehistoric route The Ridgeway, along which pilgrims and travellers have walked since time immemorial. It is an artificially shaped conical hill with a flat summit which reveals slashes of bare chalk. This, according to legend, is where the Dragon's blood fell, causing the spot to become barren. Overlooking the hill is the famous chalk-cut figure of The White Horse, thought to be the oldest of its type. There is some disagreement between archaeologists and historians as to whether it is really a horse, for its strange beak-shaped head and lively posture suggests to many that it is more likely to be a stylised Dragon. It has all the qualifications to be a place where Dragon rites were enacted, for it is positioned overlooking the fertile Vale below and is close to other prehistoric monuments like the Neolithic chambered barrow of Wayland's Smithy. Directly above the White Horse/Dragon are the earthworks of Uffington Castle hillfort.

Many people consider Dragon Hill to be one of the foremost centres of mystical power in Britain. If St George, or his Druid predecessors, performed ritual acts associated with Dragon slaying there, they were in good company. Amongst a host of important sites clustered around it is a series of ancient terraces known as the Giant's Stair above a deep combe called The Manger. Did the giant St George mythically stride up here to the Dragon's Lair millennia ago? In the valley bottom is a church dedicated to his rescued damsel, Our Lady or St Mary (where there are a number of carved dragons). Whether this superbly sculpted and minimalistic chalk-cut image, with its great round eye watching the centuries come and go, is a horse or a Dragon, the legend is still relevant. If it is a Dragon then it confirms the reputation of the great ritual hill below. As a horse it fulfils the role of St George's white charger that carries him into the underworld. Whatever the truth we can be sure that this place, with its central role in the native traditions of Britain and its position in an area studded with antiquities, was a very important ritual site. It is ideally placed for those attending ceremonies to access it from The Ridgeway in their thousands and assemble in the valley below or on the crest of the hill above, where they could have observed every detail with exceptional clarity.

The Dragon Hills

A notable but overlooked feature of the British landscape is the great number of similarly flat-topped conical hills which exist in surprising profusion throughout the land. No-one knows for sure when they were built or why, but

it is certain that they are amongst the oldest man-made structures in existence, pre-dating many megalithic remains. They are as likely to be found in open country as right at the heart of what was once an ancient settlement. Wherever there is a syllable 'ton', 'tor' or 'tot' in a placename it signifies a sacred

The Tynwald Hill on the Isle of Man   mound and place of assembly or ritual, as at Totnes in Devon, or the now-vanished mound of Tothill in London's Westminster, likely to have been the original 'Gorsedd' giving rise to the present seat of government. At least one such artificial hill is still used for this purpose, the Tynwald on the Isle of Man, where each year on St John's Day disputes are settled and laws proclaimed. Some authors have noted that these 'Tot' hills may relate to Thoth (pronounced *Tot*), the Egyptian God of Magic. At Lewes in Sussex such a mound has been sliced away to accommodate a bowling green, whilst one at Christchurch in Dorset is right next to the Priory (which also has a collection of dragons carved on the base of its columns). Other examples exist within the precincts of the Law Courts of both Oxford and Cambridge, showing that they were important centres even in prehistory. One Victorian writer refers to over 70 'Tot' hills even in his day.[1]

These distinctive mounds must have been among the most significant features of the prehistoric landscape, and appear to have been used as centres for ceremonial purposes, as well as the proclamation of laws, enthroning kings or chieftains and any attendant rituals. Many of them

Marlborough mound

are specifically associated with legends of Dragons, which are said to coil themselves around the ancient earthworks. They had spiral pathways to the summit (the spiral is the earliest symbol for the dragon), and ritual processions may have been part of their function. Merlin's Mound, in the grounds of Marlborough College, is a remarkable example of this, where the wizard Merlin is said to be buried. This mound gave its name to Marlborough (Merlin's Barrow). All the evidence points to these enigmatic monuments being Dragon Mounds.

When Edward III decided to build a castle (and later St George's Chapel) at Windsor, the site he chose was one of the most famous of this type of truncated earthwork. The mound was then a large conical hill with a flattened summit encircled by a deep trench. It was always believed that this ancient table mound was the site where King Arthur held court, one of the great Round Table sites mentioned in the old chronicles. In the Bardic tradition it was known as the site of the Gorsedd, or *Great Seat*, the focal point where Druids and Bards gathered to proclaim the laws of the land and hold their ceremonies. This was probably why it became a meeting place during Arthurian and later times, for it apparently had always been known as a place of royal power. In a curious way it *is* a Round Table, made of Earth, a miniature version of the wider environment. These mounds would have made ideal observation platforms for measuring the movements of the stars and planets, that other endlessly revolving heavenly Round Table.

Later ages continued the use of these mounds as focal points of administration and influence when invading Anglo-Saxons built wooden palisades on the larger ones for defensive purposes. The Normans later erected stone towers, turning them into castle mounds or 'Motte and Baileys' from where they could control the surrounding country. Thus the places of spiritual power became redefined as those of earthly dominion. The example at Windsor however, and the building of St George's Chapel, emphasises not only their royal associations but another link with the old Dragon legends, as Edward invoked the old Pendragon dynasty. Once places where Druids and their precursors enacted open air rites and mystery plays, this sacred function was superseded in later times by more utilitarian functions. Nevertheless these Dragon mounds still lay at the very heart of the local community.

There may even have been a deeper and more magical dimension to these mounds, for in the Egyptian Creation Myth the first land to appear after the flood is the Mound of Creation. This marks the symbolic beginning of life on Earth, as the land rises from the waters of the abyss, and paintings show the Mound with the head of Atum, the first god-man, on its summit. All Egyptian temples symbolised the original Mound of Creation, making such places of prime importance in their cosmology. It cannot be far off the mark to suggest that they may have had a similar mystical role in Britain and Europe, as places where magical ceremonies connected with the Dragon powers of the land were enacted.

If there was indeed a prehistoric cult of the Dragon which was later absorbed into the legend of St George, we can probably assume these Dragon Hills were the focal points, erected at significant geomantic locations such as the crossing of dragon currents—where the male and female energies of nature come together and 'mate'. Such a proposition would entirely explain why places such as Dragon Hill or the Round Table Mound at Windsor were of such importance. The Welsh name for these mounds is 'Pen-y-Byd' (The Head of the World), and it is known that the Druidic Gorsedds represented a microcosmic Earth rising out of the sea, as in the Egyptian myth.

Besides these examples we cannot ignore the greatest of all in this class of monument, Silbury Hill at Avebury, the Serpent Temple of ancient Britain. This is the largest artificial hill in Europe, designed like its smaller counterparts as a flat-topped conical mound, and surrounded by water in winter months. This massive mound, supposedly the burial place of King Sil in his golden chariot, is certainly no ordinary heap of earth. As large as the pyramid of Khephren, it is constructed with a highly sophisticated understanding of soil mechanics. Inner walls of chalk support its bulk, infilled with at least thirty-five million basket-loads of loose material. It is one of the greatest archaeological enigmas ever. Its interior is of stepped circular construction with a core of clay and flint transported from other parts of the country. The infill is alternate layers of organic and inorganic material, and such a specialised construction has caused many researchers to speculate that it is in fact a gargantuan 'Orgone Accumulator' similar to the devices developed by Wilhelm Reich. He believed he had found one of the basic forces of the universe, an invisible energy he called 'Orgone' because of its similarity to the sexual forces released when the two polarities unite. This essential Life Force, he concluded, also had a negative form causing decay and death, much like the poisonous breath of the legendary Dragons.

Whatever the reason for this incredible example of Neolithic engineering, its links with the great Serpent Temple demonstrate that it must have had some profoundly important function. Recent archaeological work has revealed that it too once had a spiral pathway to the top, emulating the coils of a dragon. Was it the greatest Dragon Mound of all, a place of Creation and re-Creation?

Green Jesus

The other famous St George site, besides that of Dragon Hill, is at the small, isolated church at Brinsop in Herefordshire. Here there is an impressively-carved 12th century tympanum of the saint with his spear thrust into the gaping mouth of a serpentine dragon, with an arch of astrological symbols. In the boggy ground

next to the church is the site of Dragon's Well, from where the beast is said to have emerged. It can be no coincidence that the next village is called Wormsley. Inside the building are a number of draconic accoutrements, including a fine sculpture of the saint performing his sacred duty in full armour. But what particularly catches the eye is the blue-and-gilt altarpiece, which is very unusual indeed and depicts Jesus Christ on the cross, yet this cross is a living tree, carved with

extravagant flourishes of flowers and greenery. It is a striking image of an aspect of Christ's persona that is rarely shown, but which is very enlightening for our understanding of him as the inheritor of pre-Christian tradition. For here, in a

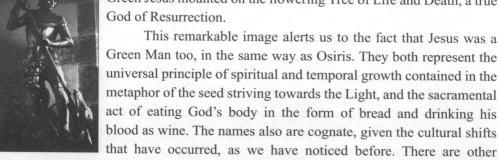

place where George, the Green Man, slew a dragon, is an image of Green Jesus mounted on the flowering Tree of Life and Death, a true God of Resurrection.

This remarkable image alerts us to the fact that Jesus was a Green Man too, in the same way as Osiris. They both represent the universal principle of spiritual and temporal growth contained in the metaphor of the seed striving towards the Light, and the sacramental act of eating God's body in the form of bread and drinking his blood as wine. The names also are cognate, given the cultural shifts that have occurred, as we have noticed before. There are other correspondences too. One almost hesitates to mention that in certain areas of France there was (and is rumoured to still be) a cult of Jesus as a priapic fertility god, where a wooden pole was inserted through the back of a statue to create an ithyphallic image, in what must be a very early form of Christian worship. This was done only at certain times, and was roundly condemned by Church authorities who tried to stamp it out. But the local people evidently persisted with the practice until it ended up as a secretive underground offshoot of traditional religion.[2] The correspondence here with the wooden phallus of Osiris, made by Isis to bring about the conception of their Sun-God son Horus, is apparent. It seems France may have inherited another aspect of the old Egyptian ways besides the Marian/Isis worship that became so prevalent in this part of Europe.

Shining Knights

Besides Uffington and Brinsop there are many other locations in the British Isles that have a distant memory of St George and his dragon-slaying activities, even though they may not be so well-known. A number of early medieval carvings commemorate this, some, like the one at Brinsop, being impressive works of art (for instance a similar tympanum can be seen in the Forest of Dean).

Equally significant are the great variety of other dragon-slaying and dragon-taming legends that haunt mainland Britain. It is impossible to recount them here for they would fill a large volume. The very density of such tales show the power of this archetypal battle, and they exist in every country. Famous British legends include the Lambton Worm (worm is an Anglo-Saxon word for serpent or dragon). The story tells how when John Lambton caught a weird-looking worm in a river and tossed it into a nearby well, it grew into a monstrous creature. Here the tale begins to betray its real roots, for at this point our hero becomes a Knight of St John and travels to Rhodes (one-time headquarters of the Order, and site of another dragon legend—here a Grand Master, Dieudonné de Gozon, is said to have slain one in a cave on the island's north coast). Whilst he was away, the creature grew huge and slept coiled nine times around an artificial mound called Worm Hill. Its diet was mainly lambs but it was also partial to cow's milk. Lambton the elder decided to lay a trap; a stone trough was filled with the milk of nine cows and the worm duly drank of it each day. Any less than this amount and it tore trees from the Earth in a fit of rage. Attempts were made to kill it, but in vain—lives were lost, but it magically reassembled itself when cut in two.

Seven years later John Lambton returned to find his estate a wasteland, and, despairing, consulted a wise woman. She told him to have a special suit of armour made set with sharp blades. He should lie in wait, but must swear to kill the first living thing he sets eyes on should he be successful. Setting off to fight the worm he told his father he would sound three blasts on his horn if things went his way, and that his favourite hound should be let loose to run to him. The battle with the worm went well; it coiled itself around him and was cut to pieces. When he blew the horn though, his father, overcome with relief, ran towards him instead of releasing the hound. John was forced to break his vow, but it brought a heavy price: the Lambton family was cursed for nine generations, that no Lord would die in his bed. Extraordinarily, the curse seemed to work, for historians have observed how the prophecy was fulfilled until Henry Lambton, the ninth in succession, died in a coaching accident in 1761.

Allowing for the inevitable accretions that such a tale may gather over the years, the fact that John Lambton was a Knight of St John (closely linked to the Templars), and that he succeeded in ridding the country of a devastating worm or dragon which had turned it into a wasteland, is significant. It shows that returning Crusader knights resurrected the old dragon-slaying traditions of Druidic and early Christian times, and brought prosperity back to a land ravaged by some indefinable pestilence in the guise of a draconic creature connected, as ever, with a well and an artificial mound. The great majority of such dragon legends have as their central hero a knight, perhaps the most telling feature of all. Their Coats of Arms frequently bear dragons (often long before the incidents related) indicating that they were the inheritors of a more ancient tradition. Where they have tomb memorials they are often shown with crossed legs, a symbolic device showing they had been to the Crusades. At Slingsby in Yorkshire just such a memorial exists in the local church. It was here that Lord Wyvill (whose crest bears a Wyvern) killed a huge serpent over a mile in length.

The legend of the Laidly Worm, however, is concerned not with dragon-slaying, but a spell or enchantment where a young girl is trapped in a loathsome reptilian body, and saved by a kiss. Here we may have a sense of the spiritual disciplines involved, where Love, in this case for the feminine principle, may transmute negative influences. We can begin to see that many of these old myths were resurrected and injected with a new life by the Crusader Knights, who feature so prominently as the heroes.

Along with the introduction (or re-introduction) of the Green Man and the Black Madonna, the dragon rituals were reborn anew. These three components fit neatly into the St George legend. In this way the knights, especially the Templars, were responsible for reviving an entire cult of ancient religion, thrown about with a cloak of Christendom and emblazoned with a St George's Cross, a symbol of the greatest antiquity. It was as if their purpose was to challenge the orthodox interpretation of Roman Christianity and expose it for the sham it was, a deliberately-contrived and artificial religion designed largely by Constantine as an exercise in world domination. In fact this is exactly what the Templars were accused of, and the reason why the Church could no longer tolerate them. They had to be exterminated.

Other famous British dragon tales have a number of common themes running through them, and the most intriguing of all is how often the knights wore suits of shining armour studded with spikes or blades. In the story of Sir Peter Loschy of Nunnington in Yorkshire, the dragon coiled around him and was sliced up but was immediately regenerated, until his dog carried the pieces up to a nearby hill. Dogs are often another motif in these stories, as they represent mythic guardians of the underworld.

The tale of Sir John Conyers, who killed the Sockburn Worm, a 'monstrous and poisonous vermin, ask or werme, which had overthrown and devoured many people in fight' is preserved in Bowe's manuscript in the British Library. He too wore shining armour festooned with razor blades, but also had a magic sword, a falchion, which doubled as the title deed for the manor (a clue that these rituals were often concerned with preserving ancient boundaries). It was the custom that this falchion was presented to each new Bishop of Durham at a river that marked the limits of the estate. This old ritual has now been resurrected, and the present Lord of the Manor invokes the event in the following way:

'My Lord Bishop, I here present you with the falchion wherewith the champion Conyers slew the worm, dragon or fiery flying serpent, which destroyed man, woman and child; in memory of which, the King then reigning gave him the manor of Sockburn, to hold by this tenure, that upon the first entrance of every bishop into the county this falchion should be presented.'

That the 'fiery flying serpent' was not originally something to be feared, but a force of growth and fertility, seems to be indicated by close examination of the falchion, which still exists in the cathedral treasury. It has a broad blade and has been dated to the 13th century. On its cross handle are dragons. But they are not images of 'monstrous or poisonous vermin'—their tails grow into serpentine foliage. They are Green Dragons. A similar fact may be noticed about the legend of the Dragon of Wantley, near Sheffield, for the Coat of Arms of More of More Hall, who despatched his dragon with a club, shows a Green Dragon as well.

We may ask why should a specially made suit of shining armour be the required uniform for a potential dragon slayer? On the one hand it seems an obvious ploy; as the dragon coils itself boa-constrictor-like around its victim it is cut to pieces. But if we cross-reference the British dragon tradition with the Dragon-men of Chinese feng-shui, we can sense another reason. One of the most basic techniques here is the use of mirrors, which can reflect the invisible stream of unbalanced power away from its course. In **The Living Earth Manual of Feng-Shui,** Stephen Skinner notes that the places where the ch'i accumulates are known as the 'Dragon's Lairs', but that under certain circumstances they can become the focus for more deleterious emanations: *'Sha is the antithesis of ch'i, and can be translated as 'noxious vapour'. It is a form of evil ch'i and is often called sha ch'i or feng sha (noxious wind)'.* As we have observed before, such a description is suspiciously close to the idea of the 'poisonous breath' of dragons. Were these old dragon-slayers using what amounts to a scientific tool to fragment and destroy such noxious emanations? Mirrors are still used by the Dragon-men of today, so we can be sure they work. A highly-polished suit of armour would not only protect those within it, but if set with similarly mirror-like blades then it might well have the effect of fragmenting the stream of harmful energy, or 'cutting up the dragon' into pieces. Many other such legends refer specifically

to the use of mirrors. At Wherwell in Hampshire there is an old Priory (now
a private residence) with a well in its basement whose waters were famous for
bubbling and appearing highly energetic (the wher-well). Here resided one of
those very strange creatures called a cockatrice, a composite, almost alchemical,
griffin-like beast which was hatched by a toad from a cock's egg in the basement
(then a crypt). This alarming creature devoured humans and killed a number of
knights who were trying to overcome it. It was only when a local
labourer took a mirror into the crypt that it instantly fell dead upon
seeing its own reflection. Such stories indicate that far from dealing
with gross superstition we may be touching remnants of a science
that, as in the feng-shui tradition, was purposefully employed, mostly
by knights who had immersed themselves in the extant mystical
traditions of the Orient. We should not forget that the Sufi adepts who
taught at the Moorish and African universities were behind a great
deal of the magical lore that found its way into medieval Europe. The
Sufis introduced Alchemy, Tarot and the Qabalah, and it is also likely

that they were masters at understanding the forces of Nature. As inheritors of
the Persian and Zoroastrian Mysteries, they may have been aware of the oriental
Chinese traditions and the disciplines of feng-shui. There may well have been
a universal tradition of this understanding of the Earth's energies, as we have
seen in the Druidic legacy of the Celtic saints. The conclusion must be that an
important part of the mystical sciences included learning how to neutralise or
otherwise nullify the dangerous emanations that can occur from deep within the
Earth. One of the great Sufi teaching centres was at Jerusalem.

One last legend deserves our attention. Piers Shonks was a 23-foot tall
giant who lived under an oak tree on an island at Brent Pelham in Hertfordshire.
He had already rid the surrounding country of many demons, but when he was out
hunting with his winged hounds one day he came across a terrible dragon. He shot

it with an arrow, but the Devil was incensed and swore
he would steal his soul after his death, whether he was
buried inside or outside the church. Piers neatly avoided
this situation by shooting another arrow through the
church window where it became lodged in the north
wall. This was the place he was buried, neither inside
or outside, thereby keeping his immortal soul. The
elaborate grave-slab that marks the spot has, at its base,
a Green Dragon with a foliate cross sprouting from its
bearded mouth.

*Club-wielding figure clad in greenery
with Green Man shield, from Christchurch Priory, Dorset.*

The Hairy Wild Men

That the traditions of dragon-slaying extend far back beyond Crusader Knights and even Celtic saints can be seen by studying the earlier vestiges of native ritual. Much of this is preserved in old churches that have not had their interiors 'restored'. The bench ends in Crowcombe Church in Somerset are a vivid reminder that within relatively recent times (certainly the last 500 or so years) the memory of local traditions probably extending back into prehistory was still alive. Besides a number of draconic Green Men there is a bench end of two naked men thrusting spears into a two-headed dragon. This takes us back to a time when dragon-slayers were not clad in armour, but were the Wild Men of the Woods, the shamanic magicians of their day. This memory is exemplified by the story that Merlin, the archetypal wizard, was born hairy, for hairiness signifies control over the natural world, including the animal kingdom. In many churches and cathedrals there are carvings which speak of this; a misericord in Chester Cathedral shows just such a hirsute wildman (known as a Wodewose) grappling with a dragon. These images are far more common than may be imagined, but, like the ubiquitous dragons which only appear when summoned, few seem to notice

Wild Wodewose figures emerge from the ears of a Green Man at Crowcombe

them. In Brittany, two enormous Wodewoses bearing clubs guard the entrance to Quimper Cathedral, just as twin dragons appear on a number of British cathedrals. It looks as though the clubs of these shamanic magicians were the original dragon-slaying weapons that evolved first into spears and then into swords, which all mythically represent Light. One of the main characters in the Midwinter Mummers' Plays is a giant who sings:

> *'Here I come Beelzebub'*
> *And over my shoulder I carry my club;*
> *And in my hand a frying pan,*
> *And I think myself a jolly old man.*

When we realise that the earthwork known as the 'Frying Pan' (alternatively known as the Trendle), above the Cerne Abbas Giant, was the place where the old seasonal rituals took place, we can see that this may preserve a true relic of prehistory. This was where the Maypole was set

Wodewose fighting a Dragon in Chester Cathedral

up, signifying the central pole around which the heavens dance, and the site of fertility rites. Later times turned the giant into a blundering and disorderly figure, but nevertheless it looks likely that the Cerne Giant could have originally been a genuine shamanic giant, a Sun God aligned with the Stonehenge solsticial axis who tamed the dragon with his club. Rodney Castledon, who spent many years conducting a resistivity survey of the figure, concluded that the giant was also 'grasping a wild mop of dreadlocks from which is swinging a severed head'. This may be another piece of the puzzle, involving head-worship of the sacrificed god.

These hairy giants or Wodewoses are the earliest dragon-tamers of all, the shamans who could cross over the threshold from the visible world into the Otherworld, which was populated by natural forces which could be communicated with directly.

The Swiss anthropologist Jeremy Narby, in *The Cosmic Serpent*, tells of his experiences after drinking the hallucinogenic preparation *ayahuasca*, a traditional part of Amazonian shamanism; he found that serpents or dragons not only guarded the entrance to this mystical otherworld but that they possessed great knowledge and intelligence, and could communicate through speech and visions.

According to Narby he had discovered why such creatures abound in the creation myths of the world, and that they are not only the origins of all magical knowledge, but of life itself. Is this why so many Green Men have those wild, staring eyes? Have they glimpsed the Otherworld through ingesting magical plants such as Mandrake (*man-dragon*), much prized for its magical effects, which were such an important part of medieval herbalism?

Certain 'magic mushrooms', including 'Liberty Caps', contain substances such as Psilocybin and are commonly available from fields and meadows. The chemical composition of this closely replicates seratonin, the hormone produced by the brain and associated with consciousness changes and spiritual vision. This memory of prehistoric shamanism obviously lived on in remote rural areas, yet was also a feature of Templarism and esoteric Christianity. It is probably why John the Baptist, the spiritual mentor of the Templars, was so often depicted wearing a hairy coat. We have already noted the overtones of head worship associated with him. Both these link him with an older, shamanic way of life.

An excellent example of this can be seen in the 12th century cathedral at Exeter, a veritable repository of arcane knowledge, where John appears clad in animal skin as a roof boss in a side chapel. The place is also heavily populated with Green Men, including one that supports a statue of the Virgin, an eloquent statement to those who perceive the truth behind such mysteries.

It seems apparent that these traditions in the end all came together in the age of the Templars. At Altarnun Church in Cornwall there is a unique collection

of carvings which, although from the 16th century, shows that such memories lived on in the craftsmen guilds of Freemasonry. Called 'The Cathedral of the Moors' it is situated close to the old Templar route down to St Michael's Mount, a pilgrim's pathway going back to prehistory. A few miles away is the small church at Temple, where travellers across the deserted landscape of Bodmin Moor were offered shelter and refreshment.

These bench ends, which somehow miraculously survived the so-called Victorian restorations, are like a bible of the esoteric beliefs of the Templars. A repeated image is a sheaf of corn, bound in the centre, with a head protruding from the top.

The Spirit of Nature, as a bearded 'Green Man', rises from a flower, holding two stamens in his hands. From a bench end in Altarnun Church.

This is a very Osirian image, associated with the intelligence within nature, the spirit of the dying and rising god as immortalised in the folk memory of John Barleycorn. Another panel shows a head coming out of a chalice, making an unmistakable connection between the Head and the Holy Grail, both symbols of

higher consciousness. There are many Green Men with their bodies turning into foliage in the Renaissance fashion of the day. Eight dragons accompany four heads on the font.

Wherever one looks there is a story, the story of how the Spirit of Nature illuminates our understanding. It is an open book of the wisdom that was once widely understood, then lost, and subsequently resurrected by the mystical brotherhoods of the Crusader Knights.

A disembodied head, symbolising higher spiritual consciousness, rises from a Grail, from which two dragons, the twin polarities of Nature, drink. From Altarnun Church.

16

The Spear of Light

Throughout this investigation we have come to realise that the myth of St George is a true archetype, one that can mean different things according to the way we choose to perceive it. It is rather like looking at a distant scene through a telescope: one can focus on any facet of the vista and magnify it, sometimes losing the sense that each individual aspect is part of the whole. The telescope can even be reversed, when everything becomes distant and almost beyond recognition as we peer into the remote past. Then it is our own consciousness which becomes the focal point.

So far we have dwelt on the various themes of the mystery and realised that each one fulfils an important function in the scheme of things. Thus the mythology of St George is a many-faceted and multi-layered body of lore drawn from earlier gods of regeneration and renewal, as well as representing our own inner personal quest for knowledge.

It is a mystical journey that leads us right to the heart of the mystery of human potential. The Virgin of the myth is the feminine principle, that pure unsullied energy, the instinctive source of life that is ready to be married to the intellect, the bonding of which is the essence of all creativity. The Dragon symbolises the energies of Nature that are available for our own enlightenment; thereby hangs the perennial science of the Kundalini, the ch'i, the invisible but primal force of many names. That these forces were known and understood in antiquity is another of the things we have largely forgotten in the modern world. Their codification in a vast system of symbolism, which includes the various cultural interpretations of many different races, is one of the reasons they may sometimes seem difficult to decipher.

Yet there was a science of the Dragon that was at the root of all systems of initiation. Whatever religion we choose the evidence is there. Set tamed Apep, Horus, the son of the Egyptian Green Man, battled Set (and also, in the Mystery Schools, cut off the head off Isis, who in one of her guises, was a serpent). Apollo shot his magic arrows at the Python, the source of all healing and wisdom, at Delphi, and St George rescued the maiden, thus releasing humanity's true inner nature through the taming of the Earth's forces. In the Western Mystery tradition these are all known as 'spear-shakers', an idea that goes back to the earliest times. Pallas Athene was another amongst the many gods and goddesses who had the courage to challenge the prevailing attitudes by 'shaking the spear' of truth.[1]

The feet of Sir Roger North, Elizabeth the First's treasurer, rest on a dragon in Kirtling Church, Norfolk.

In the Elizabethan age the occult fraternities in particular aligned themselves with this principle, and the group of luminaries and adepts gathered around the magus John Dee were deeply committed to challenging prevailing attitudes. Francis Drake (*Drake* is an old English form of *Dragon*), when elected member of Parliament for Tintagel, appears to have consciously taken on the mantle of Arthur, who according to ancient legend had been born there. If he was born there, and was to come again, then this should be the place of his rebirth. So Drake became a maritime Arthur, invoking the old Pendragon spirit. He may well have known the secret of the old Earth Magic, for he built his fortress next to the place on Plymouth Hoe where the giant figures of Gogmagog were cut into the turf (there was also a chapel to St Catherine here, the Templar version of a Sun Goddess). As we know, there is a solstitial axis connecting Tintagel with the Hoe linking the birthplace of King Arthur (another giant-killer) with these old giants.

Sir Walter Raleigh, Philip Sydney, Francis Bacon and the other members of this secret 'Dragon Society' were all the foremost thinkers of their day, studying esoteric history and the Hermetic arts as well as exploring other unfamiliar territories. Another of these 'spear-shakers' was William *Shakespeare* (born on St George's Day), whose true identity has been the subject of much scholarly discussion, but whose name and date of birth suggests another level of meaning altogether. Edmund Spenser, yet another of this esoteric group of luminaries, in **The Faery Queen**, included **The Legend of the Knight of the Red Cross** as an allegory of this quest for enlightenment. His blow-by-blow account of the duel between the Knight and the flying, fire-breathing dragon was designed as a rollicking good tale, but concealed much arcane symbolism and esoteric formulae. St George, one of whose epithets was 'The Rose of Sharon', was also an essential feature of Rosicrucianism, and this Rose appeared emblazoned on the Red Cross as a metaphor for the aspiring adept (*Sub Rosa* means *secret*). Here the slaying of the Dragon referred to the refining of the lower energies into higher spiritual levels. Death is transformation, so dragon killing is transformation too. Alchemy is full of dragons whose meaning is that of transmutation, referring to the refining of gross matter to higher spiritual energies.[2] On one level it symbolises our inner shadows, which have to be slain before we can grow. But the dragon is also a shining, spiritual principle, so slaying it in these terms is an allegory for our own personal evolution. In the Druid tradition 'dragons' meant initiates, and the most sacred symbol was the dragon's egg, out of which hatches the newly refined individual, purified by being born again. The Virgin represents the purified soul which is released from the dragon of our fears. This is why on King Arthur's shield the Red Dragon is ultimately replaced by an image of the Virgin, representing spiritual transformation.

How precisely this process of unfoldment is achieved is the province of those prepared to commit themselves wholeheartedly to such disciplines. However, there are methods by which one can quicken the growth of the seed that lies dormant. The spirals of the dragon energy need to be awakened and made to release their imprisoned Light or it may remain forever trapped in dark matter. Then the radiant beauty of illumination (the Virgin, whose love is pure) can be freed. In this way the myth of St George becomes a personal quest that has within it the secret of both creation and transformation.

To the ancient mind, it seems that the realms of the Otherworld were not only close to physical reality, but underscored it and permeated everything. Thus one could cross over into other dimensions by achieving a different state of consciousness. Access to these spiritual worlds was particularly enhanced at certain times and at certain places: at dawn, dusk, Solstice, Equinox or other critical points in the annual cycle; at holy hill, stone circle or sacred spring. Even in the current frenetic age this quality is still preserved for those who wish to use such portals to penetrate the inner workings of Nature, and these days there are an increasing number of people with enquiring minds who seek them out exactly for this reason. The modern revival of interest in these matters shows how deeply we all thirst for real understanding, even as the world loses touch with its true roots. The 'new magic' of paganism, Wicca and 'alternative' beliefs of every shade, a re-interpretation of primordial principles, is currently the biggest growth area of Western religion, whilst many church congregations decline.

These magical inner realms beyond the visible world are forming our reality all the time, even though we may not realise it. Creation is taking place at every moment. Within the aura of the old sites are reservoirs of power that can reveal the patterns of existence whose templates structure physical life. The energetic dragon spirals of the ancient sites are always available so we can reconnect with the Earth. These reservoirs of magical energy extend to the old gods too, many of whom have later become venerated as saints, like St George. Many centuries, or even millennia, of prayer, devotion and magical ritual have built up, on the inner levels, powerful sources of pure energy which can be tapped into. 'Patron' saints are 'patterns' that operate through natural law.

Geomancy, in the true and original meaning of the term, signifies co-operation on a deep level with the spiritual and physical environment. Thus in the past the places representing the sacred life of the people were part of the divine order, chosen not by human caprice but by the gods themselves, the eternal principles and energies of Nature. In this way human life may be ordered by the magical forces present in the Earth, and brought into synchrony with the cycles of the Cosmos. The grail-like symbol of the human head (a vessel that is a receptacle of spiritual energies, and also full of blood) was frequently associated with the entrances and gateways to this otherworldly dimension, marking them out as boundaries between this hidden world of formative forces and the material realms where they become manifest. The head itself is the means by which one can enter these realms, through the organs of spiritual perception which are guarded on either side appropriately by the *Temples*.

When you look into a well, the first thing you see is a head—your own. Shimmering and undulating as if peering straight at you from another reality, your own reflection reminds you that it is with your head that you perceive such miracles. In the watery world of magic the head guards the threshold of the mysterious Otherworld which truly determines our fate. Water, the symbol of the living spirit, signifies the veil between these worlds. This is why the sacred head of worldwide tradition is associated especially with wells and springs, and also eloquence. Wherever the lairs of the Dragon exist, water and Light come together. It is how the spiritual realms may speak directly to us.

Temples of Light

The evolution of sacred sites has always reflected that of humanity, and consequently they are repositories for much of the knowledge which is at the core of mythology. The earliest were the natural springs and caves, the most ancient of all the lairs of the Dragon. But at some stage humanity made a quantum leap and began to build vast monuments whose design and complexity is the greatest historical puzzle of all time. No-one yet understands the mysteries of the pyramids, even though great numbers of books have been written about them. We may call these edifices temples or tombs, yet this only demonstrates our own limitations. However, one generally-accepted thing is that they enhance the consciousness of those within them—just as one might attend a service in a cathedral today, where the music, incense, and ceremonies, as well as the atmosphere created by coloured stained-glass and flickering candles, all combine to have a dramatic effect on the mind. This is not speculation, for modern science has shown what has always been known, that these are all specialised techniques that alter the brainwave patterns of the participants and induce an uplifting, spiritual experience. In fact all the trappings of what we call 'magic' are designed with this end in mind.

Among the earliest forms of these types of structure were circles of stone, erected over the crossings of underground streams and fault lines, the veins and arteries of the Earth which create a complex network within the planet's crust.

The stones themselves are powerful conductors of the Life Force, and when arranged geometrically according to natural law, and positioned in the landscape with reference to certain risings and settings of the heavenly bodies, they become charged with energy.

This can cause a number of effects besides the more subtle and intangible changes in the brain. Sometimes the energy can be seen as well as felt. It can even be photographed under certain conditions, and some examples of the spiralling coils of dragon energies are included in the colour section of this book. That such effects can be photographed at all can surely mean only one thing: that these energetic effects are caused, or affected, by Light.

The frequencies of this Light may normally not be visible to the untrained eye (although those gifted with clairvoyance may see it clearly), for its vibrations are beyond the spectrum of normal vision. But when it is especially intense it can register on photographic equipment (where it can often be mistaken at first to be the result of faults in the film or processing) allowing an amazing glimpse into a world that is all around us, yet usually invisible.

Light is the greatest mystery of all, and the truth is that nobody understands exactly what it is or how it behaves. We know it can apparently manifest both as energetic wave forms and as streams of particles. This initially came as something of a shock to scientists, who in the end were obliged to admit that the observer is as much a part of the phenomena being observed as the object itself. We cannot know all the mysteries of Light, but we can utilise its known properties. For instance, through mass spectrometry it is possible to ascertain the constituent elements and their proportions of stars millions of light years away by measuring the different frequencies within it. Light encodes a great mass of information which can be read if only we know how.[3]

In the mystical traditions of antiquity, everything was thought to be made of Light vibrating at different rates. Most of it we cannot sense, for the infra-red and ultra-violet regions of the spectrum are invisible to the human eye. It is only when we see a rainbow or the prismatic effects of Light reflected or refracted through crystals or water that we become aware that what we call 'white light' is composed of a myriad series of oscillations. Each colour has its own characteristic frequency and consequently its own effect upon the human mind and body—colour 'healing' has been shown to have a direct influence upon people's moods and general health. Green in particular has soothing and inspirational properties as well as being the colour of growth and the basis of earthly life.

In medieval Alchemy the Green Lion was used to signify the light-sensitive pigment Chlorophyll, the magical substance that transmutes sunlight into living matter, and those hunting the Green Man will come across Green Lions frequently. The Lion is Leo, the sign of the Sun.

But there are deeper mysteries here. Each type of Light has its own characteristics. The Light of the rising Sun at the Midwinter Solstice, when it is 'reborn', is of a radically different quality to that of a sultry summer's afternoon. Artists and photographers know this and choose their times carefully. Different times of the day and year have different colours and rates of vibration, with blue predominant in the morning and yellow later in the day. Spring and Autumn, as analogues of the yearly 'day', are the same. The quickening power of Spring sunlight has the capacity to stir the Life Force within the seed, even though it is buried in the dark earth. The seed can sense the Light even if it cannot experience it directly. This is especially true of the reflected Light of the Moon, which has a crucial influence on plant growth. The science of Biodynamics demonstrates that moonlight is a critical factor in regulating fertility.

Where is all this leading? The answer is perhaps the greatest enigma of all: why ancient people, having been content to worship at natural shrines which we know to be sources of the Earth's spirit, suddenly decided to construct huge edifices. Their design criteria certainly took account of the dragon energies, for they were always built at locations with a long history as sacred sites. But now another factor enters the equation. Light.

Egyptian Temples had many functions, as mansions of the gods, portals to the divine, and microcosms of the universe. But the most profound thing of all is how they were specifically designed so that at a certain moment in the Sun/Earth cycle a narrow beam of sunlight penetrated the dark interior to illuminate a statue of the god in his inner sanctum. The priesthood believed that this activated the gods and brought them to life, and that certain types of stone resonated with particular frequencies. Red granite from Aswan was the most prized material, and enormous quantities were transported throughout the country for pyramid and temple building. Some pyramids, including those of Menkaure and Khephren at Giza and the Red Pyramid of Snefru at Dahshur, look as though they may have been entirely covered with it, for the lower layers are still intact. Granite, of which quartz is the largest single ingredient, is particularly sensitive to Light, and quartz creates a piezo-electric effect, setting up electro-magnetic pulses (this principle is at the core of modern technology). It thus becomes 'charged' by the Light, just as the Egyptians claimed. Sometimes the power becomes so great that crystalline rocks act like condensers, and can discharge, or 'earth' themselves, as the dowser Tom Lethbridge discovered when he touched the granite megaliths of the Merry Maidens in Cornwall.

There is no doubt that both megalithic and Temple structures throughout the ancient world were designed primarily with these matters in mind. The materials were chosen because of their energetic properties and the design arranged to be in synchrony with certain times when a particular type of Light would be absorbed. In Egypt the pinnacle of this mystical science included the erection of massive obelisks cut from a single piece of red granite. At the quarry at Aswan is one of the best examples, half-cut from the rock. It would have weighed, if it had ever been finished, in excess of 1000 tons. This would have been the biggest in the world had it not been abandoned because of a natural fissure discovered when the project was nearing its end. The word *obelisk* signifies the twin ideas of fire and transmutation implied by the symbol of the serpent—*obelos* in Greek means fire, and obelisk also refers to *basilisk*, meaning a snake-like or draconic creature. Their sheer size and the craftsmanship involved in their production marks them out as energetic structures of the highest calibre; they ring like a bell when struck, and many people have reported them 'singing' or giving out a high-pitched frequency when the first rays of sunlight fall on them.

That the Egyptians had a preoccupation with the Mystery of Light is clearly apparent. The heretic King Akhenaten made it the central tenet of his mystical religion of the Aten, the Sun-Disk depicted with rays issuing from it and terminating in hands, as if they were actually touching and caressing whatever they fell upon. In his famous **Hymn to The Aten** he wrote 'Your rays suckle the fields, when you rise they live and grow for you'. The word ray also reminds us of the essential power of this idea, for *ray* is itself nothing less than the original name of the Sun-God *Ra*, which has cross-fertilised into English. But from the earliest ages the idea of a single shaft of Light has also been symbolised by a spear. In many paintings and papyri Ra sits surrounded by his compatriots in his solar barque, whilst Set, or later Horus, wields the Spear of Light to establish divine order.

The Seed of Sun and Earth

Thousands of miles from Egypt there is evidence of the same preoccupation with Light that gave rise to the great Temples of the Nile. The extraordinary thing is, though, that according to current theories the prehistoric monuments of Ireland were built long before the Great Pyramid. The hundreds of structures stretching from Galway Bay in the west to County Meath in the east are among the greatest wonders of the ancient world. They were built by a highly advanced branch of a civilisation whose ingenuity, vision and skills were breathtaking.

This legendary race, the Tuatha dé Danaan, are said to have arrived on the western shores of Ireland on Mayday or Beltane, not in normal ships but by flying through the air. They defeated the previous inhabitants, colonised the land and built great mounds of earth and stone wherever they went. They were, according to their name, 'The People of the Goddess Anu, or Ana', and their conception of the country as the living body of a fertile goddess still lives on, with *Eire* being another of the goddess' many names. Near Killarney two beautifully rounded mountains with small cairns on the summits are still known as 'The Paps of Anu', the breasts of the great mother.[4]

In the early accounts these people were incomparable magicians whose knowledge far exceeded that of any others. They 'excelled all the peoples of the world in their proficiency in every art'. They brought four great talismans: The Lia Fail, the Stone of Destiny, which shrieked when touched by the rightful king; the magic Sword of Nuadu which always guaranteed success; the Spear of Lugh, the most powerful weapon in the world, and the cauldron of the father-god, the Dagda, which endlessly replenished itself. The Tuatha were believed to be fallen gods or angels, and in ***The Book of the Dun Cow***, written about 1100, it was written that 'they came from heaven on account of their intelligence and for the excellence of their knowledge'.

The Dagda, the 'Good God', the Irish Sun-God, also known as 'The Lord of Great Knowledge', was the God of Druidism and Magic. His daughter Brigit was the inspired Goddess of Poetry, and her two sisters, who shared the same name, were deities of healing and smith-craft. Besides the Dagda the two other great leaders were Lugh with his spear of Light and the giant Ogma, the Lord of Eloquence and the inventor of the Ogham language. He had a radiant countenance, hence his title Ogma Sunface. There are over 330 chambered mounds across northern and eastern Ireland which were, according to these legends, built by this race of magicians. These are all the dwelling-places of the Sídhe, the elemental spirits of the land. They are also the entrances to the otherworldly 'Land of Eternal Youth' or Tír na nÓg. All these sacred centres are upwards of 4000 years old, and many are from an even earlier period. The people who constructed them apparently had an overriding preoccupation which guided their design—the properties of Light.

The greatest of their achievements is concentrated in a small but rich and fertile area in what is now County Meath, encircled on three sides by the River Boyne, the ancient river goddess whose flowing waters brought magic to the land. Her great 'Palace of the Boyne', the *Brú na Bóinne*, now known as Newgrange, overlooks this dramatic loop in the river like the pregnant belly of the Earth Goddess, and in fact one of the meanings of the word Brú is exactly this—*belly*. In English it is derived from Beli or Baal, one of the many names of the Sun God who gave his name to Beltane.

The monuments that these miraculous gods built are certainly among the most remarkable on Earth. They are still referred to (as are the Pyramids of Egypt) as tombs or graves, yet all the evidence suggests they were originally nothing of the kind. Bones have been found in them certainly, but the same could be said of a church, even though that was not its original purpose. The three major sites of Newgrange, Knowth and Dowth are among the finest surviving examples of this type of structure in Europe. At Knowth there are over 1600 stones weighing upwards of one ton, and many of them are exquisitely carved with a myriad of perplexing but inspiring designs, making it the greatest concentration of megalithic art in the world. An early observer who tried to make sense of them was Sir William Wilde, father of Oscar, who concluded that the carvings were in the nature of sacred hieroglyphs.[5]

A more recent researcher, the American artist Martin Brennan, who spent a number of years decoding them, has shown in *The Stars and the Stones* that they were not created for decorative or arcane religious purposes but as repositories for highly sophisticated astronomical knowledge. Those designs that have yielded to investigation show an understanding of solar, lunar and planetary cycles that modern astronomy has only recently achieved, such is the level of their technical expertise. Amongst the many 'symbols', which are more in the nature of cosmic equations and scientific formulae, are the earliest known form of sundials, accurately measuring the path of the Sun in its annual cycle.[6]

But Brennan's greatest contribution to our understanding of these structures is the idea that they were conceived as Temples of Light. Others had noticed before how at certain times of the year a thin shaft of sunlight would enter the dark passageways, but it was Brennan who, along with a team of researchers, witnessed such phenomena at first hand. On one occasion he predicted that the only remaining intact cairn at Loughcrew was aligned to the rising of the Equinoctial Sun, but after an early-morning drive from Dublin, arrived just after it had risen. 'We felt as if we were ten minutes late for an appointment made over 5000 years ago,' he wrote. On entering the chamber he found a golden shaft of sunlight penetrating deep inside the monument, illuminating spirals and other symbols carved into the stones. All these structures, even those partially destroyed, demonstrate the same characteristics of tracking the Sun. At Loughcrew it was found that originally a whole series of mounds had monitored the Sun's progress, and as the Light disappeared from one it entered another. These monuments are thus revealed, over 5000 years after their construction, as an impressive series of scientific instruments laid out across the land.

As scientific instruments they are unique, yet they replicate the effects of the Egyptian Temples, whose alignments, as Sir Norman Lockyer noted over a hundred years ago, were determined by the angle of the Sun's declination at certain times. There is evidence too that this tradition was not lost in the fog of prehistory, but formed an essential part of the Mystery Wisdom behind later church architecture. Many cathedrals, including Chartres and Nevers in France, track the Sun and mark out the Solstices and Equinoxes in a similar fashion.

Most churches face East, towards the equinoctial sunrise, but many are aligned to other directions, often to the point on the horizon where the Sun rises on the saint's day to which they are dedicated. This is because even though the churches built on the site are of comparatively late construction, they were designed to continue the original concept, having replaced stone circles whose megaliths are often incorporated into the fabric of the building.

At Newgrange (now reconstructed), the first shaft of Light from the reborn sun at the Winter Solstice enters the cruciform chamber through a specially constructed roof-box surrounded by walls of white quartz, whose aperture allows only a 'spear' of Light through. This then tracks across the floor for some minutes before striking a stone carved with a triple spiral. Then it penetrates to the deepest recesses of the chamber, where the shaft illuminated a heavy stone basin in the centre of the floor (now in a different position). Being present at this extraordinary cosmic light-show is a deeply moving experience that many have

The entrance to Newgrange before reconstruction.
The dragon spirals on the stone represent the polarities
of Nature, and its inward and outward breath. The central
line marks the Spear of Light at the Midwinter Solstice.

likened to a spiritual revelation. Visitors today are shown a simulation of the process, and even this can be very humbling.

There are many fascinating lines of investigation to be pursued here, but we must of necessity limit ourselves to the theme of the current book. One thing that should be pointed out, though, is that the design carved on the lintel of the roof-box, the functional hub of the whole structure, shows a linked series of 'St Andrew's Crosses', indicating the solar axes of the year. Exactly the same design can be seen on a number of

churches and cathedrals, and is especially noticeable on either side of the entrance at Kilpeck. This is not the only example of meaningful symbolic imagery, for the chevron design cut into the doorways of Saxon and Norman churches can also

be seen within these prehistoric monuments. One of the alcoves or recesses in Newgrange has exactly this design over it, and it occurs elsewhere too, including the reconstructed mound at Fourknocks. This chevron design is frequently compared to the Egyptian hieroglyph for water, but its presence in

5000 year-old chevron design at Fourknocks

these circumstances would suggest it refers more to waves of Light. The dramatic zig-zags certainly evoke the energetic nature of Light rather than flowing water. Curious, too, that the Sumerian god Zag, from where the word zig-zag derives, has as his symbol a double-headed axe, the 'St Andrew's Cross'.

Another notable feature of these structures is the existence of great stone bowls occuring at their very centre. These were a common feature of the Irish megalithic mounds, and something of a mystery, for although they are sometimes described as 'basins' by archaeologists, they are far too shallow to really deserve the term. Newgrange has a number of these, including one with two curious indentations, but the most stunning is at Knowth, whose chamber is aligned to the equinoctial sunrise. No-one has yet satisfactorily explained what they were used for, yet they are among the greatest enigmas of all, and the Knowth

Above, one of the Newgrange stone bowls in its recess. Below, detail of the bowl, with its two shallow indentations.

bowl is a truly exceptional example of megalithic art, carved with striking designs. Some think they may have held water, or had something to do with

The Knowth Bowl

funeral rites. But the shallowness of their design is reminiscent of other Neolithic artefacts. These are querns, used for the grinding of corn. In such a sacred context it could be that the preparation of wheat or barley had an important sacramental purpose. The one in Newgrange with its circular depressions certainly looks as if it could have held grinding stones, and many likely such stones litter the site of Knowth in particular. It seems entirely possible that rituals were performed within these chambers to infuse the sacred body of the Corn God with the Light of the newly-reborn Sun. The corn, embodying the Sun's energy, could then be ingested. Could we be touching on the true origins of the sacramental eating of the body of the dying and *rising* God?

Of further interest in this context is a unique structure at Knowth known as a 'Keyhole Corn Kiln', made from a circle of stones set into the Earth, with a fan-shaped opening banked up with soil. It was used for drying corn or barley, which would be heaped up inside and a fire lit at the entrance. The heat from the fire transmitted

The 'Corn Kiln' at Knowth

itself to the stones, which then surrounded the grain with a gentle heat which dried and 'malted' it, encouraging the seed to begin to sprout. This technique was considered of great magical significance in the ancient world, for it symbolised the awakening of the seed within the initiate. The grain was used for the making of a magical form of bread and the brewing of a dark type of beer. In Egypt this beer was known as *Zythum*, sacred to the Barley God Osiris, which was ritually imbibed during religious ceremonies (the Irish version was known as *Lionn Dubh*, a dark porter). These mystically impregnated types of bread and beer were consumed in antiquity as a sacramental act of the highest significance. The Egyptian hieroglyphic shown as a loaf of bread probably refers to this, for hieroglyphics are always used in a sacred context. This may also be the mysterious 'shew-bread' mentioned in the Bible. The close proximity of this unique Corn Kiln to the central mound at Knowth, together with the sacred bowl (or quern) enclosed within the mound, is strongly reminiscent of the prehistoric

The Knowth phallus (replica)

use of the Rock at the Temple of Jerusalem as a 'Threshing Floor'. Remarkable Neolithic finds at Knowth include a stylised serpent or dragon, and an elegant phallus, carved with spiral designs and indicating a deep preoccupation with fertility. Here the mysteries of the Light are married to those of the dying and resurrecting god, the Lord of Fertility and human evolution, in a transcendent cosmic ritual reflecting the rebirth of the Sun on Earth. Was this rite of rebirth also directed towards awakening the soul of the priest/ king initiate who performed the ceremony? Were the energetic effects of such rituals concentrated and 'fixed' within the magic mounds, invigorating the land with the powers of fertility? When Knowth was excavated by the archaeologist George Oegan he found it composed of alternate organic and inorganic layers, just like Silbury Hill and the 'Orgone' or *ch'i* accumulators of Wilhelm Reich.[7]

But what is apparent in all of this, even though much of the true meaning behind it is currently elusive, is that the prehistoric monuments of Ireland amount to physical evidence of what may be the true origins of the St George myth. Here is the Spear of St George (or Lugh, the Sun God, whose harvest festival of Lughnasa was one of the most widely-celebrated of all the old country fire rituals) penetrating the dark (artificially-constructed) cave.

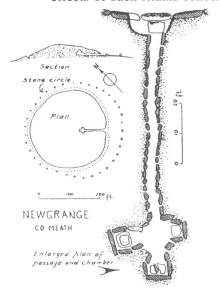

NEWGRANGE
CO. MEATH

The cruciform chamber at Newgrange, along which the Spear of Light shines at the Midwinter Solstice

What lies within? It is surely a Dragon's Lair, for the famous Newgrange Triple Spiral inside the mound is illuminated by the Spear of Light just before it reaches the innermost recesses, built in the shape of a cross. Whatever the exact nature of the rites taking place within the dark chamber at the precise moment of the Sun's rebirth, it is certain that we are not dealing here with superstition or primitive beliefs. These are the elements of a lost science of Light, which enters the man-made Dragon's cave to release the 'pure spirit' within the Earth.

The most well-known feature at the entrance to Newgrange is the spiral-covered 'kerbstone'. A central line marks the track of the Spear of Light at the Midwinter Solstice, and on either side dragon spirals spin in both directions; on the left they are anti-clockwise and on the right clockwise, or as the old pre-industrial language would have it, sunwise. These patterns of swirling cosmic imagery are a masterpiece of megalithic art, but they also speak of a profound understanding, where the year is divided by the vertical line, and the opposing directions of the spirals signify the unfolding creative force and its natural corollary. The sunwise spirals signify the outward, expanding processes of Spring; their opposite refers to the inwardly focusing energies of the declining year.

Closer examination of these patterns reveals that they come from the Earth itself. At its base, where it touches the ground, is the source of the dragon spirals; spiritual energy streams up from below, flowing freely from the Earth, released from its imprisonment by the Spear of Light.

Dragon spirals at Newgrange.

Left, the triple spiral, illuminated by the Spear of Light at the Midwinter Solstice.

Above, energy spirals emanate from the Earth on the entrance stone.

Right, a double spiral representing the polarities of Nature.

17

The Alchemical Wedding

he ruined abbey and church that stand on the summit of the Hill of Slane overlooking the River Boyne are amongst the most famous places in Irish Christian legend. They mark the site where the early missionary St Patrick lit the Easter Fire that directly challenged the power of the Druids and began the Christianisation of the country. This place is visible from both Newgrange and the Hill of Tara, the ancient seat of the Irish kings. Prehistoric earthworks surround the lower slopes, and in the ruins of the Friary church is a prominently displayed carving of a winged dragon, thought to be a fragment of the heraldic shield of the Norman overlords who became the new 'kings' of Ireland. Some of their Templar-like grave slabs still exist built into a nearby church.

At this spot St Patrick is said to have lit the Paschal Fire before the Druids lit their own on Tara as they continued a tradition that went deep into prehistory. It was the inviolable rule that the first fire was kindled at the very centre of kingship, and then all the other hills across the country would erupt into flame as far as the eye could see, purifying the land and celebrating the return of the Light of Spring and seasonal rebirth. The story goes that St Patrick lit his fire in contravention of the Brehon Laws, the ancient code of law governing the country, and that King Laoghaire, on seeing the fire at Slane from his royal residence on Tara, rode out to challenge Patrick in the company of his chief Druids. However, one man from his entourage, Erc, is said to have stood up for Patrick and 'refused to obey the words of the Druids'. He became a loyal servant and was made the first Bishop of Slane, dying around 512 AD. A curiously-shaped tomb with triangular end-blocks still exists in the graveyard and is known as Erc's Tomb. It is believed to be one of the oldest of its type in Ireland.

The monastery founded by Erc probably superseded a former Druid College, as with so many other such sites across Ireland, and may also have inherited its reputation as an important centre of learning. The French chronicler Mézeray in his **Histoire de France** of 1685 recorded that the Merovingian King Dagobert II went there to study as a child.[1] In 653, at the tender age of seven, he became a monk and entered the abbey to receive his education in preparation for kingship. This was not an uncommon practice at the time, continuing the long tradition of Ireland as one of the great centres of learning of the Druid, and later the early Christian, world. For many centuries the aristocratic families of

Europe had sent their sons and daughters to be educated there. Dagobert himself was strongly immersed in the mystical traditions of kingship, and has since been linked by Lincoln, Baigent and Leigh, the authors of **The Holy Blood and the Holy Grail**, to the legendary treasure of the Templars and the mysteries surrounding Rennes-le-Château.[2]

The ritual performed by Patrick was a powerful magical act showing that the Druids were no longer the custodians of the land, for the invocation of the Fire within the Earth now symbolised a new age, and a great shift in Ireland's fortunes. The Druid Colleges were to become Christian monasteries, and the lighting of the equinoctial fires, one of the most deeply ingrained rituals in the life of the land, carried on with a new purpose, to bring the Light of Christ. This ancient practice had taken place at Newgrange and its surrounding hills and monuments for many thousands of years, and now continued under the new ethos.

Patrick is also renowned for another challenging feat—that of ridding Ireland of its serpents, which he banished with the help of the dragon-slaying St Michael. This is a mythic way of stating that Christianity was now the moving force of the new age, and that the old dragon and serpent science, the Earth-based religions of fertility and the Mysteries of nature, had been superseded. As Christianity took hold, people began, with the encouragement of the Church, to hunt down and kill serpents, and to this day there are no snakes left in Ireland. It is interesting that the ritual act that began this process took place on the Hill of Slane (old spelling *Sláine*), as if Patrick was himself an early Irish version of St George, choosing this spot because of its geomantic powers where the old Dragon Science could be *slain*.

The Slane Dragon

The fact that the fragment of stone carved with a winged dragon still exists at this place seems remarkable in a land that came to despise all draconic and serpentine imagery. Its near-miraculous preservation seems to imply that the Norman overlords under Richard Plantagenet, Lord Lieutenant of Ireland, may have inherited an understanding of the significance of dragon-slaying, or taming, right into medieval times, despite official proscription. At the time the Baron of Slane was Richard le Fleming, who had sailed from Wales in 1169 and could well have had Templar connections. We should not be surprised at such a possibility, even though such knowledge was generally somewhat secretive because of its heretical nature, for Ireland was known as a centre of Templarism at those times. One of the reasons for the Crusaders' early success in the Holy Land, and their great prowess in battle, was due to the quality of their horses, which were bred in Ireland and could match the champion equines of the Arabic world. Significant too is that Newgrange and its satellite mounds became the property of the Cistercian Abbey of Mellifont, for this was the Order reformed by Bernard of Clairvaux, who was also behind the founding of the Templars. With their esoteric beliefs the Templars were vividly aware of the old pre-Christian ways, and the churches they built are still haunted by many a Green Man. They were also initiates into the perennial Mystery Wisdom; *'Symbolic carvings in Templar preceptories… suggest that some officials in the Order's hierarchy were conversant with such disciplines as astrology, alchemy, sacred geometry and numerology, as well, of course, as astronomy—which, in the 12th and 13th centuries, was inseparable from astrology, and every bit as 'esoteric'.'*[3] The presence of the Norman knights in the area of Newgrange and Tara (where they continued the old kingship rituals by being crowned at the former Druid centre), and especially of the young Prince Dagobert, can only lead to the conclusion that these prehistoric Temples of Light and Hills of Fire possessed some especially powerful significance. County Meath has always been known as 'The Royal County' because of its long-standing associations with kingship.

The returning Crusaders, having become immersed in the Sufi mysticism which itself preserved much of the ancient Persian/Zoroastrian knowledge of Fire and Sun worship, must have seen at Newgrange, Knowth, Dowth and Tara the reverberating echoes of a once-universal tradition that united all religions, and was their common source. The rituals and observances of the Egyptian religion too were dedicated to the same principles, adopted by the Templars and later Freemasons in their own rites of passage.

They knew that Osiris was behind the mask of the Green Man, and that the essence of all religion was based on the ever-renewing cycles of the Life Force created by the sacred Fire of the Sun. They also knew of the divine intelligence within Nature, and that the Earth, in a real and palpable sense, was a living being, whose network of currents of flowing energy vitalised the land. They left their mark on this ancient landscape too, for another curious thing about Newgrange is the existence of an unusual building very close to the great mound itself.

The walls of this are of an excessive thickness for the scale of its construction, and its large circular 'windows' and vaulted roof makes it seem just like a crypt. It is said to be a medieval dovecote, but what it is doing here no-one seems able to explain. If it is really a dovecote, then we can appreciate the symbolism, for the Dove represents the Holy Spirit which

The curious building known as a 'dovecote' at Newgrange

brings its heavenly grace to Earth at Easter-time, the moment of resurrection. The style of building is, however, unique in this context, for medieval dovecotes are invariably tall circular structures with holes at the top, whilst this one is squat with large round windows and an added chamber. It seems just as likely that it may have been some type of ritual structure built on the site of one of the oldest Temples of Light on Earth.

The Norman knights, the 'new kings' of Ireland, would have also been aware of the old legends from annals like the pre-Norman Codex *The Book of Leinster*, which was copied down in manuscript form just before the arrival of Baron le Fleming. They would have been aware that the Tuatha dé Danaan were also known as 'The Lords of Light', and that Newgrange was 'a magnificent otherworld palace or festive hall, existing in a timeless realm of the supernatural... the domain of gods, a place of perpetual festivities and a wonderful 'land' where no one ever dies.'[4] It was said to contain three fruit trees which perpetually bore fruit, as well as the famous inexhaustible cauldron of the Dagda. His consort was Boanne, the River Goddess whose source was an Otherworld well surrounded by hazel trees, whose nuts fell into the spring and provided mystic inspiration to any who drank the waters.

The Templars' identification with St George also comes into play here, for what must be one of the earliest versions of the legend is specifically attached to Newgrange. The early texts of Irish history state that the owner of the magic mounds, the Dagda, shared them out between himself, Lugh, and Ogma (all different aspects of the Sun God). We have already noted that Ogma is a prehistoric forerunner of George. That 'The Mansion on the Boyne', as Newgrange is called in these texts, belonged to the Dagda, the Father-God, seems particularly appropriate as a place of rebirth, for the word *Dagda*, or *Dadda*, is one of the first sounds uttered by a new-born child. It is also the root of 'dagger'—another form of the Spear of Light, for all these weapons were originally symbolic shafts of sunlight, representing truth and justice.

As recounted in *The Book of Leinster*, one day the Dagda was approached by his son Áengus Mac Óg, who complained that the Great Father had given all the magic mounds of the Sídhe to Lugh and Ogma. It was too late, said the Dagda, for they had already been granted to the other gods. The name Óg immediately alerts us to the fact that the youthful son-of-the-Sun God Áengus is yet another early form of George. Áengus asked for 'a day and a night in thy dwelling', and this was granted. But, in a trick of cosmological wizardy, Áengus claimed, 'It is clear that night and day are the whole world, and it is that which has been given to me'. Áengus was called Mac Óg (or Óc—the g and c are cognate), *'The Young'*, by his mother the river goddess Boanne because he had been born all in one day, a day which had magically been lengthened by the Dagda.[5]

These early stories encode elements of the cosmology of Newgrange, in particular its identity as the supernatural residence of the Sun God who is reborn within it every year. Áengus is clearly the 'Lord of Youth'—the newly-reincarnated son of the old Father God of the dying year. He is born at the time of the Midwinter Solstice, when the actual length of the days increase, just as the legend says. His observation that 'Night and Day are the whole world' is a telling allusion to the ancient division of the year into a bright half (Samh) and a dark half (Gamh), and the Light and Dark that create the cycles of earthly existence.

These 6-month periods, the ancient Summer and Winter, were marked by the Beltane fires in early May, as the Sun's light quickened the fertility of the Earth, and the Feast of Samhain, summer's end, celebrating the start of the dark wintertime. Overlaid on this 'night and day' of the solar cycle were the other great festivals of Imbolc at the beginning of February (the Christian Candlemas still retains elements of fire ritual), and Lughnasad, the Feast of Lugh, the Sun God who brings forth from the Earth the bountiful harvest. All these festivals correspond to the solar alignments of the megalithic mounds, which also operated as a comprehensive calendar of extraordinary accuracy. The transition from the Dark to the Light, the most critical point of all, takes place within Áengus' own magic mound, a cosmically determined ritual attended by the Gods themselves.

The Lord of Love

Áengus, the 'Young God' of Celtic literature, is one of the most beautiful of all the Irish gods and goddesses. He is an eternally youthful exponent of love and beauty, a sort of Gaelic Eros whose kisses become birds which hover invisibly, whispering thoughts of love into the ears of the young men and women of ancient Ireland. He inherits many of his father's characteristics, including a golden harp (The Dagda, as the 'Druid Oak King' of the Solstice, has one of oak) whose music is so sweet that anyone hearing it is obliged to follow the fairy music to his palace of Newgrange.

Áengus is thus an Irish Apollo, whose ever-youthful beauty is the Light of the new-born Sun. One night whilst he dreamt within his palace he was visited by a beautiful maiden who vanished when he tried to embrace her. She appeared again the following night, singing and playing the harp. Áengus was so love-struck he could eat nothing, and after a year of pining for her he was in danger of wasting away. The royal physicians predicted his imminent death if things were not to resolve themselves, so Boanne and the Dagda, distraught that their son might die of unrequited love, determined to find the dream-maiden. Another year passed, but then he received a message to go to a lake called 'Dragon's-Mouth', where he found her, along with her companions, in the form of a graceful white swan of unsurpassed beauty. When he proclaimed his passion for her, the virginal maiden, whose name was Caer, promised to become his bride if he too would become a swan, which he did, and they both flew to his palace of Light, reverted to their human forms, living long and happy lives.

The themes of this tale, one of the earliest legendary accounts so indissolubly linked with the great Temple of Newgrange, have a familiarity that echoes the myth of St George many thousands of years later. Áengus and George, both youthful shining Sun Gods, rescue the Virgin of incomparable beauty from the 'Dragon's Mouth'. Thus they release the true spirit within the land, symbolised here by the serene beauty of the swans, whose royal associations are still strong today. Swans are creatures of Love, and they mate for life. When engaged in their courtship ritual the shape of their necks creates the classic 'heart' shape that has become the universal emblem of loving emotions. Áengus and his bride couple within the dark cave, where the spiral dragon power is fertilised by the cosmic shaft of the life-giving Light.

The Sacred Marriage

Another legend connected with Newgrange, and written down as early as the 10th century, is the famous love story of Diarmud and Gráinne. It ends with the death of the Adonis-like Diarmud, who was brought up by Áengus, and on his demise is taken back to the magic hall of Light so that his adoptive father can 'put an aerial life into him so that he will talk to me every day'.

Gráinne, daughter of Cormac, High King of Ireland, first caught sight of Diarmud during a great banquet at Tara. He had a beauty-spot on his cheek which no woman could set eyes upon without falling instantly in love with him. Even though she was betrothed to the warrior Finn McCool she could not help herself. She passed around a jewelled drinking-horn filled with drugged wine, and all those present drank and fell asleep, except for Diarmud. She told him of her love, and put him under a magic bond to flee with her. They eloped from Tara and sheltered in a hut made of branches until Finn tracked them down and demanded entry. Fortunately Diarmud had a collection of magic weapons, including the 'Red Javelin' and the 'Yellow Javelin'. Áengus also appeared with a mantle of invisibility which Gráinne threw around herself and used to escape. Surrounded, Diarmud took a giant leap which took him to the place where Áengus and Gráinne had sought refuge.

They lived in a wood and hunted wild animals for food, but Gráinne, with child at the time, was overcome by the desire to eat enchanted berries, the food of immortality. This led to Diarmud killing the guardian and stealing the fruit, but fighting for his life again as he battled with Finn and his men who were intent on revenge. Gráinne was yet again spirited away using the magic cloak of Áengus. In the version known as ***The Pursuit of Diarmud and Gráinne*** Finn is undaunted and gives chase, causing Áengus' death when his foot is pierced by a poisoned bristle from an animal skin. (Like the Greek Achilles, the young god is invulnerable except for his heel).

This old cycle of tales, much garbled over the centuries, eventually passed into medieval romance as the ***Legend of Dermot and Graney***, but evidence suggests its true provenance is in the ages of remote prehistory. Gráinne is a Sun Goddess (the Irish word for the Sun today is *Grian*, also used as a girl's name meaning 'Brightness and Beauty'). It seems in the earliest matriarchal times the Sun was considered female. In old English, the word for the Sun, *Sunne*, was also feminine, as was the Saxon goddess Oestre who gave her name to the East and Easter, when the old New Year began at the Spring Equinox, March 25th.

Diarmud (sometimes *Diarmud Donn*) is the old god of the underworld, the later versions of the story having reduced both god and goddess to humans, albeit with magical powers. The name Gráinne, besides being a reference to the Sun of a previous matriarchal age, gives further clues to her great antiquity as her name includes Áine, Ana or Anu, the goddess of the Tuatha Dé Danaan. It also gives us grain, the fruits of the Earth's fertility.

In ***Mythic Ireland*** Michael Dames observes that megalithic 'passage graves' were formerly known as the *'Beds of Dermot and Graney'* where the two lovers were supposed to have united in nights of passionate love-making.[6] He likens the form of many of these structures to that of a stone chamber representing the body of the goddess, which was 'entered' by those seeking to know her mysteries as well as being fertilised by the Light of the Sun. Throughout Ireland these monuments were widely known for their erotic power, being favourite places for lover's trysts. Even in the early 1900s this tradition was still strong, when they were called 'Darby and Grane's Beds' because of their aphrodisiac properties and ensuing popularity with young couples. The Victorian archaeologist W.C. Borlase, in ***The Dolmens of Ireland***, noted that such Neolithic chambers were invariably associated with libidinous activity, and also believed to cure infertility. In County Clare alone he found no fewer than twenty-two such places.

At Lough Gur in Munster is one of the great Neolithic ritual centres of Ireland, whose waters have revealed a vast trove of treasures now scattered throughout the museums of the world. Here, the 'Bed of Dermot and Graney' (also known as the 'Giant's Grave') is dated to 2600 BC, and the local legend relates that upon entering the chamber, Diarmud discovered that he was in possession of a Golden Sword. Is this a memory of the real purpose of these 'tombs', of a shaft of sunlight penetrating the dark womb of the Goddess to create a 'Child of the Light', the reborn consciousness of the initiate? The Irish word *colg* means both sword and phallus, as well as the sheath around a grain of wheat. As the Light fertilises the female powers of the Dragon a similar process takes place within the individual. In the Qabalah this is symbolised by a flash of lightning (*Barak* in Semitic, *Baraka* in Sufism) which at the critical moment enters through the top of the head and shoots through the energetic centres of the body to awaken the coiled dragon power at the base of the spine. In Egyptian tradition this is represented by the Djed pillar, the spine of Osiris, the Ever-renewing God of the Underworld.

All this is part of the universality behind the Mystery traditions of antiquity. The 'beds' of the union between the Light and the Dark Matter of Earth are alchemical vessels of transmutation, just like the Temples of Egypt and the Boyne Valley. Wherever there are megalithic monuments we see evidence of this, and across the Celtic world are many thousands of Neolithic structures whose legends speak of the Giants of the Sun and Earth, or of the solar King Arthur, who later took over from them. In these later legends the weapon of Light is Excalibur, the 'Sword in the Stone', that is, the power of Light trapped within the Earth. He who understands how to draw it out discovers his true kingship over the earthly realms.

The Dragon's Treasure

In the centre of Lough Gur (notice how both the name of the place and the presiding goddess begin with the *g* letter signifying the Earth) is the enchanted island of Knockadoon, once one of the most densely populated Neolithic settlements in the country. The eastern section of the lake was drained and connected by causeways to the mainland in the 18th century, when a remarkable collection of gold artefacts and chariot fittings were uncovered, as well as hundreds of cattle skulls deposited in a ritual manner. No less than 20 bronze axes, 12 spearheads, 2 swords, a rapier, a number of daggers and 120 stone axes have been found so far. A network of prehistoric wooden trackways, similar to those at Glastonbury, also existed until they were burnt as fuel.

Before the current age of rationalism elected new gods of the mundane and prosaic, this sacred lake was one of the great portals to the underworld, and those that lived within its mystical aura recounted many strange and otherworldly experiences. Clustered around the magic lake are a number of weathered limestone caves which were believed to be entrances to the regions within the realms of the Earth Goddess. One is called the Money Hole because it was said to contain a crock of gold (as had been found in the lake bed), and another is still known as Tir na nÓg, The Land of Eternal Youth, like many others across the country. Unlike the Christian tradition that such places lead to Hell, full of fire and damnation, such caves possessed the reputation of being places of transformation. Within their womb-like atmosphere one can still be inspired by 'a strange familiarity derived from pre-natal emotions, which the unconscious mind clothes in pictures of a fairy land.' Not only the caves, the lairs of the female Dragon power, invoke such strange and archaic thoughts. The whole area was noted for its powers of enchantment, and the local people were in awe of its mystical attributes, which might lead one to enter the underworld, never to return. Reports of strange lights in the sky, and eerie 'fairy' whirlwinds over the lake, only endorsed its reputation as a place where different realities converged. The poet Fitzgerald noted in 1879 that 'even to fall asleep in daytime on its banks was considered to be reckless folly'. The entire vicinity was a mystical place of rebirth, and the sacred island was thought to be the body of the Goddess herself, with the cave of Tir na nÓg her vulva, as if the Earth was a vast Sheela-na-gig.

Caves such as those at Lough Gur have always been known for their inspirational qualities and their power to transport one into other dimensions. Edmund Spenser, the Elizabethan author of **The Faery Queen**, noted that even in the 16th century poets and bards recited their great works (which often went on for many hours, even days) whilst lying in the darkness of the cave entrances to Tir na nÓg or facing them, out of respect for the sources of their art. Their apprenticeship was deeply involved with such places, and long periods were spent within the underground chambers learning and composing sacred poems. They were the Dragon-tamers of their day, absorbing the inspirational and transcendent powers issuing from the body of the Earth Goddess, and trans-forming it, as well as themselves, into an expression of the Divine.

As Michael Dames has noted, these entrances to the Otherworld 'all led towards music (often played on a harp), a magic tree (frequently of gold and silver, from which a sacred branch was plucked), divine horses and birds of dazzling colours, a banquet where a cauldron of ale was always full, and where an unearthly kind of Time was enjoyed. Central to the vision, its source and overseer, stood the figure of a beautiful woman.' At Lough Gur there are also legends of a Wild Hunt with its pursuing hounds of death and a ghostly Druidic horse. The mythic hero Finn McCool was believed to have chased the Sun Goddess here too, (as recorded in a 12th century manuscript), arriving at the start of the Harvest celebrations.

The Harvest not only refers to the gathering of the grain to provide sustenance until the Sun is reborn the following year, but the Harvest of the Soul as well, where all the experiences of life are gathered up before the last sheaf, or 'head' is cut. As the corn is cut and dies, it gives us life, and as we die we are given life anew. The Harvest at Lough Gur is cosmologically marked on the landscape by an alignment directed to the Lughnasad, (or Lammas), sunrise. It passes through a megalith on a grassy knoll known as the 'Housekeeper's Chair' and a Neolithic circular platform on the smaller Garret Island, where there is also a tower built by the Norman family of the Desmonds.

This island is named after Geároid, a legendary figure who was responsible, along with the Goddess, for the formation of the sacred lake (note the first syllable, meaning *Earth*). Although he became a feature of the many legends that still haunt the place, Geároid was a historical person, born in 1338 and the second Earl of Desmond. He was a noted poet and mystic, and his themes were those discussed here, including the story of Diarmud and Gráinne. As the son of an invader, he may well have been of Templar inclination, for he immersed himself in the mystical traditions of the area and was known by local people as 'an enchanted magician, a periodic rider, a lost leader whose return is awaited, and a feared King of the fairy host'. He was also said to practice witchcraft, and was believed to have drowned in the waters of the lake whilst under a spell of enchantment, like a willing sacrifice to the Goddess.

His folkloric name is Gé an Oileán—the Goose of the Island. (Curious indeed that the Egyptian Earth-God Geb was depicted as a goose, and that they both in this case share the old word for the Earth—*Ge*). Having descended from a family who were said to have webbed feet, he was transformed into the bird as he stepped from the lakeside near his castle, which still stands today. The lake is now a wildfowl sanctuary and geese still inhabit it, nesting on his island. That the Desmonds were adherents of some form of Celtic Revival perpetuating prehistoric beliefs and practices is apparent; they also placed a striking carving of a Sheela-na-gig in their castle at Caherelly near the lake. She can still be seen in the Limerick Museum, but without her head.

The Lughnasad alignment running through Geároid's island also passes directly through the most impressive of all the Irish stone circles, the Lios (enclosure), at nearby Grange. The similarity of the name to Newgrange suggests it too may have once belonged to a monastic estate. However, today its preservation is not funded by any official body. It is carefully tended by local farmer Tim Casey at his own expense, with occasional donations from visitors.

The Lios' significance is not linked to the Newgrange/Winter Solstice rebirth, but Beltane and Harvest-time, or the Feast of Lughnasad, for the alignment coincides with the position of the rising Sun at both these times. At these moments in the yearly cycle the Spear of Lugh flies along this axis to enter the stone circle and create a mystical bond, the sacred marriage, between Sun and Earth.

18

Harvest of Souls

The local name for the magnificent stone circle and ritual enclosure at Grange is the Lios of Crom Dubh. The circle comprises a ring of 113 upright megaliths, yet not all of them appear contemporary. Some of them are great dressed slabs which are more reminiscent of an Egyptian Temple. The biggest of all is a cyclopean megalith in the north-eastern quarter known as Rannach Crom Dubh, the Harvest God of Lughnasad. It is the presiding presence, a god trapped in stone, and adjacent to it is a rustic shrine, a small stone altar with offerings of coins and flowers left by those who still venerate the ancient spirit of this place. The gargantuan stone stands close to the entrance, which is aligned with great precision to the Beltane/Lughnasad sunrise and its corollary, the corresponding Imbolc/Samhain sunset. This was originally noted by an early researcher into the alignments of prehistoric monuments, Admiral Boyle T. Somerville. As well as broken fragments of pottery of the 'Beaker Folk' similar to that found throughout Europe, he excavated a post hole at the centre of the circle, the remains of a central 'pole' or gnomon for determining an accurate alignment with the other sites on the Beltane/Lughnasad axis.

The great megalith of Rannach Crom Dubh, named after the prehistoric God of the Harvest

Remarkably this great ceremonial centre was originally only one of three within a very short distance of each other. The remaining stones of a second, which was even larger, but destroyed by roadbuilders, are still to be found to the west, along with the remains of a chambered cairn. A third, smaller circle can also be seen

Setting sun at the Lios of Crom Dubh, with the two 'Horn Stones' to the left, sending their long shadows into the stone circle.

to the east, with some large stones remaining. These were all part of an entire ceremonial landscape around the sacred lake. But the alignment within the Lios of Crom Dubh shows that the most significant motive behind the design of these structures was not simply to create a place of ritual; they were built as places of solar alchemy.

The main axis of the circle, aligned with the entrance passage, also points to two distinctly shaped triangular stones on the opposite side, although one has lost its tip. These stones resemble the horns of a great bull, creating a notch where the blood-red sky and its setting Sun would have been seen to sink on the horizon of a Neolithic Spring or Autumn. An observer standing at the opening of the circle would thus see the spectacle of the setting Sun vanishing between the megalithic horns. Excavations have revealed the burnt remains of bulls which were ritually eaten during the festivities. It is likely too that the sunken megaliths, all virtually touching each other, formed a bullring, for Crom Dubh was, amongst other things, a Bull God. This was an important aspect of Osiris as well, for he represented animal fertility as well that of the plant kingdom. The date of construction of these Neolithic structures coincided with the Age of Taurus, when the Sun rose in the sign of the Bull God at the Spring Equinox, so the bull represented a mystic as well as physical virility. The image of the Sun entering the bull's head at sunset would have had a profound significance, as it had been born in the constellation of Taurus at the previous Equinox.

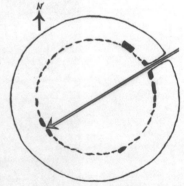

The Spear of Lugh piercing the embanked stone circle of Crom Dubh, with its tip pointing between the 'Horn Stones'.

Crom Dubh is one of the oldest of the Irish gods, his festivals later taken over by Lugh of the Tuatha dé Danaan as Lughnasad. Marie Macneill, in her classic work *The Festival of Lughnasa,*[1] studied almost 200 sites in Ireland where this annual harvest celebration took place. These were mere fragments of a once-great ritual festival that occurred right across the country to mark the approach of the end of Summer, just as the Beltane rites of the God of Spring were once universal. Crom Dubh or Crom Cruach was so popular in the folkloric tradition that it appears he may have been a truly primeval god, of such great antiquity that he was displaced by the later legends, which are themselves of considerable age. Yet Macneill found that worship of the original god was central to the rituals, and believed he was none other than a previous incarnation of the Dagda. This would make the Lios of Crom Dubh an 'ever-renewing cauldron' that endlessly repeated the cycles of the heavens, a microcosm of the wider universe.

His name means 'The Dark Bent One', because he presided over the ageing, dark half of the year. He stooped because he carried the sacred sheaf of wheat on his back, the gift of Life from the underworld forces that caused the soil to become fructile. In County Limerick his festival was still celebrated until the mid-19th century as 'Black Stoop Sunday'. Like the Dagda he also possessed a magical forked staff similar to the Uaz sceptre of ancient Egypt, and an image of this, laid out in stones, was excavated at the Lios. The widespread and persistent traditions show that Crom Dubh was once regarded as the most powerful god in Ireland until displaced by the Christian missionary St Patrick.

Like Osiris, also depicted with a black face, he was the Lord of the Underworld, and taught people the arts of cultivation, including the use of the plough and the storage of grain in granaries. As the god of the golden harvest he brought bread, the Lammas Loaf, and the dark beer known as porter, brewed from malted barley, just like his Egyptian counterpart.

They were both Bull Gods too, and brought the virile powers of the Sun into the Temples, in this case with the Spear of Light which aligns precisely with the bull's horns. The Bull mythology of Osiris and Crom Dubh may even have been incorporated into early Christianity as the symbol of St Luke, whose name so closely echoes that of Lugh. It was in the waters of Lough Gur, directly on this extended Lughnasad axis, that a Bronze Age spear inlaid with a golden sunbeam was found.

The Bull God with three Ears of Wheat or Barley, the emblem of the influential and ancient Drewe family. From Youghal Church, Co. Cork.

*St Michael's fiery sword raised heavenwards,
from a painting by George Segal*

The Sword of the Sun

Crom Dubh, as the dark god of the underworld, seems to be the earthly counterpart of Lugh, just as St George is the earthier twin of St Michael. As Lugh's popularity was universal in the Celtic world, a new replacement Christian 'god' took on his roles and attributes. Lugh the Sun God of harvest-time was thus transformed into St Michael (whose name means, 'Who is as God'), with Lugh's Spear becoming the Fiery Sword held aloft by the shining archangel. The overwhelming popularity of St Michael in Ireland seems entirely due to the fact that he is a reincarnation of Lugh.

The cosmic balance between Lugh and Crom Dubh is reflected in later times by the feast of Michaelmas, the Autumnal Equinox when Light and Dark are in equal balance all over the world. For this reason St Michael is often shown holding the scales of Libra in one hand, whilst in his other is the radiant sword. The essential difference between the heavenly and earthly twins of Michael and George is dramatically portrayed by their respective weapons of Light.

Michael's Sword is often shown pointing heavenwards, symbolising victory, whilst George's Spear is directed towards the Earth—in fact into the Earth, and its caves and wells inhabited by the female Dragon Power, the Feminine principle in Nature which later ages did so much to vilify. Michael's intimate connection with his earthier brother was still remembered, though, in the traditional eating of the Michaelmas Goose, the sacred bird of the old Earth Gods.

Michael's sword is of the Sun, and he became the new presiding deity right at the beginning of the Christian age, taking over the sanctuaries of the old Sun Gods of former times. Like Lugh's Spear, Michael's 'Sword' can be seen as a series of aligned sites that are cosmically oriented, determined by the rising and setting Sun. These may be localised as at Lough Gur, but other Sun-Lines extend for great distances. Evidence points to the fact that they exist all over the world, the remnants of a prehistoric science that was dedicated to the Forces of Nature. In Britain what has become known as the St Michael Line runs for some 360 miles from the very westernmost tip of Cornwall, via Glastonbury and Avebury, to the east coast of Norfolk. In its path are a great number of significant sites dedicated to St Michael, St George, and the Virgin St Mary.

Glastonbury's reputation as the first Christian Church in the West, dedicated to St Mary, and its associations with both St George and St Michael—whose tower stands on the famous Glastonbury Tor pointing heavenwards like a sword—preserve a strong memory of this science of natural cycles.

The axis of the sacred hill corresponds with the countrywide alignment which is directed towards the position of the rising Sun at Beltane. This was the time of the old May Rites which (like those preserved at Helston) included both St Michael and St George taming the Dragon, the female powers of the Earth. This axis also corresponds to the Harvest Festival of Lughnasad, for due to the extraordinary symmetry of the solar cycle the Sun sets at this time beyond its western extremity.

This alignment, or 'corridor', created by the blade of Michael's Sword, as well as passing through a wealth of churches overwhelmingly dedicated to these three saints, also runs straight through the entrance stones of the great Serpent Temple of Avebury, where the Norman font in the church portrays the Dragon-taming Bishops. This was the centre of the May Rites of prehistory, taking place at exactly that time when the Sun and Earth created a heavenly and terrestrial axis linking all these places together, and shooting the lightning flash of the rising Sun along the mystical axis of Southern Britain.

Also on this line is Ogbourne St George, reminding us that George and the old Celtic Sun God are one and the same. The Neolithic sacred centre of Stowe's Hill on Bodmin Moor in Cornwall is also accurately aligned, and marks the crossing point of the St Michael Line with that leading between Tintagel and Plymouth, another solsticial 'Sword of Light', this time linked with the solar King Arthur. Close to its eastern extremity lies the ruined Abbey of Bury St Edmunds with its large Norman tower bearing prominent Dragon's Heads, exactly like those at Kilpeck.[1]

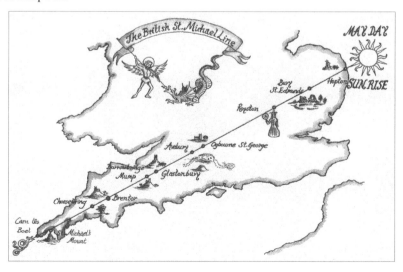

A further, perhaps even more striking example of Michael's cosmic Sword bringing the Sun's power to Earth, is the 'Apollo/St Michael Axis' which runs right across Europe, taking in its path the major St Michael centres of antiquity, as well as a great many other notable places. These include the island sanctuary of Skellig Michael, just off the coast of Ireland, St Michael's Mount in Cornwall, Mont St Michel in Normandy, Sagra di San Michele in the Alps, Monte Sant' Angelo on the 'spur' of Italy, and the Temple of Apollo at Delphi in Greece. Here it becomes clear how the Dragon-slaying St Michael absorbed the character of former Sun Gods like Apollo, who despatched the Python with his golden arrows. This alignment, originally discovered by the French researchers Jean and Lucien Richer, also leads to Mount Carmel in the Holy Land, the place of an early fire-duel between the prophet Elijah and the pagan priests of Baal, signifying the very beginnings of Biblical Christianity.[2]

The entire Earth is covered with a network of these Sun-Lines that were set by the seasonal cycles of fertility, marking the interaction between the Sword of Light from the Sun and the topographical sites where the Earth's Dragon energies are naturally concentrated. This alchemical reaction between the Heavenly and Earthly realms was always understood to have a powerful effect upon the fertile seeds within the soil, and a corresponding quickening power over humanity's own spiritual development. This is the true meaning of the Green Man, and the spirit of earthly renewal in all its forms. Thus St George and his heavenly twin St Michael are the two great symbols of cosmic order, as well as the eternal guides of humanity, who beckon us to tame our own Dragons and resume our true role as guardians of the Laws of Nature.

Thanksgiving

A century or so ago, harvest-time would have been a memorable and much-celebrated occasion in the countryside. In ***Hones Every-day Book*** of 1826, a gentleman farmer describes the moving effect it had upon him when 'on a fine still autumn evening' the sound of local people performing a timeless rite had 'a wonderful effect at a distance'. He tells of a countryside where the people are part of its living traditions, and how he would hear upwards of twenty men—often joined by maids, women and children—'Crying the Neck'. Standing on a high hill it was possible to hear six or more groups of harvesters in the distance performing the ceremony: 'They are heard throughout the quiet evening air, at a considerable distance sometimes. But I think that the practice is beginning to decline of late, and many farmers and their men do not care about keeping up the old custom. I shall always patronise it myself, because I take it in the light of thanksgiving'.

To be present at such a rite would have left a strong impression. In the last field of corn there would have been an air of intense excitement and anticipation, for the field had been harvested down to its last small patch of standing corn. As it is cut, the last handful of living crop containing the spirit of the harvest god is grabbed by one of the elders who fashions a mannikin, binding it at the waist and neck with gaily-coloured ribbon. Around him move the reapers in a circle, and as the figure is lowered to the ground they remove their hats and their fingers touch it with reverence. A long, melancholy cry is uttered as they raise themselves upright. This is repeated three times, each time with greater abandon. The long lamenting cry of 'The Neck' is replaced by 'The Neck! The Neck! The Neck!' and then 'We Have 'Un! We Have 'Un!' accompanied by irrepressible laughter and hats now flung high into the air. In the ensuing merriment girls are kissed and there is good-natured larking in general. After a scuffle, the 'Neck' is snatched by a young man who runs off with it towards the farm, where, waiting for him, is a milkmaid with a pail of water. Her task is to throw the water over him and the Corn God as he enters the house.

This ritual is exceedingly ancient; even Herodotus reports the same thing occurring in his day, accompanied by exaggerated melancholy and repetitive cries. The Corn God is dead! Earlier times no doubt witnessed a far more alarming scene, for the effigy replaced a real sacrificial victim whose blood was believed to fertilise the fields, magically impregnating them with the spirit of the God for the next season. Perhaps a dim memory of such ritual murder explains the reluctance shown in some rites in Wales, where the participants were loath to assume responsibility for the God's death. After cutting the last sheaf they would throw scythes at it from a distance, thereby sharing the responsibility.

The joy of Harvest—the completion of the summer cycle, with its bounty to see the country through to next Spring—must have been tangible throughout the land. After the anxieties of wind and weather the relief must have been profound. The corn is in, the waggon and horses garlanded with ribbons and flowers, and seated upon the leading horse is a pretty maid dressed in white over whom is triumphantly raised a single sheaf of the best corn in the field, arranged and decorated to resemble a human shape. The Harvest homecoming was accompanied with fiddles, pipes, drums, songs and laughter, and the diarist John Aubrey comments, 'It is donne with great joy and merriment'. A celebration banquet ensued with much cakes and ale consumed by the local people, dressed in their best. With a shining Harvest Moon lighting the silver fields, the effigy, now called a 'Corn Baby', in recognition of its rebirth the following year, was hung from the rafters, where it slowly turned like the seasons of the year, from Lammas to Lammas.

How poignant that today the end of Harvest is accompanied by nothing more than the sound of tractors and combine harvesters, some as big as a house. No voices can be heard above the roar of the machinery, and otherwise the fields are silent and deserted, as if lamenting the days when the countryside, and the fertility of the land itself, was so closely bound up with humanity. Man may be able to live by bread alone, but it is a life of shallow pleasures and spiritual disharmony. We have gained a dubious abundance but lost our roots in the Earth, the source of our being. Joyless, mechanical, we no longer honour the old spirits of the land. Will we be surprised if the spirits of the land no longer honour us? Even in the 19th century the passing of such rituals was lamented, and in the summer of 1843 Robert Stephen Hawker, the Vicar of Morwenstow in Cornwall, reinstated something of the old ways by introducing the Harvest Festival. Although it takes place later in the season it is at the very least a prayer and thanksgiving for the Fruits of the Earth.

As we sow, so shall we reap.

Postscript

The Awakening Power

At the core of all true religions are unseen mystical forces that are the essence of transformation and the continuous process of creation. Throughout history they have been given as many different names as there are languages, but whatever they may be called these forces are responsible for the spiritual evolution of the individual and humanity as a whole.

In the Christian tradition the Holy Spirit is the purest form of this universal energy, which can descend like a revelation, changing one's perspective instantly. In Sufism and the Qabalah this is symbolised by a flash of lightning striking down from the topmost crown of the Tree of Life to bring its heavenly power to Earth.

In these traditions this power is known as Baraka or Ruach. It descends from the ever-present Breath of God, the Pneuma of the Greeks. This Breath pervades all things, invisibly and continuously flowing between them. In the Oriental systems it is the ch'i or prana, the Life Force. It circulates throughout the human body as well as the body of the Earth, and is concentrated at certain organs or nexus points where it both regulates and creates a reservoir of essential energies.

On an earthly level this universal spiritual energy is known as Kundalini or Shakti, and is symbolised by a snake or Dragon. Tibetan yogis call it Tumo, an inner heat or fire that rises up from the lower regions, creating often miraculous effects. It can be transmitted from one individual to another through touch or mental direction, and can be used for healing.

More recent researchers who have studied the various forms of these energies have called them by the names Vril, Odic Force or Orgone energy. Within a dark room or cave these can be seen as a shimmering bluish haze emanating especially from crystals, magnets, living creatures and fissures in the Earth itself. Wilhelm Reich believed that Orgone, as he called it, was the fundamental energy of life, and that its blockage or misuse was the cause of ill-health and disease. He also noticed that when streams of energy converged, they usually formed spirals.

All these different categories of energy are manifestations of the one true Spirit. In the Veda at least ten types of prana are noted within the human body, whilst the Taoists found over thirty. The science and study of these subtle energies was, in the past, one of the most important, for they were known to be at the very root of all earthly Life.

When certain types of this universal energy come together the effect can be transformational, even explosive, and in the Indian tradition the arousal of the Kundalini is a discipline for experienced practitioners. The Dragon power, if unleashed too soon, can overwhelm the consciousness of the individual. Yet this force, in all its forms, is the motive power behind all existence and evolution.

The Holy Spirit, in the form of a Dove, descends to Earth at Easter-time on Good Friday, and brings resurrection and renewal. The Dove and the Dragon, as symbols of the heavenly and earthly powers that bring rebirth and spiritual awakening, are twin aspects of the Holy Spirit that create life and inspire us to look beyond the visible world to a greater reality.

The science of the Dragon Power was a major consideration in early church building. First the exact site was selected, invariably a place where the forces of Nature had already been honoured for a great length of time. Then a tower aligned to the four cardinal directions was built. Its construction was deliberately heavy, with thick walls so that the weight of the building created a strong pressure on the Earth below; this caused the energy to rise up and concentrate in the space within. To facilitate this even further, a specially tuned bell was hung in the tower. The craft of bellfoundry is closely allied to alchemy, and the amalgam of metals used was of great significance. A pit was dug at the base of the tower for the smelting, and the bell was made on site, for during the process it absorbed certain emanations that increased its resonance.

When the bell was hung in the tower and struck, it sounded a particular frequency that set the building vibrating, for this was understood to raise the Dragon power more efficiently. The sound of the bell and shaking of the thick walls combined to create an intense atmosphere within. Later developments led to the buildings being extended, with Naves (from the word navel) forming an umbilical connection with the source of the energy. This new building was aligned on a current of natural force which, when activated by the bells, swept along its axis and through the congregation, their song and prayer raising the long-wavelength frequencies to a higher pitch. As this current of energy passed beyond the area of the rood screen it entered the Choir, where trained vocalists chanted sacred anthems and invocations specially composed to refine it even further.

By the time this flowing current of Dragon power reached the eastern end of the building it had been 'tuned' to a high level and become a form of pure spiritual energy available for transmutation. The priest performed a magical ritual designed to transform this into a higher form altogether, where the altar became a reservoir of spiritual energies which could *alter* the consciousness of those present. At that moment, the Sun rose directly in the East and a shaft of Light illuminated the altar, charging the golden chalice and other ritual objects with mystical force. The wine within the chalice, and the sacred bread that had been specially prepared, absorbed this energy and became imbued with a power that, when eaten and drunk by those present, manifested a profound spiritual experience and feeling of being at one with Creation itself, born of the Sun and Earth.

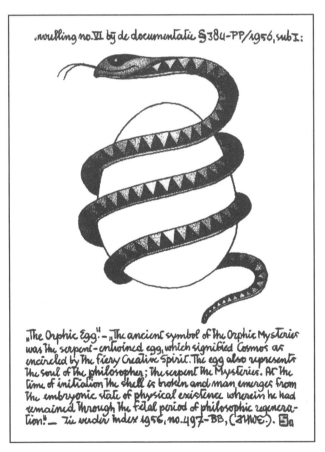

THE SUN AND THE SERPENT
Paul Broadhurst and Hamish Miller

In the late 1980s two researchers into ancient mysteries began a remarkable journey of discovery across southern Britain. Their quest began at St Michael's Mount, and led them to Glastonbury, Avebury and the east coast, and included a great number of ancient sites, some famous and many that had almost been forgotten. Their discoveries as they travelled along the St Michael Line, a countrywide alignment of sites dedicated to St Michael, have deep implications for our understanding of why these places have been so important in previous ages, and why so many people are drawn to visit them today. This account of their adventures and discoveries, written by researcher and photographer Paul Broadhurst, details their quest for a rediscovery of the forces of Nature that create the 'spirit of place'. With maps and plans by dowser Hamish Miller, this book provokes a realisation that in former times, the Earth was understood to be a living being whose powers were considered sacred.

> *'The Sun and the Serpent is one of the strangest, most stirring books I have ever read, and it may prove through its implications to be one of the most important. For if the authors are correct in what they affirm, they have uncovered in the English landscape the most remarkable of ancient secrets'*
>
> *John Michell*

216 page paperback , b/w and colour illustrations £12.95 plus £3 pp

THE DANCE OF THE DRAGON
Paul Broadhurst and Hamish Miller, with Vivienne Shanley and Ba Russell

The Apollo/St Michael axis is a remarkable alignment of sacred sites stretching from Ireland, through Cornwall, France, Italy, Greece and Israel, marked by sanctuaries dedicated to the Archangel Michael and Apollo, the Greek God of Light. Over ten years, the authors travel the length of this 2,500 mile axis exploring the significance of earth energies in the siting of these sanctuaries. Rediscovered in this book is a profound principle that takes us back to the very roots of religion, encoded in legend and myth. This demonstrates that earth energies were once at the core of a highly developed Natural Science responsible for determining the position and character of ancient sites.

> *The romance of this extraordinary journey so permeates every page that the reader is drawn, exquisitely and irrevocably onwards, as if on the crest of a wave. And yet, having travelled so far, the dazzling nature of each revelation emerges to underscore the romance, and at the journey's end I wanted to start all over again... To have started from Skellig Michael off the coast of Ireland and to have ended up at Armageddon is no mean feat and ten years of labour have flowered into a beautiful, sometimes lonely, oftimes revealing, pilgrimage of the hidden and, for so long, now, neglected pathways of the Earth.*
>
> *David Elkington*

378 page paperback, b/w and colour illustrations, £18.50 plus £5 pp

Both available direct from
MYTHOS, Box 888, Launceston, Cornwall, PL15 7YH, U.K.

References and Bibliography

1: A Legend Obscured
1. *St George* E.O.Gordon *Swan Sonnenschein & Co Ltd 1907*
2. *op cit*
3. *op cit*
4. *Calendar* David Ewing Duncan *Avon Books 1998*
5. *St George op cit*
6. *op cit*
7. **English Folk Heroes** Christina Hole *Batsford 1948*
8. **Lives of the British Saints** S. Baring-Gould & J. Fisher *London 1907*

2: Lord of Sun and Earth
1. *The Four Seasons and the Archangels* Rudolf Steiner *Anthroposophical Society 1985*
2. *Calendar op cit*
3. *op cit*
4. *Earth Rites* Janet & Colin Bord *Book Club Associates 1982*
5. *The Avebury Cycle* Michael Dames *Thames and Hudson 1977*

3: Green George
1. *Where is St George? Pagan imagery in English Folksong* R.J.Stewart *Moonraker Press 1977*
2. *Opinions vary amongst researchers, with the ratio ranging from ten to one into hundreds.*
3. *Green Man* William Anderson *HarperCollins 1990*
4. *Gawain and the Green Knight Brian Stone* Pendragon Magazine, 2002
5. *The Devil* Peter Stanford *William Heinemann 1996*

4: The Name of the God
1. *In the Name of the Gods* David Elkington *Green Man Press 2001*
2. *The Sumerians* Leonard Woolley *Norton Library & OUP 1965*
3. *History of the Kings of Britain* Geoffrey of Monmouth *Folio Society 1969*
4. *Tintagel and the Arthurian Mythos* Paul Broadhurst *Pendragon Press 1992*
5. *Examples of these found on site by the author.*
6. **The Mysteries of Britain** Lewis Spence *Rider & Co. 1970*

5: The Mystic Way of St George
1. *The Sufis* Idries Shah *W.H.Allen 1964*
2. See Postscript
3. *A Life on the Edge* Robert Graves Miranda Seymour *Doubleday 1995*
4. *The Sufis op cit*
5. *The Rise of the Gothic* William Anderson *Hutchinson 1985*
6. *The Arabian Connection* Dr Kasem Khaleel *Knowledge House Publishers 2000*
7. *op cit*
8. *The Sufis op cit*
9. *The Golden Bough* J.G.Frazer *Macmillan & Co 1933*
10. Private correspondence
11. *Qutub* Andrew Chumbley *Ignotus Press*

6: St George and the Mysteries of Albion
1. *St George* E.O. Gordon *op cit*
2. *Glastonbury's Temple of the Stars* Katherine Maltwood J*ames Clarke & Co. 1929*
3. *St George op cit*
4. *The Romance of St George's Chapel, Windsor* Harry Blackburne *Raphael Tuck 19335.*
5. *St George op cit*
6. *St George op cit*
7. *The Golden Bough op cit*
8. *The God of the Witches* Margaret Murray *Oxford University Press 1952*
9. *Hey John Barleycorn* Helen French *The Cauldron August 2002*

9: The Assembly of the Wondrous Head
1. *Myths and Legends of the Celtic Race* T.W. Rolleston *George Harrap & Co. 1912*
2. *The Templars and the Assassins* James Wasserman *Inner Traditions 2001*
3. *The Head of God* Keith Laidler *Weidenfeld and Nicholson 1998*
4. *op cit*

8: Message from the Templars
1. *In the Name of the Gods op cit*
2. *The Rise of the Gothic* William Anderson *Hutchinson & Co 1985*
3. *Green Man op cit*
4. *St George op cit*

9: The Dragon Power
1. *The View over Atlantis* John Michell *Garnstone Press 1969*
2. *The Pattern of the Past* Guy Underwood *Abelard-Schuman Ltd 1973*
3. *The Power of Ch'i* Michael Page *Aquarian 1988*
4. *Feng-shui* Ernest J. Eitel *Trubner & Co. 1873*
5. *The Power of Ch'i* op cit
6. *The Chakras* C.W. Leadbeater *Theosophical Publishing House 1927*
7. *The Old Straight Track* Alfred Watkins *Methuen & Co 1925*
8. *The Parish Church of Kilpeck* James Bailey *Five Seasons Press 2000*
9. *Quoted at the Hundertwasser Museum in Vienna*

10: Heavenly Treasures
1. *Rosslyn* Tim Wallace-Murphy and Marilyn Hopkins *Element 2000*
2. *The Stone Puzzle of Rosslyn Chapel* Philip Coppens *Frontier Publishing 2002*
3. *op cit*
4. *Stonehenge and other British Stone Monuments Astronomically Considered*
   Norman Lockyer *Macmillan & Co 1909*
5. *Megalithic Sites in Britain* Alexander Thom *OUP 1967*
6. *The View over Atlantis* op cit
7. *Greek Myths* Robert Graves *Penguin 1960*

11: The Dragon of Revelation
1. *The Cult of the Black Virgin* Ean Begg *Arkana 1985*
2. *The Holy Blood and the Holy Grail* Baigent, Leigh and Lincoln *Jonathan Cape 1982*
3. *The Mysteries of Chartres Cathedral* Louis Charpentier *RILKO 1988*
4. *Points of Cosmic Energy* Blanche Merz *C.W. Daniel 1987*

12: A Search in Secret Egypt
1. *The Setian* Billie Walker John *Ignotus Press 2003*
2. *Gods of Ancient Egypt* Barbara Watterson *Bramley Books 1996*
3. *Conversation with David Elkington*
4. *Occidental Mythology* Joseph Campbell *Souvenir Press 2001*

13: The Green God of the Nile
1. *Greek Myths* op cit
2. **Op cit**
3. *Gods of Ancient Egypt* op cit
4. *op cit*
5. *Where is St George?* Op cit

14: The Art of Dragon Taming
1. *The Life of St Sampson of Dol* Thomas Taylor *Llanerch 1991*
2. *British Dragons* Jacqueline Simpson *Batsford 1980*
3. *Science and Civilisation in China* Joseph Needham *Cambridge University Press 1956*
4. *The Earth Spirit* John Michell *Thames & Hudson 1975*
5. *Celtic Heritage* Alwyn and Brinley Rees *Thames and Hudson 1961*
6. *The History of the Kings of Britain* op cit

15: Return of the Dragon Slayers
1. *Prehistoric London* E.O.Gordon *Covenant Publishing 1932*
2. *St Priapus* Ian McNeil Cooke *Men-an-Tol Studio 2002*
3. *Dragons of the West* Nigel Pennick *Capall Bann 1997*
5. *The Cosmic Serpent* Jeremy Narby *Gollancz 1998*

16: The Spear of Light
1. *Arcadia* Peter Dawkins *Francis Bacon Research Trust 1988*
2. *Op cit*
3. *The Sun* Georg Blattmann *Floris Books 1985*
4. *Celtic Myth and Legend* Charles Squire *Newcastle Publishing 1975*
5. *Beauties of the Boyne and the Blackwater* Sir William Wilde *McGlashan and Gill 1849*
6. *The Stars and the Stones* Martin Brennan *Thames & Hudson 1983*
7. *Knowth 10 Ages* William Battersby *1999*

17: The Alchemical Wedding
1. *Slane* C.E.F. Trench *An Taisce 1976*
2. *The Holy Blood and the Holy Grail* op cit
3. *Op cit*
4. *The Stars and the Stones* op cit
5. *Myths and Legends of the Celtic Race* op cit
6. *Mythic Ireland* Michael Dames *Thames & Hudson 1992*

18: Harvest of Souls
1. *The Festival of Lughnnasa* Marie Macneill *Oxford 1962*
2. *The Sun and the Serpent* Paul Broadhurst and Hamish Miller *Mythos 2003*
3. *The Dance of the Dragon* Paul Broadhurst, Hamish Miller, V. Shanley and B. Russell *Mythos 2000*

Additional Bibliography:

Appavou, Kintia, and Mougeot, Régor, La Vouivre *La Table d'Emeraude 1993*
Anderson J.J. Sir Gawain and the Green Knight *Everyman 1996*
Avalon, Arthur, The Serpent Power *Dover 1974*
Graves, Tom, Needles of Stone *Turnstone 1978*
Graves, Tom, and Hoult, Janet, The Essential T.C. Lethbridge *RKP 1980*
Heath, Robin, Sun, Moon and Stonehenge *Bluestone Press 1998*
Huxley, Francis, The Dragon, Nature of Spirit, Spirit of Nature *Thames & Hudson 1979*
Leick, Gwendolyn, A Dictionary of Ancient Near Eastern Mythology *RKP 1998*
Narby, Jeremy, The Cosmic Serpent *Phoenix 1998*
Newman, Paul, Lost Gods of Albion *Sutton Publishing 1997*
Olsen, Oddvar, The Templar Papers *New Page 2006*
Roberts, Jack, The Sacred Mythological Centres of Ireland *Bandia 2000*
Screeton, Paul, The Lambton Worm and other Northumbrian Dragon Legends *Zodiac House 1978*
Sellers, Jane, The Death of Gods in Ancient Egypt *Penguin 1992*
Spence, Lewis, The Myths of Ancient Egypt *Harrap & Co 1922*
Wright, Brian, Somerset Dragons *Tempus Publishing Co. 2002*

Index